ALSO BY JAMES ROMM

Dying Every Day: Seneca at the Court of Nero

Ghost on the Throne: The Death of Alexander the Great and the War for Crown and Empire

The Greek Plays: Sixteen Plays by Aeschylus, Sophocles, and Euripides (editor)

The Landmark Arrian: The Campaigns of Alexander (editor)

THE SACRED BAND

THREE HUNDRED THEBAN LOVERS
AND THE LAST DAYS OF GREEK FREEDOM

JAMES ROMM

SCRIBNER

New York   London   Toronto   Sydney   New Delhi

Scribner
An Imprint of Simon & Schuster, Inc.
1230 Avenue of the Americas
New York, NY 10020

First Scribner trade paperback edition June 2022

SCRIBNER and design are registered trademarks of The Gale Group, Inc.,
used under license by Simon & Schuster, Inc., the publisher of this work.

For information about special discounts for bulk purchases, please contact Simon &
Schuster Special Sales at 1-866-506-1949 or business@simonandschuster.com.

The Simon & Schuster Speakers Bureau can bring authors to your live event.
For more information or to book an event, contact the Simon & Schuster Speakers
Bureau at 1-866-248-3049 or visit our website at www.simonspeakers.com.

1 3 5 7 9 10 8 6 4 2

Library of Congress Cataloging-in-Publication Data has been applied for.

ISBN 978-1-5011-9801-4
ISBN 978-1-5011-9802-1 (pbk)
ISBN 978-1-5011-9803-8 (ebook)

For Eve, Abby, and Jonah

The only general who's never been beaten is Eros.

—Pammenes, leader of Thebes (as quoted by Plutarch)

Contents

A Note on the Archival Drawings   xiii

Preface   xv

1. Love's Warriors (August 382–January 378 BC)   1

2. Boeotia Rising (378–375 BC, plus background 400–382 BC)   31

3. Philosophers in Arms (375–June 371 BC)   63

4. *Otototoi!* (July 371–370 BC)   91

5. The Three Free Cities (370–367 BC)   123

6. A Death in Thessaly (367–364 BC)   153

7. A Death in Arcadia (364–359 BC)   185

8. The Sacred Wars (358–335 BC)   219

Acknowledgments   255

Guide to Further Reading and Notes   257

Image Credits   277

Index   279

THESSALY

Malian Gulf

*Aegean
Sea*

Pass of
Thermopylae

LOCRIS

PHOCIS

Cephisus R.

BOEOTIA

Euboea

Mt.
Parnassus
Delphi ⚏ ✛

Orchomenus   Tegyra ⚔

Chaeronea ⚔

*Lake
Copais*

Aulis

Coronea ⚔⚔

Haliartus

Thebes

Thespiae

Asopos R.

Corinthian Gulf

Plataea

✛ Mt.
Cithaeron

ATTICA

Athens

Corinth

*Saronic
Gulf*

Salamis

PELOPONNESE

Aegina

Mt.
Parnassus
Delphi 🏛 +

Euboea

Thebes. Asopos R.
Leuctra ⚔.

Corinthian Gulf

ACHAEA

+ Mt.
Cithaeron

Megara.

Athens.
Piraeus

ELIS

Corinth.

Salamis

ATTICA

Elis

PELOPONNESE

Olympia 🏛

Argos.

ARCADIA

Scillus.

⚔
Mantinea

Aegean
Sea

Megalopolis.

Tegea

Ionian
Sea

Mt.
Messene. Ithome

Eurotas R.

MESSENE

Sparta.

LACONIA

+ Mt.
Taygetus

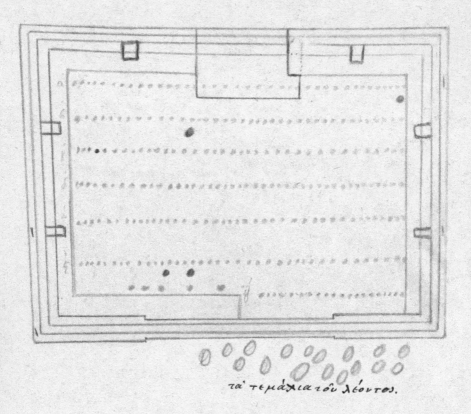

Stamatakis's plan of the mass grave, with each dot standing for a member of the Sacred Band. The larger shapes at bottom are labeled by Stamatakis "pieces of the lion," since the marble statue had not yet been reconstructed.

A Note on
the Archival Drawings

The discovery of a mass grave is a rare event in archaeology, often publicized by dramatic photographs. Yet somehow during the brief time in 1880 when the grave of the Sacred Band, at Chaeronea near Thebes, was open to view, no photos were taken. With 254 skeletons laid out in rows, this was the largest, most vivid mass burial known from the ancient world. The grave was soon covered over again, most likely forever.

The chief excavator at Chaeronea, Panagiotis Stamatakis, never published his findings, and the notebooks he had kept soon disappeared from view. While working for this book, researcher Brady Kiesling spotted a fleeting reference to these excavation notes and discovered that the archivists of the Greek Archaeological Service had located and inventoried them. We were astonished to find, as we examined them, that Stamatakis had made detailed drawings of every skeleton, marking their many wounds and fractures, and had also depicted the layout of the entire grave. With generous help from a branch of the Hellenic Ministry of Culture and Sports, the Department of Historical Archive of Antiquities and Restorations, good-quality photographs of these drawings were obtained. A selection of these are presented in this book—their first time in print.

The final image in this series (page 218) presents a composite made by digital illustrator Markley Boyer, in which all the remains drawn by Stamatakis have been reassembled in their findspots. This painstaking work of reconstruction, based on notes and measurements found in the log, allows us to see the grave of the Sacred Band as it was laid out by the Thebans in 338 BC and as it was revealed, briefly, in 1880.

Preface

To visit Thiva in modern Greece, the site of ancient Thebes, is a lonely journey for modern tourists. They'll likely be the only out-of-towners leaving the train there or driving up the hill of its Cadmea, the city center. They'll find no tourist maps or postcards in its kiosks, no multilingual menus in its cafés. As they walk down the strangely named streets—Pelopidas Street, Epaminondas Street—they'll have to look hard to find any trace of the city's classical past.

Meanwhile in the Plaka of Athens, a thousand T-shirts flutter on the walls of a hundred souvenir shops. The Athenian owl is seen on them in every conceivable pattern, as is the crested helmet of the Spartan infantry soldier. No icon evokes the memory of Thebes. Athens and Sparta, the antagonists of the great Peloponnesian War, loom over our imaginative landscape like twin colossi. Yet Thebes, which once held its own against those two cities combined, is nearly absent from that landscape.

The eclipse of Thebes from the modern mind would delight a man named Xenophon, an ancient Athenian soldier and essayist, who did much to bring it about. Xenophon chronicled the era of Theban greatness in his *Hellenica*, the sole surviving history composed in this time. But he was hardly an impartial observer. He was repelled by Thebes, since it had dared to challenge Sparta, the state he saw as Greece's natural leader. In his writings he downplayed Theban successes or, often, omitted them altogether. The single greatest triumph of Thebes over

Sparta—its founding of Messene, a city that sheltered Sparta's escaped slaves—is not even mentioned in *Hellenica*.

Xenophon also obscured another Theban achievement, its creation of a unique infantry corps composed of male lovers fighting in pairs. The Greeks called this corps the Sacred Band, but Xenophon refused to use that inspiring name. Instead he referred vaguely in *Hellenica* to the "chosen men" of the Thebans and mentioned them only once. He passed in silence over their first major action, a battle in which, as another historian claimed, they astonished all Greece by defeating a Spartan force that outnumbered them two to one. In another work, *Symposium*, Xenophon disparaged the Theban strategy of stationing lovers side by side in battle, claiming this showed only that both members were tempted to turn and run.

Fortunately Xenophon's silence and scorn are partly offset by Plutarch, author of the famous *Parallel Lives*, a set of paired biographies contrasting Greeks and Romans. Two of those biographies concerned Theban leaders who commanded the Sacred Band and led it in its victories over Sparta. One of those two biographies, of Epaminondas, has been lost to the ravages of time, but the other, of Pelopidas, survives. Two precious paragraphs of that work describe the Band and trace its origin to 378 BC, the start of Thebes's rise to superpower status. For forty years thereafter, Plutarch claimed, the Band remained undefeated in combat, until in 338 it faced an implacable foe, Alexander the Great.

Those four decades—the age of the Sacred Band, as I'll call them—are the focus of this book. These were years of crisis and decline in mainland Greece. Leadership shifted unpredictably among Athens, Sparta, and Thebes; the turbulence aided warlords and dictators in smaller cities, some of whom attained enormous strength by hiring mercenaries. War-ravaged, the Greeks sought a security framework, a Common Peace in their terms, but each of half a dozen efforts came to naught. The

Great King of Persia intervened to stop the unraveling, but he himself was weakened by rebellion and palace intrigues.

Amid the confusion, democracy somehow flourished. The uniquely Greek system of assembly rule had arisen at Athens in the fifth century BC, but in the fourth it spread as never before. Hopes for Greek freedom were never higher, but dangers were never greater. The science of war was evolving, and innovations created instabilities. Philip of Macedon, father of Alexander the Great, developed new tactics that allowed him to control all of mainland Greece, but his inspiration, in part, came from the years he had spent in Thebes.

It's often said that history is written by the victors, but the case of Thebes defies that axiom. Xenophon, in *Hellenica*, wrote of the Theban ascendance from a Spartan viewpoint; other accounts of the era, both ancient and modern, tend to center on Athens. My admittedly narrow focus on Thebes, and on its Sacred Band, springs from my sense that little-told stories are the ones that most need to be told, especially when—as in the Theban case—the protagonists had no historians of their own.

Xenophon himself, ironically, supports me in this approach. "If one of the great cities has done something noble, all the historians record it," he wrote in *Hellenica*, "But it seems to me that, if some small city has accomplished many noble deeds, this is even more worthy of being made public." Thebes was not a small city in his day, but it has become one in ours. I hope in what follows to partly restore what's been lost.

THE
SACRED
BAND

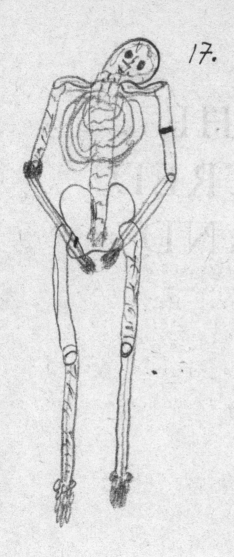

17.

CHAPTER 1

Love's Warriors

(August 382–January 378 BC)

Like many a traveler in modern Greece, George Ledwell Taylor carried with him a copy of Pausanias on June 3, 1818, when he rode out on horseback from the village of Lebadea. An Englishman on the grand tour, an architect with a special interest in antiquities, Taylor was looking for ancient Chaeronea,* site of the most consequential battle fought on Greek soil. Three English friends and one Greek acquaintance accompanied Taylor. Suddenly his horse stumbled over a stone.

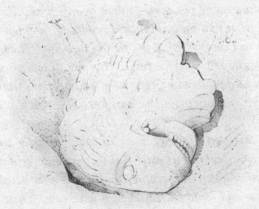

Taylor made this sketch of the lion's head at Chaeronea before he and his friends had it reburied.

* Pronounced "kay-roe-NAY-ah," with four syllables.

The stone had a curious, whitish appearance, so the party dismounted and started to dig, using their riding crops for lack of better tools. As they dug, one of the party read aloud from the notes they had copied the previous night out of Pausanias. In that ancient Greek travelogue, they had seen the following passage:

> *As one approaches Chaeronea, there is a tomb of the Thebans who died in the battle with Philip. No inscription adorns it, but a monument stands over it in the form of a lion, the best emblem of the spirit of those men. It seems to me the inscription is lacking because their fortunes were not equal to their courage.*

Bit by bit, with the help of nearby "peasants" (as Taylor termed them), a giant carved stone was cleared from the soil. It was indeed the head of an enormous lion, nearly six feet high from the shoulder to the forehead, hollow yet weighing perhaps three tons. Several previous British travelers had searched for this statue in vain. Taylor's horse and Pausanias's text had led to the discovery of a lifetime.

"Their fortunes were not equal to their courage": any British antiquarian knew what that meant. Ancient armies of enormous size had clashed at this spot, in 338 BC, and that of the Greeks had lost. The destiny of Hellas had changed forever; its city-states, small, independent units, had knuckled under to a single ruler, an imperious warrior-king. In their own eyes, their freedom had been lost. This lion was a signpost of defeat.

Unable to transport the huge stone fragments, Taylor simply had them reburied and went on his way. But they came to light again and were seen by other nineteenth-century tourists. Several noted that the pieces were large and could be reassembled with ease. There was talk of restoration, even offers from Britain to subsidize the project. These were rejected by the Greeks; the lion, after all, was a symbol of Hellenic resistance to foreign domination.

Local lore sprang up around the broken lion. It was said that during the Greek War of Independence, in the 1820s, a general had smashed the statue's base, looking for treasure or weapons to fight the Turks. Inside, the legend went, he'd found a scroll with this mysterious sentence: "The lentils need some oil." That showed, the rumors said, that the stonecutters who built this monument had not been adequately provisioned.

As the modern state of Greece connected to its past, the lion assumed new importance. In 1880, a sculptor was sent to Chaeronea, in hope that the lion could be reconstructed. Testing the firmness of the ground beneath, he found rows of skeletons, a few of which he removed for further study. An archaeologist, Panagiotis Stamatakis, was put in charge of excavating the site. Soon a startling set of finds was announced.

The lion had stood in the center of an enclosure formed by low stone walls, a rectangle seventy-four feet long and forty-four wide. Within that space, Stamatakis uncovered a polyandrion, or mass grave. Two hundred fifty-four men had been buried there in seven rows, as though formed up for combat in an infantry phalanx. Few weapons were found with them, but many strigils, metal scrapers for removing sweat and oil from the skin, and hundreds of tiny bone circles, apparently the eyelets from long-decayed sandals. A few ceramic cups had been buried there too, as though to nourish the dead in the afterlife.

The skeletons revealed the marks of violent deaths. One skull showed a laceration all across its forehead, suggesting the man's face had been sheared clean off. Another bore a squarish hole where a sharp object had been driven into the brain. On shinbones and arm bones, gouges, grooves, and hacks spoke of the strokes of swords and spears. Clearly, these men had died amid the fury of all-out war.

The New York Times, on January 8, 1881, reported to the English-speaking world "the discovery of 260 corpses" at Chaeronea, then added a mysterious clause: "Some forty only of the glorious dead are missing." The full complement, the Times implied, ought to have been three hundred. Already the remains had been linked to the Sacred Band, an elite corps of Theban infantry, three hundred strong, who died fighting at Chaeronea. Their valor, celebrated by ancient writers, *seemed to be reflected in the marble lion—"the best emblem of the spirit of those men," as Pausanias put it.*

Ancient writers claimed the Band was destroyed to the last man, but the group in the grave, as the Times pointed out, was well shy of three hundred. That left room for doubt. With so few grave goods to go by and no inscription, the tomb's occupants could not be identified with certainty. But over the decades, most scholars have agreed they are indeed the Sacred Band of Thebes.

A few pairs of skeletons were found with arms linked at the elbow, an intriguing arrangement given the nature of the Sacred Band. Ancient reports of the Band—largely accepted today, though occasionally doubted—say that it was composed of male couples, stationed in pairs such that each man fought beside his beloved. The erôs or passionate love they felt was a spur to their courage in battle, as each sought to excel in his partner's eyes.

The story of this corps began exactly twenty-two hundred years before Taylor's horse kicked that fateful stone. On a summer morning in 382 BC, in the city of Thebes, an episode unfolded that stunned the Greek world, all except those who had planned it. On that day a Spartan army seized control of Thebes in a sudden coup, setting off a forty-four-year chain of conflicts and struggles, of sporadic and futile attempts at peacemaking, and of power grabs by warlords with hired militias, leading finally to the decline and demise of the freedom of Greece.

That morning began the age of the Sacred Band.

It was a hot day. Thebes was in the midst of the Thesmophoria, a summer festival in honor of Demeter, goddess of grain and agriculture. The citadel called the Cadmea, the Theban acropolis, had been cleared of all men; only women could celebrate the secret rites or make offerings of phallus-shaped cakes, tokens of fertility, to the goddess. The governing council of Thebes, which normally met on the Cadmea, had to shift ground that day and meet in the marketplace, well below the fortified hilltop. This change of venue was crucial to what was about to take place.

Ismenias led the council that day, as he had for the past two decades. Thebes had changed course under his leadership, tilting away from Sparta, its long-standing ally, in the direction of Athens, its former foe. A cadre of young progressives had backed this policy shift, looking to Athens as the beacon of democracy and resenting Sparta, the reigning superpower, for bullying the Greeks. But others in Thebes despised this new alignment. These Laconists, as they were known,* had gone along, grudgingly, as their city dealt insults and slights to the Spartans they favored.

One such insult was being delivered that very day. A Spartan army, commanded by a certain Phoibidas, was camped outside the walls, headed north to Olynthus, its apparent target. Olynthus had defied the terms of a Spartan-led treaty, and Sparta had declared war on behalf of the treaty's signers, including Thebes. Troops had been requested from all quarters, but Thebes had forbidden its citizens to serve. Now that the enforcement squad was on their very doorstep, the Thebans continued to ignore it, but also made no effort to block its passage. Ismenias and his party might resent Spartan power, but they were not strong enough to challenge it—not yet.

Ismenias was one of three Theban polemarchs, magistrates who, by yearly election, were chosen to run the city. This triumvirate had, in recent years, been politically split. A staunch pro-Spartan, Leontiades, was also part of that board and had been since well before Ismenias came on the scene. Son of a Laconist father, grandson of a great war hero, this man had watched in dismay the rise of an opposition that leaned toward Athens. He did not like sharing power, especially when his own share was on the wane. He needed a bold stroke to regain

---

* So called after Laconia, the Spartans' home region.

control and bring Thebes back to the Spartan fold. So, with Spartan help, he'd devised one of history's boldest.

By a prearranged plan, Phoibidas and his Spartans, in the plains outside Thebes, began marching off that morning, heading for Olynthus. Then around midday they turned and dashed toward a gate in the walls of Thebes. Leontiades was waiting there to admit them. He ushered the troops through streets made nearly empty by summer heat. Up they ran toward the Cadmea, a stronghold unguarded on this day alone. Once inside, they were handed a *balanagra* or "bolt puller"—a metal sleeve that slid over the bolt that secured the Cadmea's gate, then caught it with a protruding stud and pulled it free. In modern terms, this was the key to the city. The Spartans cleared the women from the Cadmea, then locked themselves in and locked all opponents out.

The takeover happened so fast that, down in the lower city, the council meeting went on undisturbed in the market square. Suddenly Leontiades appeared to announce the change of regime. A few of his fellow Laconists had arrived shortly before and quietly stationed themselves—with armor and weapons—around the council venue.

"Do not despair that the Spartans have seized our acropolis," Leontiades intoned, meaning the Cadmea. "They are enemies only to those who are eager to fight them." Then he pointed to his rival Ismenias. "The law allows polemarchs to arrest anyone who does things that merit death. Therefore I arrest this man, on the grounds that he fomented war. You captains there, get up and seize him and take him away to the place we discussed." Ismenias was led off to the Cadmea, now the headquarters of a Spartan army of occupation. Leontiades and his Laconist friends took control of Thebes.

Greek cities had known overthrows before, even covert troop insertions by "foreign" powers—that is, by other Greek cities. No previous coup had had such complete success. In only an hour or two, the new regime was installed, backed by an unassailable garrison force. Not a single blow had been struck.

The followers of Ismenias, those who'd "Atticized," or sided with Athens, had suddenly become enemies of the state. Many made haste to flee, in a pattern seen often in Greek party strife: losing factions went into exile in cities that shared their views. In this case, Athens, the obvious place to seek refuge, could be reached by a two days' walk or a single day's ride. Three hundred Thebans made their way there, including Androclidas, a leading Atticizer who'd escaped arrest, the fate that awaited hundreds of his comrades.

Among these exiles was one whose name, though yet obscure, was soon to be heard everywhere. At around thirty years old, Pelopidas was among the youngest and most ardent of the group—a man of *thumos*, high-spirited anger and pride, as Plutarch termed him. Appalled by the Spartan seizure of his city, he longed to strike back, even if the effort took years—as indeed it would.

Messengers from the Spartans arrived at Athens, demanding Athenians banish the Theban exiles. To these envoys Athens turned a deaf ear. It welcomed the Thebans by official decree and made room for them amid its broad porticoes, bustling streets, and crowded agora, or marketplace. In those venues the exiles gathered and talked of events back home. Through friends and allies in Thebes, they kept a close eye on Leontiades—while he, as they would soon enough learn, was keeping an eye on *them*.

The Cadmea, the hill that now housed a force of fifteen hundred armed men, had been named for Cadmus, the mythic founder of Thebes. A prince of Phoenicia (in modern Lebanon), he had arrived in the region, according to legend, pursuing his sister Europa, abducted by Zeus. The oracle of Delphi told him to give up that quest and instead find a cow with moon-shaped marks on its flanks, follow its wanderings, and settle on the spot where it first lay down. That cow, called *bous* in Greek, led Cadmus to a region that then got the name it still bears today, Boeotia.* Cadmus made his home where the cow took its rest and set in motion the tragic history of Thebes.

A nearby spring, the best source of water, was guarded by a dragon, so Cadmus slew the monster and planted its teeth in the ground. From those teeth sprang a crop of armed warriors, who fought one another until only five were left. (Some of the same teeth found their way to Colchis, land of the Golden Fleece, where they again sprouted armed men in the tale of Jason and the Argonauts.) Those five, the Spartoi or "sown men," begot the lines of the leading families of Thebes. With the help of these dragon-teeth men, Cadmus built the enormous walls of the Cadmea and, at the top of the hill, a palace for himself.

Cadmus was now king of the land, and the gods gave him a queen, Harmonia, daughter of the adulterous union of Ares and Aphrodite. The Muses themselves sang the couple's wedding hymn, at a spot later shown to tourists by Theban guides. But Harmonia brought a curse as her dowry. Aphrodite's husband, the blacksmith god Hephaestus, hated the offspring of his wife's love affair. He crafted a charmed necklace for Harmonia's wedding gift that would bring youth and beauty, but also dreadful misfortune, to those who owned it.

This necklace would pass through the hands of generations of Theban rulers, enacting its doom on each in turn. The sufferings of this royal line became famous throughout Greece. Their horrific fates were staged, over and over, in tragedies composed by playwrights in classical Athens. Thanks to the

---

* Pronounced "bee-OH-sha," with the first *o* silent. The Greeks called it Boiotia (first syllable "boy"); place names are given here in their more familiar latinized versions.

survival of those plays, the myths of Thebes still claim a place in our collective consciousness.

The necklace passed first to Semele, daughter of Cadmus and Harmonia, a beautiful young woman whom Zeus took to bed. Semele conceived a child by Zeus, but after jealous Hera planted doubts in her mind, she worried that her "divine" lover was only an ordinary man. She demanded that Zeus appear to her in his true form, and the god obliged by descending as a thunderbolt—instantly scorching her to death. Her fetal child was rescued from the ashes and sewn into Zeus's thigh. It matured there into Dionysus, a god who was thus, in a sense, born at Thebes. Euripides opened his play *The Bacchae* with the return of Dionysus to his native city, where his mother's grave was still smoldering, many years later.

Next the necklace came to Agave, Semele's sister, whose son, Pentheus, had come to the throne of Thebes. *The Bacchae* tells the story of this wretched pair, aunt and cousin, respectively, to the god Dionysus. Though Agave believed her sister's son had been fathered by Zeus, Pentheus scoffed, declaring that Semele had only invented the tale to explain her pregnancy. Dionysus was determined to prove his divinity. Working a spell on both Agave and Pentheus, he caused the mother to see her son as a lion and hunt him to his death on Mt. Cithaeron, then tear him apart with her hands. In the play's harrowing last scene, she awakes from her dream and sees that the trophy she holds is her son's severed head.

The necklace came next to Jocasta, wife of King Laius (great-grandson to Cadmus), who gave birth to a doomed son, Oedipus. Frightened by a prophecy about the boy's future, the royal couple exposed him as an infant. Rescued by a shepherd and reared by adoptive parents, Oedipus grew up unaware of his origins. To avoid a prophecy that he'd kill his father and marry his mother, he ran away from those he thought had given him birth. An old man he slew in a chance encounter on the road turned out to be his father, King Laius, and the woman he married—her youthful appearance preserved by the necklace—was Jocasta. In Sophocles' immortal drama *Oedipus Rex*, he discovers the truth and, in anguish, puts out his own eyes.

The two sons of the blinded Oedipus fought for the right to succeed their father. A war began for the right to rule Thebes, stoked in part by the necklace. One son, Polynices, used the necklace to bribe an ally to help him invade Thebes, where his brother, Eteocles, reigned. In the ensuing battle—imagined by Aeschylus in his play *Seven against Thebes*—the two brothers killed one another in single combat, leaving the city leaderless. That brought an interim ruler, Creon, to power.

Creon sought to reestablish order after this civil war. Unsure of support, he adopted a desperate measure: he decreed that the body of the invading brother, Polynices, be left unburied, a putrescent warning to other attackers and rebels. But the sister of Polynices defied the edict and tried to bury the corpse. Creon shut her in a prison of rock to starve, but she hung herself there instead. Her story inspired another timeless Greek play, Sophocles' *Antigone*.

The royal line begun by Cadmus thus came to an end, and so, for a long time, at least, did the trail of destruction wrought by Harmonia's necklace. Those who received it next sought to quash its power forever: they dedicated it to Athena in her shrine at Delphi, as one of the sacred treasures set aside for the goddess. There it remained, safely out of circulation, for centuries. But it finally emerged, as we'll see, to add further disasters to the story of Thebes.

Through the legends of Cadmus's line, Thebes became known as a landscape of suffering. Visitors were shown the grave of Semele, the fountain where Oedipus washed off the blood of his murdered father, the seven gates where the Seven against Thebes had perished in combat, one at each gate. A rut in the ground came to be called Antigone's Drag Track: here the intrepid girl had supposedly dragged the body of her brother, too heavy to lift, in an effort to get it onto a nearby pyre. And towering in the distance, looming over the whole region, was the savage mountain, Cithaeron, where Agave, driven mad by Dionysus, had dismembered her own son with her bare hands.

Other mythic figures too had landmarks at Thebes. Heracles (called Hercules by the Romans) was thought to have been born there, and the ruined house of his parents stood outside a southern gate. The graves of Heracles' children—killed by their father in a fit of madness—were found there as well, as was the stone called Sophronistêr, "Wiser-Upper," allegedly thrown at Heracles by Athena to stop him from also killing his father. Penance for these murders took Heracles south, to the Peloponnese, so cities in that region also thought Heracles was "one of their own." But only the Thebans could boast he was born and bred among them.

Thebans also claimed the tomb of Iolaus, the nephew of Heracles and, as many thought, his *erômenos*, younger beloved. The two men had sojourned together on many adventures, with Iolaus squiring for Heracles, driving his chariot, or aiding him in combat. Iolaus stood beside Heracles in the battle with the Lernaean Hydra, cauterizing the creature's necks as Heracles lopped off its heads, thereby preventing two new ones from growing out of each wound. The Thebans honored this heroic/erotic partnership with a set of athletic games, and the tomb of Iolaus became a pilgrimage site for male couples. According to Plutarch, who cites Aristotle as his source, men pledged their love for one another beside that tomb, as if the bond between Heracles and Iolaus were their model.

In no other Greek city do we hear of such vows, but then, Thebes was unique in how it regarded *erôs*, sexual love, between men. Male *erôs* took many forms across the Greek world, as Plato attests in his meditation on the subject, *Symposium*. In

Athens and Sparta, male *erôs* was "complicated," as Plato has one of his speakers, Pausanias, declare. But among the Boeotians, Pausanias claims—referring principally to the Thebans—male pair bonding was embraced and even encouraged by law. "No one there, neither young nor old, would say it is shameful," Pausanias says, adding that this cheerful acceptance was also seen in Elis, in the Peloponnese.

Two other Greek writers, our principal sources for classical Thebes, confirm this phenomenon. Xenophon, a contemporary of Plato's, claims that "among the Boeotians, a man and a youth live together *suzugentes*"—"yoked together," a word that elsewhere refers to a bond of lifelong marriage. Many centuries later, Plutarch, himself a Boeotian, gave a similar account. Theban lawgivers, he says, "gave *erôs* an outstanding place in the *palaestras*"—athletic arenas where men wrestled and court-

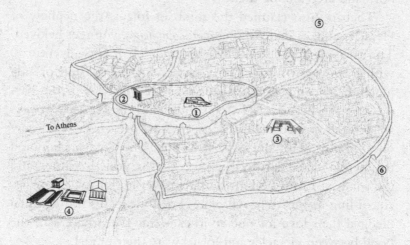

Classical Thebes, with the Cadmea at center and crucial sites highlighted: (1) the ancient palace of Cadmus, already in ruins by this time; (2) the temple of Zeus Hypsistos at the Cadmea's highest point; (3) the agora; (4) the district sacred to Heracles, with temple, athletic complex, and Sophronistêr stone; (5) Antigone's Drag Track; (6) the tomb of Iolaus and fountain of Oedipus (likely locations).

ship often took place. This official support of male *erôs* improved all of Theban society, Plutarch says, since the ardor of younger partners, the *erômenoi*, was mixed with the wisdom of older lovers, whom the Greeks called *erastai*.

Who were these lawgivers, whom Plutarch does not name? Aristotle tells of an early statesman, Philolaus, who's a likely candidate. This man emigrated to Thebes along with his *erômenos*, an Olympic athlete, Diocles. The pair had fled their native Corinth to protect their bond when it was threatened by Diocles' mother (we're not told how). In Thebes the pair lived out the rest of their lives and after death were buried together, in graves that, on their instruction, faced each other. These graves were later shown to visitors at Thebes. Perhaps it was Philolaus, so devoted to *erôs* himself, who drafted the laws that encouraged it in others.

Tombs, monuments, and landmarks kept the myths of Thebes alive and also channeled for Thebans the power of *erôs*. Only in Thebes, it seems—some sources name the Peloponnesian city of Elis as well—did men make vows to each other, live together as though wed, and seek to preserve their union even in death. While in Athens and Sparta *erôs* was "complicated," in Thebes it was natural, straightforward, and bolstered by solemn vows.

Such was the city the Spartans entered in 382 BC, and such was the fortified site they occupied. Phoibidas had evicted the "sown men" from the hill that had nurtured their "roots," where the charred ruins of Cadmus's palace—set afire, it was said, when Zeus came to Semele as a thunderbolt—still stood after centuries. Such moves, in the Greek mind, were demonstrations of hubris, arrogant pride. If they succeeded, they called down the wrath of the gods.

"One might tell many stories, of both Greeks and non-Greeks, that show how the gods do not ignore the wicked or those who

13

do unholy things," Xenophon writes, in a solemn passage of *Hellenica*, his history of these times. The "story" he then tells is the sequel to the Spartan takeover of Thebes. It's clear from his context who had done the "unholy things": Phoibidas, first and foremost, and his Theban collaborators. And along with these, perhaps, Xenophon meant to accuse Agesilaus,* one of Sparta's two kings and, quite likely, the architect of the invasion of the Cadmea.

Agesilaus despised the Thebans, who had dealt him a personal blow (as we shall see in the next chapter). He was also a strong proponent of Spartan machtpolitik—expansion of influence, or of empire (as some saw it), by military force. He'd carried Spartan arms farther in mainland Greece than any monarch before him, and even beyond the Aegean, into lands of the Persian Great King. The seizure of Thebes fit in perfectly with his ambitions, and many suspected he had planned and authorized it, using Phoibidas as his agent. Today's scholars largely concur with that view, though the truth may never be known.

Not all Spartans admired Agesilaus or approved of the Cadmea seizure. The Spartan ephors, a board of five who guided policy, were outraged that Phoibidas had acted without their approval. They summoned him back to Sparta for trial, a proceeding watched intently by Greeks everywhere, most of all by the Thebans. Would Sparta punish one of its own for an act of aggression and a violation of standing treaties? Would it give back control of the Cadmea and remove its choke hold from Thebes?

At the trial the ephors kept asking who had given the orders, perhaps expecting the answer "Agesilaus." But Phoibidas took sole responsibility for his act. The court seemed inclined to convict him, as clearly it should have, but then, Agesilaus

---

* Pronounced as five syllables ("ah-gess-i-LAY-us"); either a hard or soft *g* is correct.

intervened. "If what he did was bad for Sparta," the king told his countrymen, "he could be justly punished; if it was *good*, there's an ancient law that permits him to act on his own authority. We must look *only* to whether the things he did are good or bad." This naked appeal to self-interest, and expansion of Spartan power, carried the day. Phoibidas was let off with only a fine, and Agesilaus (according to some reports) obligingly paid it for him.

With a lack of contrition that shocked later ages, Sparta retained possession of the Theban citadel. What was more, it put the whole region under its power, setting up garrisons and installing puppet regimes in the cities surrounding Thebes. The Spartan lion, it seemed, meant to swallow Boeotia whole. With bases in Plataea, Thespiae, and Orchomenus,* the Spartans established a ring of force around occupied Thebes.

Ismenias, leader of Thebes's pro-Athenian faction, was put on trial in Thebes by Spartan judges. Accused of misdeeds that went back decades, he was convicted and summarily executed. Taking his place was a Laconist named Archias, a henchman serving Leontiades. New tools of repression kept the city in line: spies and secret police, arrests and detentions, torture of dissidents. But three hundred Thebans had escaped before those weapons were deployed. Living in exile in Athens, official guests of the state, they planned and bided their time.

It must have seemed to many Athenians that history was repeating, but in reverse. Twenty years earlier, just after the war they'd lost to the Spartans—the Peloponnesian War—they too had endured a Spartan garrison force and a puppet regime, called the Thirty. *Their* dissidents too had gone into exile, and most had landed at Thebes. Now *Theban* exiles had fled Spartan puppets and landed in *Athens*, a mirror-image inversion of

---

* All principal Greek sites are shown in the maps at the start of this book.

those events. The symmetry was clear to the Thebans as well, and it gave them hope.

In the earlier episode (403 BC), Athenian exiles had staged a covert incursion to retake their city. With help from the Thebans, a squad of seventy had struck out across the border and seized a fort in the Attic countryside. The Athenian people had rallied to their cause, for the Thirty were widely disliked. Supporters soon gathered in numbers such that even the Spartans could not oust them. The Thirty were driven from power and democracy was restored, less than a year after it had fallen.

If such a thing could be done by Athenians leaving from Thebes, perhaps a similar plan could work for Thebans leaving from Athens. The Theban exiles began to talk in secret of a mission to retake their city. Fast walkers, after all, could get from Athens to Thebes within a long day, or, more to the point, a long night. Sympathizers in Athens would help them, just as, two decades earlier, supporters in Thebes—Ismenias, now executed—had helped the Athenians.

The exiles' plans took on new urgency when, in their third year in Athens, a team of dagger men arrived to attack them. The junta back in Thebes, headed by Leontiades, had sent these men to rub out the most prominent exiles, launching what he must have seen as a preemptive strike. Several exiles were targeted, but in the end only one life was lost—that of their senior member, Androclidas. Among those who escaped was Pelopidas, the high-spirited man of *thumos*, and he now stepped into the vacant leadership role.

Foreseeing that more attacks might be coming, the exiles decided to act. Thirty signed on for the mission, led by Pelopidas and another young firebrand, Melôn. Winter, with its long nights, was then approaching. The winter solstice, the longest of nights, was a festal day in Thebes, the Aphrodisia—a day to honor Aphrodite, goddess of sexual love. That day would serve the plotters well, for they knew how the junta liked to celebrate it.

Sympathizers in Thebes were informed of the plot and given supporting roles. A man called Charon—ominously named for the ferryman of the underworld—would conceal the returning exiles at his home. Others in Charon's circle would lend their hands: Gorgidas, Simmias, Epaminondas, men respected in Thebes for authority and sound judgment. One man in particular, Phyllidas, would play a critical part; by concealing his Atticist leanings, he'd risen to high rank within the junta, as chief of staff to the polemarchs themselves.

Secrecy was paramount, for such plots often failed when betrayed by informers. In this case, a leak *did* occur, just as the exile squad was making its way toward Thebes. An Athenian priest in Eleusis, not far from Attica's border with Boeotia, somehow learned where these Thebans were headed and what they intended. He scrawled a quick message and sent it on to Thebes, with instructions that the polemarchs there must read it immediately. None of the exiles guessed they had been detected.

Pelopidas and his small column halted as they crossed into Boeotia. Only a dozen would go forward from there, a group small enough to attract little notice; the rest would wait until sent for. These twelve dressed as hunters and shouldered gear—poles for beating brush and nets for snaring game—so their presence in open country would not seem odd. Other disguises awaited them at their destination: women's dress and veils, secured at the home of Charon.

Then, bidding their comrades take care of their parents and children in case they never returned, the twelve set out for seven-gated Thebes.

A cold wind was blowing that day in Thebes, and a thin snow was falling. For those gathered at Charon's house, a half dozen or so, there was little to do but wait—and worry. Spartan troop movements in the region gave hints their plot was known or at least suspected. Yet neither the polemarchs nor their Spartan masters had made any move against them. There had been no dread knock on the door—though one was soon coming.

The events in Thebes on that day and the one that followed, in late December of 379 BC, were described, five centuries later, by Plutarch, a native Boeotian, in two different works. His accounts were no doubt embellished, but also, quite likely, informed by primary sources he'd read and researched. The same two days were also recounted by Xenophon in *Hellenica*. The three versions, taken together, give us more detail about these forty-eight hours than any other similar span in all Greek history, but they differ among themselves on various points. What follows is based largely on Plutarch's texts.

One member of Charon's group was more worried than the rest. A friend had told him of a strange dream he'd had the previous night: Charon's house had appeared to be pregnant and laboring to give birth, but instead of a child, it produced a jet of flame. That fire spread and consumed all of Thebes, except, significantly, the Cadmea, the hill where the Spartans were camped. In the dream, that fortified base had survived, wreathed in black smoke, while the rest of the city burned—an omen perhaps of disaster for Thebes and victory for the Spartans.

The group around Charon was unaware of this dream and of what was taking place elsewhere in Thebes at that moment. The man who had learned of the dream was attempting to call off the plot. He'd ordered a neighbor and confederate, a man named Chlidon, to ride out into the plain, find the exiles making their way from Athens, and tell them to turn back. Chlidon was just then searching for his horse's bridle but failing to find it. His wife finally told him she'd lent it to a neighbor. Chlidon was cursing and shouting, and his wife was shouting back, attracting a small crowd of curious onlookers.

While the couple bickered, the group at Charon's house

went out and headed for the home of Simmias, not far away, to join another cell of conspirators. As they walked through the streets of Thebes, they ran into two men they dreaded: Archias, one of the Laconist polemarchs, and Lysanoridas, the Spartan garrison chief. The pair were walking down from the Cadmea, attended by soldiers. Archias called out to one of the group, the seer Theocritus, and drew him apart in private conversation. The others looked on nervously, but Archias was merely seeking advice about a religious rite. Theocritus explained the whole tale to the group as they walked on together:

It seems that the Spartans based at nearby Haliartus, acting on orders of King Agesilaus, had opened the tomb of Alcmene, the mother of Heracles. The king wanted the woman's remains brought to Sparta, so he could tap into the mystical powers he thought they possessed. No bones had been found in the tomb, but several strange objects emerged, including a bronze tablet inscribed with an unknown script. Soon after this exhumation, the crops had failed in Haliartus and a flood had ruined the fields. Now the garrison chief, Lysanoridas, was setting off to Haliartus, to close the tomb and appease the ghost of Alcmene. Clearly Spartan overreach, Theocritus said, had angered the gods.

Charon's group arrived at their destination and greeted Simmias. He too, they learned, had just had an anxious encounter: Leontiades, chief of the junta, had come to his home that morning to discuss a detainee, Amphitheus, an Atticist rounded up in a recent purge. Simmias had pleaded for leniency—banishment rather than death—but Leontiades had stood firm. The man was scheduled to die the following morning. "What cruel and barbarous natures!" Simmias exclaimed, in disgust, to the others.

Simmias then told his guests of a curious stranger seen in Thebes the previous day. The man had performed a sacrifice at the tomb of Lysis, a sage of the Pythagorean school, and had slept by that grave, in the open, on a bed of heaped-up branches.

No one knew of this man, and his arrival in Thebes, at such a tense moment, seemed somehow significant. One of the plotters, Epaminondas, was sent out to find this man at Lysis's tomb. Epaminondas and his brother Caphisias, who was also there at the house, had grown up as students of Lysis and knew where the grave was; indeed they had dug it themselves, not long before.

These two brothers were at odds over the plot now in motion. Caphisias had joined eagerly and was ready to act, though action, he knew, would require the shedding of blood. Epaminondas disliked the Spartan occupation as much as his brother but did not approve of bloodshed. Epaminondas explained his demurral in medical terms: No doctor would resort to surgery, or to painful cauterizations, if a disease could be cured with drugs or diet instead. Just so, Epaminondas believed, the ills of Thebes could be cured without knives and flames. He sought a gentler remedy, though what this might be was unclear.

Not present at the home of Simmias, but foremost in everyone's thoughts, was Phyllidas, the mole. He was on duty at the *polemarcheion*, headquarters of the regime, arranging the schedule for the upcoming fest. He'd told his fellow plotters just what those arrangements were. Archias, one of their targets, would drink and carouse with his cronies, and with women, at the *polemarcheion*. But one of the women was a respectable lady who insisted on discretion. To avoid embarrassing her, Leontiades, the head of the junta, would stay home. That divergence would complicate the task ahead.

Epaminondas returned to Simmias's house, accompanied by the stranger he'd found at Lysis's tomb. This man was Theanor, a Pythagorean from south Italy, who'd come to ensure that Lysis received proper burial rites. He'd been relieved to learn that these had duly been performed by Epaminondas and his brother. Theanor offered the youths a cash reward for this service, and for their care of Lysis in old age, but the two refused to accept it. Though their family was not well-off, the brothers were known for restraint and moderation, qualities learned not only from Lysis but from their sober-minded father.

Then Chlidon arrived, in a fret over his missing bridle and the noncompletion of his assignment. So the plotters just then learned of how one of their number had nearly gotten the mission scrubbed before it began. A force that we might call luck, but the Greeks would link to the gods, had seen to it the bridle was not where it ought to have been, so the plot could go forward. The exiles were still on their way, and nothing could stop them.

As they crossed Mt. Cithaeron, Pelopidas and the exiles he led abandoned their hunting gear, changed into peasant clothes, and divided into groups of two and three. The gates of Thebes would be watched, but small groups such as these, apparently coming back from work on nearby farms, would be inconspicuous. The wind and blowing snow allowed them to wrap up their faces, and they passed through the gates undetected. Some saw a flash of lightning, not followed by thunder, just as they entered the city—an omen, they thought, of their mission's "brilliant" future.

Inside the walls, confederates were waiting. Guided by these men, the exiles slipped through the streets to their rendezvous point, Charon's house. At last all twelve had arrived. Some three dozen others were gathered there too, the inner circle of anti-Spartan resistance.

Just then a pounding was heard at the door. Two of the junta's soldiers were outside, demanding that Charon accompany them to the *polemarcheion*. It seemed that something had leaked. Charon would have to obey the summons, but his comrades worried he'd give them away under torture. Charon produced his fifteen-year-old son and offered the boy as a hostage, but Pelopidas, seizing the leadership role as his *thumos* bid him, dismissed the need for such pledges. So Charon went off with the soldiers, while those in the house grew more tense. One of their circle, they noted, was missing—the same man who'd earlier tried to abort the plot—and they assumed he'd betrayed them to save his own life.

At the *polemarcheion*, Archias was already drunk and anointed with scented oil; the Aphrodisia was getting underway. A highborn woman was soon to be brought to him, one he had long desired; Phyllidas, his trusted aide, had arranged the assignation. Other willing partners—beauties and women of standing—would pleasure his staff. The regime's top command would enjoy a night of carefree carousal, in honor of Aphrodite. "That's the kind of men they were," remarks Xenophon, with disapproval. Lack of self-restraint, as he saw it, was the downfall of leaders and soldiers, especially when it came to the sex drive.

"We hear some exiles have entered the city and are being hidden here," said Archias as Charon came into the room. Archias's speech was sloppy, as was his strategy, for he'd given away what he knew—and that wasn't much. His informants had spotted exiles arriving but did not know their purpose. Charon, relieved, feigned outrage: "Who are they?" He promised to report any news he could find of such men. Phyllidas, standing by nervously, chimed in, "Yes, do that, Charon, and leave no stone unturned." With that, Charon was dismissed. Phyllidas hastened to bring Archias back to the business at hand: feasting and drinking, and then, the rites of Aphrodite.

As Charon departed, a messenger from Athens was brought in. He carried the letter from the Athenian priest who had somehow learned of the plot. The messenger tried to convey the letter's timeliness: "The sender bids you read this right away, for it concerns urgent matters." *"Urgent matters tomorrow!"* said Archias merrily, tucking the note beneath the pillow of his banqueting couch. He was too intent on the coming carousal to read it.

Soon after, the women arrived.

Claps and cheers rang out from those in the *polemarcheion* as finely dressed women came into the room, accompanied by what seemed to be their maids. But as the group entered, a certain Cabirichus, who held a ceremonial priesthood, recognized a male form beneath the female clothing. "Isn't this Melôn?" he asked, grabbing an arm.

It was indeed Melôn. He spun away from Cabirichus, drew a dagger, and charged straight at Archias, his target. Drunk as he was, Archias had barely discerned what was wrong before Melôn cut him down with a heavy blow. All over the room, as junta officers dropped their goblets and reached for weapons, the conspirators threw off disguises and went on the attack.

By chance, Cabirichus was holding the sacred spear, a Theban emblem of priestly authority. One of the plotters seized this weapon and tried to wrest it away, while urging Cabirichus to join the liberation. But Cabirichus too was drunk, and in his confusion he held stubbornly on to the spear. Another plotter came up from behind and stabbed him to death, then snatched the hallowed staff from a pool of blood.

The hall quickly turned into a slaughterhouse. On one blood-spattered couch lay the letter, still unopened, that would have revealed the plot and changed history. But power and pleasure had made Archias blind to approaching danger. "Urgent matters tomorrow!" had been his reply. The phrase became a popular tagline, repeated by devil-may-care Greek revelers for centuries after this night.

Elsewhere in Thebes, Pelopidas was leading a second squad of commandos to the house of Leontiades. This group had but a short time to act. Word of the attack at the *polemarcheion* would quickly spread. It had not yet arrived, though, when Pelopidas reached the house and found it locked, but fortunately not guarded.

With grim double meaning, Pelopidas announced himself

This gold vessel of the fourth century BC, found in
Bulgaria in a large cache of such vessels, may well
depict Pelopidas's attack on the house of Leontiades,
though other theories have been proposed.

as an envoy come from Athens. A slave undid the bolt and
opened the door a crack. Pelopidas and his companions threw
it wide and rushed in, then hurried toward the *andreion*, the
men's quarters. There, Leontiades was already arming himself
and preparing to meet them with force.

A plotter named Cephisodorus was first through the door
to that room. Leontiades dispatched him with a sword thrust
to the side. Pelopidas entered second and began tussling with
Leontiades, who was shouting for his household slaves to come
to his aid. But Cephisodorus's body blocked the door, leaving
the two to fight it out unaided. After taking a blow to the head,
Pelopidas drove his blade home. Leontiades, mastermind of the
Spartan takeover and head of the rightist regime, fell dead at
Pelopidas's feet.

By prearranged plan, the groups led by Melôn and by Pelopidas, their targets eliminated, rendezvoused in the street and made their way to the prison. Over a hundred members of their faction were confined there. Phyllidas, not yet revealed as a mole, tried to gain the prisoners' release by staying in character as a junta official. "Archias orders you to bring Amphitheus to him," he said to the jailer, naming the dissident due to die the next day. But the jailer grew suspicious and demanded some token of authority. "Here's my authority!" Phyllidas cried, as he ran the man through with a spear. Then all the internees were set free.

The plotters now made their first public pronouncement, crying aloud in the streets that "the tyrants" were dead. They asked all Theban patriots to come out of their homes. Some did so; the plotters issued them weapons taken from smithies and from the market square, where arms captured in a long-ago battle were hung as a memorial. Others held back and stayed indoors, uncertain of the plot's chances or, perhaps, supporting the Spartan side.

The shouts reached the Cadmea, two hundred feet above, and alerted the Spartan garrison troops encamped there. From their lookout posts they could see lights inside homes, torches carried through the streets, dusky shapes gathering in the marketplace—the signs of a revolution in progress. The time had come for them to do their duty. Yet as crucial hours slipped past, the gates of the Cadmea stayed shut. The garrison chief, Lysanoridas, was away at Haliartus, resealing Alcmene's tomb; his two officers, Herippidas and Arcesus, were frightened by the commotion and unwilling to act without their superior's orders.

By the time the sun rose, the Spartan position was clearly deteriorating. A squad of Thebans who helped guard the Cadmea, the Kreittones ("Mighty Men"), deserted and went over to the insurgents. Some sort of smoke screen was used to conceal the plotters' movements; in this way, the dream that preceded the coup was fulfilled, in a different way than expected. The Cadmea *was* wreathed in smoke, but the "flames" that consumed the city were the ardor of Pelopidas and his comrades.

The Cadmea was by now surrounded and under siege. The question of outside intervention became paramount. During the night the Spartan chiefs had sent a distress message to Plataea, a garrisoned town ten miles away, perhaps by fire signals. Cavalrymen had ridden out from Plataea to help, but Theban horsemen had stopped these troops and turned them back to their base. Meanwhile, the besiegers, Pelopidas and his crew, had sent messages of their own. As the day wore on and the siege cordon tightened, fresh forces arrived to help the Thebans maintain it—an army from Athens.

Athenians had been of two minds about helping liberate Thebes. They wanted to pay back the help Thebes had lent to their own liberation two decades before, an effort they saw as the "sister" of this one. But they also did not want to risk a clash with Sparta. It's not clear whether they authorized these troops or whether their generals, informed of events in Thebes, took matters into their own hands. However that was, the troops were invaluable now. They crossed the border, where they'd been awaiting a summons, marched into Thebes, and took up siege positions, preparing to assault the Cadmea's walls and offering rich rewards to the first man to break through.

The siege went on for days, perhaps a week. The garrison might have held out had it been made up solely of Spartans, famous for preferring death to defeat. But most of the Cadmea troops were conscripts from Sparta's allies who had no hatred of Thebes. Finally the two Spartan chiefs agreed to withdraw from the region under a truce. Accompanied by a column of their Theban collaborators, they led their forces off the Cadmea and out through the gates of Thebes. The families of those they'd killed or imprisoned stood by as they left; some could not help lashing out in revenge, despite an official promise of safe passage.

A gloomy march took these troops over Cithaeron and onto the Isthmus, their route back to the Peloponnese. At Megara they encountered a Spartan army heading north, led by a young

Spartan king, Cleombrotus, less than a year on the throne and conducting his first known campaign. This force had been sent out a few days before, by Sparta, to break the Cadmea siege and rescue the garrison troops. Relief, these troops now saw, had been one day away when they chose to surrender.

After exchanges of news, each army went on its way, in opposite directions. The garrison troops headed south to the Peloponnese, to face the wrath of the Spartans. Their two commanders, Herippidas and Arcesus, were arrested in nearby Corinth, evidently trying to flee. Cleombrotus meanwhile continued on toward Cithaeron with the relief force. His goal was no longer rescue but reinforcement of Spartan posts in Boeotia, and, if possible, punishment of Thebes. (We'll pick up his trail in the chapter that follows.)

In Sparta, Agesilaus had a cold welcome prepared for the garrison chiefs. Herippidas and Arcesus, whose inaction was held to blame for the loss of Thebes, were tried and executed. No doubt they were hurled into Caeadas chasm, a grim abyss outside Sparta, its floor by this time strewn with human remains. The officer in charge, Lysanoridas, was assessed a fine too great to be paid and went into exile. He'd been off the scene on the solstice night, but the ire of the king demanded that scapegoats be found. It seems that the Spartans took further revenge by killing the man's mother, Xenopeitheia, considered the most beautiful woman in the Peloponnese.

Sparta's anger inspired fear in all who had aided the Thebans. The Athenians quickly took steps to repudiate their involvement. In a move that oddly mirrored the executions at Sparta, they condemned to death the two generals who had led their troops into Thebes. The Athenians' support of the liberation movement had lasted a week, perhaps two, before a total reversal. Thebes would stand alone, without their support, to face future Spartan armies. In time, as we'll see, Thebes would face those of Athens as well.

• • •

27

At Thebes, Pelopidas and his comrades reckoned up their stunning success. They had retaken their city from a Spartan-led army, in a short time, with light losses. Their plot had barely escaped discovery when Archias put aside his urgent letter, yet had succeeded completely. It was, wrote Plutarch in one of his loftiest sentences, "the night when Pelopidas, with no fort, no walls, no citadel, but merely by bringing twelve men home, loosed and struck off the shackles of Laconian power, which had seemed impossible to loosen or break."

A counterblow, however, was surely coming. The new regime turned its attention to defense. One leading member, Gorgidas, stepped forward with a remarkable proposal.

Gorgidas had served as a Theban hipparch, or cavalry commander, before the Spartan takeover and had stayed in Thebes during the occupation. His unyielding spirit had helped inspire the resistance. Though he knew the site of a sacred Theban landmark, the tomb of Dirce—a secret place revealed only to hipparchs at their swearing in—he refused to take the Spartans to it when they wanted to open the tomb to harness its power. As Plutarch reports, the Spartans were so awed by his proud bearing, they did not even try to interrogate him.

Though he'd trained as a cavalryman, Gorgidas knew any struggle with Sparta would be an infantry match. The heavily armed foot soldier, or hoplite, was the Spartans' main combat weapon, honed to a razor edge by rigorous training and drill. Thebes could not compete with that training program, the *agôgê* as it was called, which relied on a huge number of helots, or state-owned slaves. But the Thebans could draw on a strength of their own, state-sponsored male *erôs*.

Just as Gorgidas had sworn his oath of office at Dirce's tomb, so Theban male lovers swore oaths of loyalty at the tomb of Iolaus. Their pledges were sober commitments, made in the presence of a powerful ghost. A pledge of love, Gorgidas reasoned, might support the new Theban state as much as his old pledge of service. Thinking along these lines, he embarked on an experiment. He recruited male couples, three hundred men altogether, and formed them into an infantry corps: the Sacred Band of Thebes.

Thebes housed the Band on the Cadmea, the innermost part of the city, so some called them the City Band. Their upkeep and training were provided at state expense. Initially, Gorgidas served as their captain; later, Pelopidas, whose high spirit fitted him for command, would take over that role and reorganize the Band into new formations. A third Theban leader, Pammenes, contributed to the endeavor and put into words the concept behind the Band: "A squad held together by *erôs* cannot be dispersed or fragmented, since lovers and their beloveds feel shame if they disappoint one another; they stand firm against all dangers on one another's behalf."

Plutarch deploys an equine metaphor to explain the strength of the Band. He notes that, contrary to what one might think, chariots pulled by two-horse teams run faster than single horses. The reason lies in the rivalry of the team. As they run side by side, the chariot horses spur one another's *thumos*—the part of the soul that seeks honor, victory, and glory. *Thumos*, Plutarch claimed, could be spurred in paired soldiers as well as paired horses. When that happened, both men became braver and fiercer than either would be on his own.

The Sacred Band of Thebes was formed in the wake of the solstice plot and drew on energies unleashed by that liberation. It posed a distinctively Theban answer to Spartan values: instead of machtpolitik and the cult of the state, the Band relied on a native tradition, the view of male *erôs* as a long-lasting, privileged bond. The Band was built to defend a new government, run by young men who'd succeeded against all odds but who knew that those odds were still against them. Its strength would be tested, and soon, against Sparta, the sternest test any army could face.

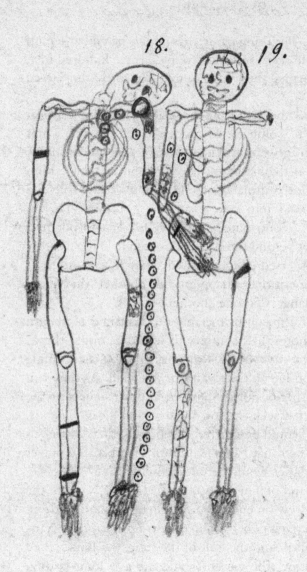

18.   19.

CHAPTER 2

Boeotia Rising

(378–375 BC, plus background 400–382 BC)

At the center of ancient Boeotia stood an enormous lake, Lake Copais, supposedly created by the god Heracles. From it came two products for which Boeotia was famous: a species of eel the Greeks found delicious, and a variety of reed that, when cut into strips and treated, gave to the aulos, a sort of double-chambered oboe, its finest musical tone. But the lake also made the surrounding air heavy and humid, and this was thought to affect the brains of Boeotians. Other Greeks found them slow or blockheaded and sometimes spoke with contempt of "Boeotian swine."

The Athenians, known for their quickness of wit, were especially harsh on this score. Even the orator Demosthenes, generally well disposed toward the Thebans, nonetheless calls them *anaisthêtoi*, lacking in perception or insight, and *bareis*, literally "heavy," overbearing in a sluggish sort of way. Plato lampoons them for lacking fine words, though he also puts two Thebans, Simmias and Cebes, into a dialogue with Socrates about the immortality of the soul (the *Phaedo*). The comic playwrights spoofed the Boeotians for eating too much and thinking too little, and called them *kroupezophoroi*, "clog wearers," a hit on their rustic wooden shoes, designed for crushing olives to render oil.

The dialect of Greek spoken by Boeotians did not help their image, especially in Athens. They used broad, flat *ah* sounds, giving an effect perhaps like that of a Scots brogue, where

31

Athenians said *ee*. (Thus Theban personal names often end in -*das*, Pelopidas, where Athenians bear the more familiar -*deez*, Euripides.) The quaint way that Thebans exclaimed "God knows," *ittô Zeus*, was widely mocked as a mark of rusticity, as was their habit of swearing by Heracles or Iolaus—local heroes, as we've seen—rather than by more refined deities.

The torpid air of Boeotia was thought to block the intellect but also to promote strength of body, stolidity, steadiness. "Thick and strong," said a Roman, Cicero, of the Boeotians (where "thick" means both stout and mentally slow)—not a bad combination in infantry warfare, the primary means by which cities of Hellas competed. "They had more strength than cleverness," wrote Cornelius Nepos, who composed short biographical sketches of great Greek leaders. The most extensive comment of this kind came from Ephorus, a Greek historian whose works are now lost. In his eyes the Boeotians lacked *paideia*, higher learning, and *logoi*—a complex word encompassing speech, thought, and literary style. Without these intellectual assets, he said, it was hard for the Thebans to lead the high-minded Greeks.

Thebans were not the only objects of such disdain. The Spartans too were lampooned, especially at Athens, for slow minds, clumsy speech, and rustic dialect. But Spartans were also known for moral rigor, thanks to their iron control of their citizens' lives. Their ascetic law code banned private pleasures and enlisted all males into full-time military service. Thebans, by contrast, enjoyed their feasts and dinner parties, and, as we've seen, their male-male love affairs. They had no year-round boot camps, no *agôgê*, to astonish other Greeks with the strength of the cult of the state.

Thebes was stained by one further dishonor in the eyes of the Hellenes. During Greece's great early crisis, an invasion by Persian forces in 480 BC, the Thebans, alone of the major Greek states, had gone over to the invader. Partly this was due to geography, which left Thebes more vulnerable than states farther south, and partly to the self-interest of its governing clique, who foresaw a prosperous future under Persian rule. The larger population, the *dêmos*, demurred for a time, until the location of the city—right in the line of the Persian advance—made resistance impossible. Thebes fought *for* the Persians, *against* their fellow Greeks, in the crucial land battle that drove the Persians out—the Battle of Plataea, fought on Boeotian soil.

The shame of *medism*, collaboration with "Medes," or Persians,* lay heavy on Thebes. In the aftermath of the final battle, Athens and Sparta wanted the Thebans punished for this policy choice. A combined Greek army surrounded Thebes and besieged it for twenty days, ravaging fields and assaulting the walls. Finally the wealthy men who had forged the Persian alliance surrendered themselves. They counted on their money to protect them from retribution, but a Spartan commander had other plans. He whisked them away to Corinth and had them swiftly and stealthily killed.

Weighed down by Greek prejudice, Thebes had always been a second-rate power, compared with wealthy, literate Athens and iron-discipline Sparta. As these two states vied for supremacy throughout the fifth century BC, Thebes stayed in the background and even endured, in the middle of that century, a decade of subjection by Athens. But as it emerged from that decade—long before the worse humiliation we've witnessed, the occupation by Sparta—Thebes found its own, distinct path toward strength and social progress. It devised the first federal state on European soil: the Boeotian League.

Boeotia contained many poleis, or city-states, each separately governed, but sharing an ethnic identity and common strategic concerns. A union of these poleis, the Thebans saw,

---

* Though the peoples they denoted were distinct, *Mede* and *Persian* were synonymous terms to most Greeks. History teachers enjoy punningly telling their students that "one man's Mede is another man's Persian."

would benefit all, especially the city that led them—Thebes. Guided by unknown statesmen, the Thebans forged Boeotia into a league, an ethnically based superstate that transcended the bounds of the polis. Member cities still governed themselves within their own walls, but came together—in Thebes, of course—to form a larger whole, and, what was important, a far larger army.

The structure of the League is understood today thanks to a lucky papyrus find. Seven administrative regions each chose a representative, a boeotarch, to serve on a governing board; Thebes itself chose four, giving it a large, but not a majority, stake. This board met at Thebes, as did a council, to which each region sent sixty councilors. Thebes also hosted meetings of an assembly, at which debates could be held and votes taken. A common currency was adopted by all members, stamped *BO, BOI,* or *BOIΩ* (for "Boeotia") in place of individual city names. Military levies were apportioned evenly, and in round numbers: a thousand heavy infantry and a hundred cavalry from each sector, plus twice that number from Thebes. That made for an army of nearly ten thousand, impressive by Greek standards.

A federation of this kind was so new to the Greeks that they as yet had no word to describe it. For lack of a better term it was called a *koinon,* a "common thing"; later, Greek writers devised a new term, *synteleia*—roughly, "collection of contributions." It was neither a tributary empire, such as Athens had built, nor a hegemony like Sparta's vise grip on its peninsula, the Peloponnese. It emphasized common interests rather than hierarchy; it privileged shared ethnicity—Boeotianness—over city-state affiliation. That ranking, as we shall see, was not always shared by its members.

The strength of the Boeotian League counterweighted the weakness of Thebes in culture, learning, and language. Sparta and Athens gradually came to see the League as a threat, as its cohesion grew over the late fifth century. Ultimately these cities sought, through legal or military means, to nullify the League. Its existence would become a crucial point of debate when the mainland Greeks began, in the fourth century BC, to craft a universal treaty framework—in their terms, a Common Peace.

The new leaders of Thebes, Epaminondas and Pelopidas, would one day head diplomatic teams attending the Common Peace conclaves. Each would in turn defend the League, in speeches that thrilled those who heard them. Through their *logoi*—words, arguments, higher reason—these Thebans would prove, as we'll see, that Boeotians, despite their thick air, were more than mere swine.

The Spartan relief force that entered Boeotia, just after the Cadmea fell, was behaving strangely. It made no assault on Thebes, but wandered vaguely about the rest of the region, doing little. Its sole engagement was with a squad of 150 Thebans it met near Plataea, the same men who'd been sprung from prison the night of the solstice plot. This squad the Spartans entirely destroyed. Those Thebans had tasted freedom for just a few days, then gave their lives to defend it.

The Spartans in the relief force were grumbling about their commander (as one of them later reported to Xenophon). King Cleombrotus was new to the Spartan throne, having succeeded a brother who died of illness the previous year, and he seemed oddly lacking in initiative. How differently things might be going, the troops must have thought, if their other monarch, Agesilaus, had been in command. Under Sparta's unique constitution, two kings reigned at the same time, so the shortcomings of the weaker always stood out when compared with the stronger. In this case, Cleombrotus seemed so passive that the men wondered whether they were even at war with Thebes.

Cleombrotus was far younger than Agesilaus, more than young enough to be his son. He'd grown up in the shadow of the senior monarch, watching as his mild-mannered brother, who then reigned, got wheedled, cajoled, and strong-armed. Agesilaus had deftly neutralized this young man, diverting his interests toward love affairs instead of affairs of state. "Knowing that he was captive to matters of *erôs*, Agesilaus was always talking with him about youths who were then in their bloom," Plutarch reports. Now that Cleombrotus had taken his brother's place, it was *his* turn to deal with the older man's manipulations.

After sixteen aimless days Cleombrotus led the troops homeward, but the march proved a difficult one. As they went through a high pass between mountains and sea, a violent wind swept down from the ridge above them. Some pack animals were blown right off the cliff and into the water. The men could not hold on to their shields and had to leave them behind on the ground, weighted down with stones. They retrieved them the next day, but the episode had an uncanny feeling. It was as though the gods themselves were forcing the Spartans to put down their shields.

Back in Sparta, Agesilaus could not have been pleased by the outcome of this expedition. Yet he'd declined to lead it himself, for unclear reasons. He'd just reached sixty and claimed he'd aged out of service, but even Xenophon, his former lieutenant and tireless admirer, knew he was lying. Perhaps, as Xenophon claims, he feared political backlash from Sparta's campaigns in Boeotia. For not all Spartans, and certainly not all their allies, believed in his war against Thebes, a war that had come to seem, increasingly, like a vendetta.

How had this one man become so incensed against this one city, so much as to alarm his fellow Spartans? The answers lie deep in the fabric of who Agesilaus was, and how relations between Thebes and Sparta had broken down during his reign. A look back in time, to the start of that reign—twenty-one years before the time of the solstice plot—will help us extract them.

400 BC

Few in Sparta expected Agesilaus to become their king. He was short and lame in one leg, huge drawbacks for a monarch, and he was not in the line of succession, which passed through his brother, King Agis. But the Spartans had doubts about Agis's only son. Agis's wife, Timaea, had engaged in a notorious affair with an Athenian turncoat during the great Spartan-Athenian War (or as it's now known, the Peloponnesian War). It appeared that her son might not be the offspring of Agis. Or so, at least, Agesilaus could claim.

The Peloponnesian War had ended four years earlier, and Sparta had won. After decades of Spartan-Athenian struggle, a single superpower had emerged, and a single political system—rule by the *beltistoi* (best men), the rightist rich whom Sparta supported, and not by the *dêmos*, the masses, favored by Athens. As one of the results of the war, Sparta had gained a navy and Athens had lost one, so Greek cities in the Aegean, even on the west coast of Turkey, came under the sway of Sparta for the first time. Sparta's power expanded as never before. Pro-Spartan regimes were installed throughout the Aegean, led by small boards of *beltistoi*; one of these took power in Athens itself, though it was soon ousted, as we've seen, by Athenian exiles operating from Thebes.

Not all Spartans favored this postwar expansion, which relied on ships, money, and garrison forts—the tools of imperialism—rather than Sparta's traditional strength, the courage of infantrymen. A move overseas, these men thought, would erode Spartan values. Others, however, foresaw Spartan power going global, with outposts in Asia along with new strongholds in Europe. In time it might even challenge the Great King of Persia, Artaxerxes, as Greeks of old had once challenged Priam of Troy. A Spartan-led army had shown the way to that goal, in 401 BC, by defeating the Persians on their own turf (the episode of "the Ten Thousand," soon to be more fully discussed).

Agesilaus belonged to this expansionist faction, as did Lysander, his *erastês*, or older male lover.* The two had formed a typically Spartan male bond, part love affair, part political alliance, starting when Agesilaus was in his teens and Lysander in his twenties. Lysander went on to become a swashbuckling admiral, the hero of the war against Athens and the architect of Sparta's Aegean empire. Agesilaus became his apprentice and protégé, perhaps continuing as his *erômenos*, or beloved, as well.

Not only Sparta's conservative faction balked at the city's expansion; old allies were also disturbed. Foremost among these was Thebes, the head of the Boeotian League. In the Peloponnesian War, Thebes had fought by Sparta's side against Athens and had been well rewarded, but now, in the postwar years, Theban allegiance was wavering. The Atticists of Thebes, as we've seen, were gaining strength, in part from dislike of how fast Spartan power was growing. Lysander and Agesilaus, in some Thebans' eyes, stood for an arrogant Sparta, the bully of Hellas; Athens now looked like a valuable counterweight. Ismenias, leader of these pro-Athenian Thebans, defied Spartan orders by helping Athenian exiles reclaim their city—a defiance for which, as we've seen, he paid with his life.

The limits of Spartan power were still under debate when King Agis became ill and died. His son should have taken his place, but Lysander stepped in and stirred up old doubts about the boy's parentage. He urged that Agesilaus be made king instead. Many opposed this move; some pointed to an oracle warning against "a lame king" who would bring down on Sparta "a wave of man-destroying war." Lysander countered that Agis's son fit the prophecy too: with one Spartan parent and one (as it seemed) Athenian, he was "lame" or limping in

---

* The Spartans, uniquely, used the term *eispnêlas*, "inspirer," in place of *erastês*.

his lineage. Backed by Lysander, Agesilaus, in his midforties, ascended the empty throne.

By this time, the future leaders of Thebes—among them the high-spirited Pelopidas and the high-minded Epaminondas, and others who would take part in the solstice plot—had reached their late teens or twenties, the age of idealism and independence. They'd grown up under fathers who truckled to Sparta, but their own path was bending toward Athens and its democracy. The rise of Agesilaus in Sparta accelerated that turn. A generation older than they, determined to enforce Sparta's will on all Greece, this lame king cut a patriarchal figure, ideal for rebelling against. Yet strangely, within the next fifteen years, they'd find themselves fighting *for* him.

At the Olympic Games of 396 BC, the first since Agesilaus had taken the throne, the collective Greek world got a glimpse of the new order of things. The king's sister, Cynisca, entered the winning team in that year's chariot race—the first time a woman had won this high-profile event. A statue of Cynisca was set up at Olympia, with a verse inscription on its base, known from literary sources, that asserted proudly, "I am the only woman in all of Greece to take home this crown." Both the win and the statue helped amplify the power of Agesilaus, who seems to have put her up to competing in the race. In 1879 this stone block, no longer bearing its statue, was discovered at Olympia, with a portion of Cynisca's boast still legible on it.

395 BC

In his first major action as king, Agesilaus made ready to sail for the eastern Aegean. Sparta was deeply engaged there, fighting the satraps (provincial heads) of the Persian empire. Greek cities along the Turkish coast, subjects of Persian rule, had called for Sparta to free them from these oppressors. With his political muscle, Lysander got the as-yet-untested Agesilaus assigned to lead a fresh army there and also arranged his own appointment as one of thirty royal attendants. Recruits were summoned from all over Greece; eight thousand assembled. The Thebans, however, refused to take part, as did the Athenians.

As the ships and men were gathering for transport east, Agesilaus and his thirty attendants put in at Aulis, a port on the coast of Boeotia. He was trespassing there, perhaps in an effort to show the Thebans he could. His larger purpose, though, concerned the symbolic importance of Aulis, the harbor from which, according to myth, King Agamemnon had sailed at the start of the Trojan War. Agesilaus prepared a ritual sacrifice in a temple there, in imitation of his mythic forerunner. His message was clear, and grandiose: This war on Persia was the new Trojan War. He was the new Agamemnon, the lord of all Greece.

From a distance of an hour's ride to the west, the leaders of Thebes noted, with dismay, the arrival of this brazen king. He'd breached their sovereignty, and his planned sacrifice contained a further insult, for only Boeotian priests could conduct such a rite at that shrine. They moved to prevent the transgression. A cavalry squad rode out to Aulis from Thebes, arriving to find smoke already rising from the burning sacrifice. Before the eyes of the horrified Spartans, the squad threw the bones and fat off the altar and onto the ground. Agesilaus sailed off in a rage, his glorious gesture dashed and turned to humiliation. He headed to Asia without the blessing of Aulis's gods.

This incident at Aulis ignited the hate that later drove Agesilaus to make war on Thebes. The affront it dealt was deeply personal, directed not at the Spartan state but at its grasping king (and perhaps at Lysander as well, for he must have been there, as part of the royal contingent). It cast a pall on Sparta's Asia campaign, so when that campaign later failed, the blame seemed to lie with Thebes. The Thebans too believed that the incident had done real damage. They spoke of it thirty years later in a diplomatic parley, according to Xenophon, when demonstrating the ways that they'd hindered the Spartans.

The new antipathy between Thebes and Sparta was noted in far-off Susa, in what's now Iran, in the heart of the Persian empire. The Great King who ruled there, Artaxerxes Mnêmon,* had no wish to fight the Spartans invading his coast, having nearly lost his throne to them once before. He much preferred to set Greeks fighting each other, a time-honored Persian stratagem. As Agesilaus began boring into his western flank, Artaxerxes sent agents to Thebes and Athens, dispensing money to those who would foment war. His funds found their way into many Greek hands, including those of Theban Ismenias, already looking for ways to thwart the Spartans.

Meanwhile Agesilaus was managing the Asian campaign well enough, but his former (or perhaps current) lover, Lysander, proved harder to manage. The role of kingmaker and royal attendant did not suit Lysander; he sought to become king himself, as was learned in papers discovered after his death. The Greeks of the Turkish coast were already treating him like a king, for he'd been sole commander on his previous tours there. Agesilaus, newly installed in rule, could not tolerate this rivalry. He stripped Lysander of rank and made him a royal meat-carver, so that all who attended camp meals would observe the abasement. Finally he sent Lysander home to Sparta and carried on with the war.

Back in Greece, the Thebans had stirred up new conflicts with Sparta, perhaps with the help of persuasive Persian gold. Lysander, returned from the East, was eager to teach the upstart Thebans a lesson and persuaded the Spartans to send him into Boeotia with an army. He marched down from the north and planned to link up, at the city of Haliartus, with a sec-

---

* To us, Artaxerxes II. The Greeks used epithets, rather than numbers, to distinguish kings of the same name.

ond Spartan force arriving from the south. But the Thebans intercepted his message arranging the rendezvous. Knowing his plans, they laid a trap at Haliartus and killed Lysander in a sudden assault. Here was a second spur to Agesilaus's hatred.

Two other major Greek cities, Athens and Corinth, had by this time allied with Thebes to form an anti-Spartan coalition. (That Corinth was willing to join—a state that usually toed the Spartan line—shows how far Spartan overreach had gone.) Just as the Persians had sought, the Greek world was riven by war—the Corinthian War, it's now called (though one ancient writer termed it the Boeotian War, since it began there).

The Spartans found they could not fight three combatants at once with so many men overseas. They sent a dispatch to Asia to recall Agesilaus and his army. The campaign against the Great King would have to be called off.

Agesilaus was making slow progress in Asia when word of the recall arrived. His dreams of a new Trojan War had once again been dashed, and again, as he saw it, by Thebes. He headed for home, by a land route, since the fleet that had brought him east had dispersed. That route took him straight through Boeotia, and gave him a chance for revenge.

394 BC

The Thebans, Agesilaus knew, would oppose his homeward passage, meaning a fight would result. And so it turned out, at a place called Coronea, where the Spartans had to pass through a narrow defile at the shore of Lake Copais. The Boeotians arrayed themselves to block off the defile, and the Spartans deployed to engage them. Xenophon, who was on the scene and in arms that day, gives a vivid account of the battle and claims, without explanation, it was "like no other of my time."

Both sides, following age-old conventions, placed their

strongest units on the right of their lines. Thus Spartans and Thebans, each on their own right wing, did not face one another but the allies that filled out their coalitions. The two lines clashed, and both right wings prevailed; the Spartans punched through their opponents, who ran rather than face them, but on the opposite wing, the Thebans also broke through. They reached Agesilaus's baggage train, in the rear of his line, and started plundering his Asian spoils.

Agesilaus was donning a wreath of victory when word came to him that the battle was not done. He ordered the Spartans to turn to the rear and re-form, and the Thebans did likewise. Each side ended up facing opposite its initial position. With their allies out of the fray, Thebes and Sparta confronted one another at last.

The Thebans now had the lake to their backs and needed a breakout. The obvious move for Sparta was to part ranks and let them pass through, then attack their flanks and rear as they did so. Agesilaus would that way be guaranteed a modest number of kills. But he still simmered with rage over his profaned sacrifice, perhaps too over the death of Lysander, and certainly over being here in Boeotia at all, instead of on his glorious Asian campaign. He wanted a mortal blow. He kept his ranks closed and advanced.

The struggle became fierce as the Thebans refused to give ground. "There was no uproar, and no silence either, but that certain type of noise that results from anger and battle," Xenophon memorably reports. "Clashing shield on shield, they were shoving, fighting, killing, dying." Agesilaus was carried out of the fray, badly wounded. Finally the Spartans parted ranks, as they'd earlier declined to do. The Thebans dashed through their midst, and the battle ended.

On the following morning, Xenophon surveyed the corpses, including *three hundred* Spartans—a huge casualty figure. "One could see the ground stained red with blood, the bodies of friend and foe lying side by side, splintered shields, shattered spears, and daggers bared of their sheaths, some on the ground, others stuck in the flesh, still others still gripped in men's hands." Sparta put up a trophy on the battlefield, a formal declaration of victory. But in truth the results had been mixed.

Recovering from his wounds, and wary of further engagements, Agesilaus withdrew and took ship for home, instead of proceeding by land. His first clash with the Boeotian League had not gone at all as he'd planned. His anger was unappeased. He still needed revenge.

387 BC

Did Pelopidas and Epaminondas fight at Coronea, where Thebes showed it could withstand a Spartan assault? By now they were likely in their twenties and old enough for war, though their birth dates, and early history, are unknown. The first glimpse we have of them is in a different battle, some ten years after Coronea, and six years before their solstice plot helped liberate Thebes. Surprisingly, though, they were then fighting *for* the Spartans. Thebes was subject by then to the terms of a path-breaking treaty, a pact Agesilaus had forced it to sign: the King's Peace.

This was a first try at a Common Peace, a treaty framework embracing all mainland states. By the 380s BC, the Greeks were aware that they needed such a pact. The Corinthian War had dragged on for seven years indecisively, and the earlier Peloponnesian War had lasted four times as long. Constant fighting wrecked economies, destroyed livelihoods, and created a class of soldiers for hire who profited from conflict. Unwilling to trust one another, the Greeks were ready to let an outsider save them from themselves, even a lofty monarch in far-off Persia.

The Great King, Artaxerxes, had paid the Greeks to fight one another, but in the long run, such wars were not in his interest. They soaked up skilled military manpower, making it harder for *him* to hire Greek soldiers. As he and all his fellow rulers had learned, heavily armed hoplites, fighting in phalanx formation, could defeat any other infantry, and even most cavalries, since horses would shy from their spears. But this precious Greek export became scarce when demand increased. Only when Greece was at peace could the King* count on getting his share.

Working with a Spartan diplomat named Antalcidas, Artaxerxes devised a remarkable document, a blueprint for Common Peace in mainland Greece. The scroll was opened before an assemblage of envoys, in 387, and its terms read aloud. Hostilities would cease and armies return to their borders. In future, all states would have the right to autonomy—noncoercion, the freedom to choose their own path. This principle was guaranteed by Artaxerxes himself, who vowed to send ships and use money against all transgressors. So he *said*, but in practice, everyone knew he was too far away to police mainland Hellas. A local enforcer was needed, and that was where Sparta came in.

The conference to sign the King's Peace was held at Sparta, with Agesilaus presiding. Both the venue and host sent a message to all: the Spartans, who had helped draft the treaty, would act as Persia's Greek partner. Sparta would now have the right to break up the leagues of its rivals, above all—and this, for Sparta, was crucial—the Boeotian League. "Autonomy" might, in the hands of Agesilaus, become a club with which to smash this Theban-led superstate. He'd at last get revenge for the slapdown at Aulis, nearly a decade in the past but hardly forgotten.

Sparta's strategy became clear at the conference itself. The Thebans declared they would sign for all the Boeotians, a

* When capitalized, "King" refers to the Persian Great King (a standard convention).

A portion of the pact by which Thebes allied with Athens in the 390s. This Athenian copy, like its twin at Thebes, was broken in pieces when the pact was later abrogated.

privilege they claimed as long-standing head of the League. Agesilaus refused to permit this. Insisting that each state sign on its own behalf, he sent the ambassadors back to Thebes to seek new instructions. Then, as though pouncing on a long-awaited pretext, he mustered an army of invasion and began to march north, toward Thebes. He'd reached Tegea, on his way to the Isthmus of Corinth, when he met the returning Theban envoys, who'd come to offer submission to his will. Though it meant giving up their League, the Thebans backed down. They signed the King's Peace as Thebans only, allowing other Boeotian states to sign in their own names too.

At Thebes, this humiliation brought a swift political reversal. Ismenias and his Atticist party fell into disfavor; the Laconists, supported by Sparta, gained control of affairs. The Thebans repudiated their defense pact with Athens, signed eight years before "for all time"; they overturned and smashed the stone on which it was inscribed (a standard Greek signal of foreign policy shifts). Their newly pro-Spartan government agreed to defend the King's Peace and uphold "autonomy"—that hallowed word, now merely code for Spartan machtpolitik. And so Theban soldiers, among them Epaminondas and Pelopidas, set off for the Peloponnese to fight for Agesilaus.

385–382 BC

The target was Mantinea, a recalcitrant neighbor of Sparta's. Protected by its thick curtain wall, Mantinea had long leaned democratic and had allied with Sparta's foes. Worse, it had injured Agesilaus's pride. Some ten years before, when a Spartan force had been thrashed and the king was leading it homeward, Mantineans had stood atop their walls to mock the defeated men as they marched past. Agesilaus was forced to travel at night, in the dark, to avoid being laughed at. Now, empowered by the King's Peace, he struck back. He demanded the Mantineans pull down their wall. They refused to comply, and the Spartans went into action.

The Spartans held the right wing in this battle, as they always did. Epaminondas the thinker and Pelopidas the fighter, along with the other "allies," were posted on the left, where they faced the enemy's right—the strongest troops the Mantineans could field. Such weaker left wings were prone to collapse when phalanxes collided, and so it turned out in this case. The two Theban youths, standing side by side, watched as their comrades turned and ran for safety, leaving them stranded and exposed. There was little to do but lock shields together and fight it out.

The two men were now surrounded by Mantineans, who

jabbed at them with spears and slashed with swords. Pelopidas received seven wounds and began to succumb, sinking down onto the pile of corpses mounting up by his feet. Epaminondas took a spear thrust to his chest and was cut by a sword on his arm, but, strengthened perhaps by the lessons of his Pythagorean master, refused to give ground. He stood over Pelopidas, protecting his fallen comrade, and fended off the attackers. Then suddenly, the Spartans were at hand, driving off the Mantineans. They had won on the right, then moved leftward to "roll up the line," in time to save the beleaguered Thebans.

The rest of the campaign is recorded by Xenophon in *Hellenica*. The Mantineans took refuge behind their stout walls. But the Spartan commander had his troops dig a channel and divert a nearby river, such that its waters swirled around those walls. Made of mud bricks, these melted away at the base and the structure toppled. The Mantineans surrendered and suffered a *dioikismos*, "division of habitation." Their populace was driven out and dispersed to unwalled towns spaced widely apart. Without fortifications, they'd never again laugh at Sparta.

A harsh resolution—too harsh for many at Thebes. Such strong-arm measures made a mockery of the King's Peace, the document under which Sparta claimed to be acting. It seemed clear now the Peace was a pretext for further expansion of Spartan power. When Epaminondas and Pelopidas returned to Thebes, they found a second reversal underway: Ismenias was back in control of policy, again aligning with Athens to counter Sparta. The Sparto-Theban entente had lasted for just one campaign. No such rapprochement was ever again attempted.

The next time Sparta requested troops to enforce the Peace, three years later, the Thebans refused to take part. That drew the Spartan riposte we have already witnessed: the seizure of the Cadmea by Phoibidas, and the execution of Ismenias. Our look back in time has brought us back around to the starting point of our tale.

379 BC

The Cadmea seizure marked the high-water line of Sparta's fortunes, as Xenophon, in *Hellenica*, recognized. "Sparta's rule was well and securely established," he says, in large part because "the Thebans and other Boeotians were completely in their power." Officially, the Boeotian League was dissolved by the terms of the King's Peace. But then, when Pelopidas and his commandos won back the Cadmea, the tide of history turned.

The men of '79, masterminds of the solstice plot, took the title of boeotarch when elected to leadership posts, a signal of what they intended: to restore the Boeotian League. They began looking for ways to liberate neighboring towns, such as Thespiae and Plataea, where Sparta had installed garrison troops and puppet regimes. Piece by piece, over the next six years, the League would gradually be reassembled.

Athens began reasserting itself at just the same time. Perhaps emboldened by the Cadmea liberation—an effort that it had aided—Athenians began to rebuild their Aegean naval alliance, a power base that meant as much to them as the League did to Thebes. But they kept to the terms of the King's Peace, unwilling to risk an open break with the Spartans. They would only recruit, not coerce, the states of the Aegean, so as not to violate the autonomy clause.

With Sparta and Thebes now at war, Athens hoped to stay neutral and alienate neither side. Much better to keep to the sea and let her two rivals fight for control of the land. Then, something happened that changed that plan—something no one expected and no one, from that day to this, has understood.

Thespiae, near Thebes, was the main Spartan base in Boeotia, headed by Sphodrias, a harmost, or garrison chief. On an evening in spring 378, this man gave his troops an early dinner, then led them, as night fell, toward Athens, more than forty miles away. It was later claimed he meant to destroy the dockyards in Piraeus, the harbor of Athens, but the distance was too great for even an all-night march. Daybreak revealed the squadron crossing the Thriasian Plain, on Attic soil, still far from their target.

As alarms went up all over the countryside, the Spartan force halted, seized some trivial plunder, reversed course, and returned to Thespiae. It had done little harm, except to the fabric of the King's Peace, and to Athenians' peace of mind. Piraeus was the seat of their naval power. Had Sphodrias succeeded in his presumptive plan, their Aegean ambitions would have been quashed.

What prompted Sphodrias to mount such a harebrained march? The Greeks were vexed by the question. Athenians at first thought he'd acted on Sparta's orders and they arrested two Spartan ambassadors then in Athens. But these men pointed out they would never have been there, in the arms of their foe, had they known the attack was coming. Others believed that Sphodrias had simply gone rogue, but Spartans, with their hidebound chain of command, hardly ever did that. Still others, including Xenophon, thought the *Thebans* had urged Sphodrias on, seeking to drive a wedge between Athens and Sparta. The whole affair was a mystery and has remained so.

Everyone waited to see how a Spartan court would deal with this breach of the Peace. In a previous trial, as we've seen, Agesilaus outraged the Greeks, including many at Sparta, by getting Phoibidas, captor of the Cadmea, let off with a meaningless fine. Now the king intervened once again, with a new form of statist logic. "Sparta needs such soldiers," Agesilaus declared, referring to the distinguished career of the errant Sphodrias. To the horror of Hellas, the court acquitted the man and returned him to active duty. "To many," Xenophon concedes, "this seemed the most unjust legal decision ever taken at Sparta." (He goes on to give Agesilaus a tender motive for his perversion of justice: the king was obliging his heartbroken son, Archidamus, who was in love with the son of Sphodrias.)

More than ever, Sparta stood revealed as a tyrant city, and its hallowed treaty, the King's Peace, as a cloak for imperial designs. Thebes and Athens drew closer together than ever. Thebes joined the Athenian alliance,* and its name was inscribed on the so-called Decree of Aristoteles, a kind of alliance charter. The name ΘHBAIOI on the stone proclaimed, for all to see, the restored partnership. Thebes and Athens, the Greek world's leading democracies, were on the same side once again.

How much this partnership benefited Thebes was seen that very spring. Athens sent to Boeotia a precious military asset: its general Chabrias, a man of great skill and daring, the first of a new breed of Greek condottiere. The twists and turns of this man's career reveal his own complexities as well as those of the new age, the age of the Sacred Band.

In the past, Athenian leaders had been both public speakers and soldiers, combining the roles of general and politician. In the days of Chabrias, those paths had begun to diverge. While Athens had been at war, it elected Chabrias to the office of *stratêgos*, one of ten military commanders, many years in a row. But when the King's Peace was signed, Athens had little use for his talents. With no political role to fall back on, Chabrias went to Egypt, with a crew of experienced troops, to fight, for pay, for the pharaoh Acoris. So valuable were these Athenian soldiers in the Egyptian theater that Acoris had coin dies imported from Athens to pay them in their native currency. His goal was to gain independence for Egypt from Persia.

Money and warfare made a natural combination for Chabrias. He was famous in Athens for his extravagant lifestyle, for his wastrel son Ctesippus, and for his devil-may-care indiffer-

---

* If it was not already a member. The precise chronological sequence is a matter of debate.

ence to public opinion. Once when he and another commander had been put on trial for treason, Chabrias was seen leaving the court each day to visit the gymnasium and eat lunch. His co-defendant warned him that this might look bad to the jurors. Chabrias replied that Athens was likely to convict them both, but at least *he'd* go to his death well exercised and well fed. In the end, both men were acquitted.

After five or six years, Chabrias reached the end of his lucrative Egyptian employment. The pharaoh, his paymaster, had been fighting for freedom from Persia; when the Persian Great King saw an *Athenian* campaigning against him, he invoked the King's Peace and forced Athens to issue a recall. So Chabrias, now in his forties, returned to Athens and to government service. He was again elected *stratêgos*, in the very year that Athens remade its alliance with Thebes. The Athenians sent him, along with five thousand troops, to help defend Boeotia against the Spartans. He'd one day return to Egypt, after several more twists of his soldier-of-fortune career.

The Spartans marched into Boeotia that spring with massive force: an army of nearly twenty thousand, far more than Thebes could muster against them. At their head, this time, was Agesilaus, now seeking revenge in his own person rather than by proxy, nearly twenty years after the incident at Aulis. If he couldn't take Thebes by assault, he might at least starve it into submission by destroying its rich farmlands. With no way to import food, Thebes would have to surrender, turn over the leaders of its revolution, and come back to the Spartan fold. Or so Agesilaus hoped.

But Chabrias and the Thebans had prepared for this onslaught. They'd built an enormous stockade of brushwood and pointed sticks, fronted by a ditch, to protect precious croplands. It stretched for over ten miles, punctuated by exit ports for cavalry sallies. Stockades of this kind had been built before, to surround army camps, but never on this scale, to fence off an entire region. The Theban-Athenian army, including the Sacred Band, went forth to defend it, while Agesilaus advanced.

For a long time there was no contact between the armies, only an edgy stalking back and forth. Both sides watched one another across the fence. The Thebans were first to cross the stockade to engage. The attack was launched at evening, while Spartan forces were occupied with preparing dinner and pitching camp. A Theban cavalry corps dashed out through one of the sally ports and charged a body of men who were moving back from the fence to retire for the night. Two Spartans were cut down, along with several Thebans, Laconists driven out the previous year, now fighting on Sparta's side.

Agesilaus, far ahead with the main body of troops, learned of the attack and turned back to meet it. The Theban horsemen retreated but then paused, hoping to make a spear cast before recrossing the fence. As the Spartans approached, these men stood their ground—"like men who have drunk too much at midday," wrote Xenophon, implying they were not patient but frozen with fear. Whether or not that was true, they misjudged their timing. After casting their spears, all of which fell short, they turned and fled, but their Spartan pursuers, now at full gallop, caught up and cut them down. The stalemate resumed.

At last Agesilaus achieved a breakout. The Thebans, he noted, always took breakfast behind the lines before coming out to the fence. So he brought up his own troops at dawn and got the jump on them. He made a move toward a point in the fence, and the Thebans, disturbed by this sudden onrush, dashed to defend it, abandoning other guard posts in their haste. That was what Agesilaus expected. He signaled a unit to peel off from the rear and seize one of the abandoned posts. In a moment, the Theban stockade had been punctured, and Agesilaus was leading his men into the rich farmlands of Boeotia.

The generals leading the Theban-Athenian force—from Athens, swashbuckling Chabrias, and Gorgidas from Thebes, creator and now commander of the Sacred Band—fell back to a nearby hill. From there they could launch attacks on "ravagers," Spartan contingents sent out to destroy cropland. They were not strong enough to meet the Spartans on flat ground, but they hoped, from this perch, to limit agricultural damage. Agesilaus, for his part, could not accomplish his mission while threatened by raids and harassments; he had to dislodge that force. He ordered his twenty thousand to form up for battle and move up the hill.

Atop the ridge, the defenders beheld a sight that often inspired terror: a fast-approaching wall of red-cloaked troops, each bearing a shield with a red Λ—lambda for "Lacedaemonian," the mark of the Spartan-trained soldier. "A solid mass of scarlet and bronze"—that was Xenophon's description of Agesilaus's phalanx. But Chabrias, who'd fought Spartans before, was not intimidated. At his signal, the Thebans and Athenians dropped shields to the ground and rested the edges against the tops of their knees. This collective "at ease" stance—planned and practiced beforehand—declared they were certain they would not need to engage. They were calling the Spartans' bluff. Agesilaus broke off his advance and returned to the plain below.

No fighting had taken place, yet this episode was later hailed as Chabrias's greatest exploit. When Athens commissioned a statue and asked him his preference, Chabrias chose to be portrayed in this moment of insouciance. The statue, now lost except for fragments of its base, depicted Chabrias with his shield propped casually against one knee.

Agesilaus accomplished little on that first march into Boeotia. A second one, the following year, was also largely a failure. His allies, the Peloponnesian troops that made up the bulk of his army, began to get restive. They muttered about leaving farms and homes to serve in *Sparta*'s wars. That had always been true, but they saw less point in fighting Thebes than they had in other campaigns.

A reconstruction of Chabrias's memorial statue in Athens (based on the work of John Buckler). The base has survived, with carved victory wreaths and inscriptions naming the allies and fellow soldiers who contributed funding.

Back in Sparta, officials doubted the wisdom of Agesilaus's crusade. When the king showed a wound he'd received in Boeotia, Antalcidas, the diplomat who'd helped draft the Peace, shook his head. "That's a nice tuition fee you've gotten for teaching the Thebans to fight," he remarked. It was part of the Spartans' code to avoid a sequence such as this: repeated attacks on the same target, effectively training their foe in how to resist.

Agesilaus was nearly seventy now. Two marches across Cithaeron in two successive years, and two tough campaigns in Boeotia, were taking a toll on his health. On his march home from the second invasion, while climbing a hill in Megara to talk with the magistrates there, he was struck by a violent pain in his good leg. The limb began to swell alarmingly. A doctor was summoned and the leg was lanced below the ankle. The resulting hemorrhage could not be stanched, and it seemed Agesilaus would die from loss of blood.

Then the king fainted and the flow of blood somehow stopped. Agesilaus was carried back to Sparta on a litter, desperately weak. He'd survived, but he'd have to rely on Cleombrotus, his junior fellow monarch, to fulfill his designs against Thebes. That man, it was known, did not share his anger or hatred.

In 376 BC, with Agesilaus bedridden, Cleombrotus led the army again into Boeotia, but never made it over Mt. Cithaeron. He tried to force his way through the mountain passes, but Theban troops, hidden in some high rocks, ambushed his advance guard and killed about forty. That was enough for Cleombrotus. He turned around, perhaps with relief, and, once back in the Peloponnese, disbanded the army. The Spartan war on Thebes came to a halt. Sparta moved instead to efforts to counter Athens, which was now rebuilding its naval alliance. That was the goal many Spartans had preferred all along.

Agesilaus watched helplessly from his sickbed as Sparta began building ships and hiring crews. Sea wars, in his eyes, were craven affairs, fought with timber and cash, not body and mind. The Spartan way, the way he believed in, was the clash of heavy infantry, the great test of courage and strength. Belief in that test propelled him always toward Thebes and the "dancing floor of Ares," the open Boeotian plains, flat spaces that allowed deployment of phalanxes. But now, with his good leg phlebitic, he had no way to get there.

Since the Cithaeron route was now closed, Sparta could no

longer support its garrisons in Boeotia. Thebes began attacking those cities one by one, starting with Thespiae, then moving on to Tanagra, Plataea, and Haliartus. Several top Spartan commanders, including Phoibidas, the captor of the Cadmea, were felled in these attacks. In 375, four years after its liberation, Thebes turned its attention to Orchomenus, Sparta's strongest outpost in the region and the one base it could resupply by ship (plus a short march). Thebes had a plan to take this asset from Sparta—a plan that relied on the strength of its Sacred Band.

It had been four years since Pelopidas, on the day of the winter solstice, led eleven men across Cithaeron to begin the liberation of Thebes. Since that time, he'd become leader of a different cohort. Command of the Sacred Band had passed to him from the hands of Gorgidas, who had brought the corps into being. What caused the change is unknown, but its consequences were swift and profound. The Band, in the hands of Pelopidas, was to become a far more potent weapon, tapping more directly into the power of *erôs*.

Pelopidas himself was filled with *erôs*, as Plutarch meaningfully says—a "passion" to see Thebes flourish, and to drive Spartan troops from the region. Still perhaps in his thirties, now married with young children, Pelopidas was zealous for the Boeotian cause. His friends chastised him for neglecting his farms to serve his city instead. "You'll need the money," they told him, but he pointed to a nearby blind beggar and said, "*He* needs the money, not I." His wife received a similar brush-off when she asked him, as he left the house for a battle, to look after himself: "You ought to say, to a leader and general, to look after the *citizens*," he reproached her.

The spirit that drove the solstice plot was strong in Pelopidas. Plutarch describes his nature as defined by *thumos*, the quality Plutarch ascribed to rivalrous chariot horses. (Our *thyme*, according to one theory, derives from this Greek word, reflecting a folk belief that the herb gave a spur to courage.) *Thumos* was largely a virtue in Plutarch's eyes, but it also required *logos*, reason, to rein it in. Without such restraint, *thumos* could become mere rage. Epaminondas, trained in philosophy, would soon add *logos* to Pelopidas's *thumos* to form an ideal leadership team.

Being ruled by *thumos* meant wanting to run straight at one's foe, rather than use delays or stratagems. Thus Pelopidas, during the exile in Athens, had convinced his fellow Thebans not to play politics—fawning on orators who might sway Athens to back their cause—but to march toward Thebes, in disguise, and fight their foes with their own hands. Now that he had the Sacred Band as his striking arm, Pelopidas was again prepared to run huge risks in pursuit of huge rewards. His target, Orchomenus, was manned by over a thousand Spartan troops.

Orchomenus had been a problem for Thebes since mythic times. Legend held that its people were Minyans, an ancient, indigenous race, and that its early kings had subdued Thebes in war and imposed a yearly tribute (a hundred oxen). The god Heracles, a Theban by birth, reversed that power dynamic, leading the Thebans to victory and imposing a tax twice as large. Whatever the basis of that story, Orchomenus ever after resented—and often defied—Thebes's lead. Its topographic position, defended by water and hills, stiffened that defiance. Now the city was also defended by a huge Spartan-led force.

Through his informants, Pelopidas kept a close watch on these garrison troops. When he heard that they'd left their base and gone on a raiding mission, he dashed northward with the Sacred Band and a small contingent of horsemen. He hoped to occupy Orchomenus before the Spartans returned, locking them out of the walled town. Perhaps, after that, a larger Theban force could be sent to crush them. At the least, they would need to take ship back home and be gone from Boeotia.

The Theban intelligence network was not all it might have

been. It had spotted the garrison force departing Orchomenus. But a new one, arriving by ship to replace it, had gone unobserved. The Spartan departure, it seems, had not been only a raiding excursion but also a troop rotation. Pelopidas arrived at Orchomenus to find it strongly held by fresh soldiers. There was little to do but head home.

Turning to leave the region, Pelopidas and the Sacred Band made their way around the shores of Lake Copais. At a place called Tegyra, they came to a small temple, abandoned, but touted by locals as the spot where Apollo was born. Here too, it seems, Orchomenus had sought to compete with Thebes, the birthplace of Heracles and Dionysus, by claiming an even greater native god. The flooding of a nearby river constricted the army's track, squeezing them between marshlands and rocky hills.

Suddenly they spotted the Spartan raiding party, coming through a narrow defile, directly ahead. They were trapped, outmanned by a force at least double, perhaps four times as large. A Theban soldier gave voice to his panic: "We have stumbled into our enemies' hands!"

"Why not say *they* into *ours*?" Pelopidas coolly replied. With minutes in which to deploy, he formed up the Sacred Band for battle, packing them densely together. He would never have sought this fight, but since it had been thrust upon him, he meant to win.

The Spartans too were surprised by the sudden encounter. But their lifelong training program prepared them for moments like these. At a word, file leaders detached from the column of march and assumed phalanx formation. The two Spartan polemarchs leading the squad, Gorgoleon and Theopompus, took their place at the front of the line.

What happened next is best recorded by Plutarch. As the two sides met, Pelopidas and the Sacred Band charged the two polemarchs, visible on the Spartan right wing. Both were felled within minutes. The Spartans were rocked back on their heels.

They had not fought the Sacred Band before, had perhaps not heard of its existence. This first contact made clear they faced a formidable weapon.

In a normal battle, the Spartans would have relied on their numbers, outflanking the Sacred Band to attack from the side. Now, though, they parted ranks, as though to let the Thebans go through and get clear. Dismayed by the loss of their leaders, they wanted a disengagement; perhaps too they planned to close ranks and attack from the rear as the Thebans went past. This, as Xenophon said of the Battle of Coronea, was the safest, most sensible way to gain a small win and save face.

Pelopidas was having none of that scenario. He marched the Band into the midst of the Spartans, then turned and led them again on the attack. The Spartans were unnerved. Stripped of leadership, divided into two half armies, they withdrew from the fight, moving off at speed toward Orchomenus. Pelopidas chased them as far as he dared, then broke off pursuit, wary of being lured into a trap. He led the Band back to the battlefield. There they despoiled the Spartan dead and made a trophy of their captured weapons, a signpost proclaiming Thebes's victory.

The Battle of Tegyra had lasted perhaps an hour or two, but its impact was huge. No land army had stood up to the Spartans as the Sacred Band had done, especially when outnumbered and taken by surprise. Plutarch—himself a Boeotian—marks the moment's significance. "This battle taught the other Greeks that warriors and fighters are not made only on the Eurotas, nor in the place between Babykê and Knakion," he wrote, naming landmarks of Sparta. The Spartans were invincible, he writes, when they *seemed* so; their reputation had been their greatest weapon. That reputation had been dealt a huge blow by the Sacred Band.

The chronicler Diodorus reaches a similar conclusion about Tegyra. "Never had this happened in previous times," he writes of the Theban victory, meaning that never before had an outnumbered force beaten Sparta. "As a result, the Thebans were filled with high spirit, and their courage was more widely proclaimed, and they clearly positioned themselves to compete for the headship of Greece." It was, Diodorus opines, "a deed worthy of memory." But another historian, the Spartophile Xenophon, disagreed; he tried to expunge Tegyra from the record, by omitting it altogether from his *Hellenica*.

Pelopidas learned from the outcome of Tegyra. Unlike Gorgidas before him,* who had spread the Band out at the front of a larger phalanx, Pelopidas had kept them together, had indeed taken them on the march as his sole infantry squad. Their concentrated mass—a spearhead formed of men—had been hurled at a single point in the Spartan line, causing the deaths of two polemarchs at the point of impact. After this projectile hit its mark, the tide of battle had turned.

From this point on, Pelopidas kept the Band together in close formation, even when they fought in the larger Boeotian army. Their strength, he now knew, lay in this dense array, a cohesion cemented by *erôs*. It was just as Pammenes, another Theban leader, had said, when discussing a passage of Homer's *Iliad*. That passage advised forming up soldiers by tribes and by clans, with neighbors and kin side by side. Much better, said Pammenes, to form them up in couples, "so that, out of love for their *erômenoi* or shame before their *erastai*, they would stand fast against dangers for one another's sake."

Pelopidas remained in command of the Band. The Thebans selected him, year after year, to fill that high post, an assignment well suited to a man of both *thumos* and *erôs*. It would be Pelopidas, four years hence, who would lead the Band to its sternest test, when Agesilaus resumed his fight with the clog-wearing Thebans.

---

* Gorgidas disappears from the historical record after 378, perhaps killed in action.

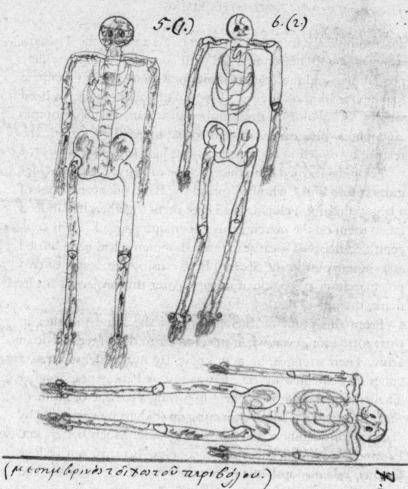

5. (1.)   6. (2.)

(μεσημβρινὸς διὰ τοῦ περιβόλου.)

(οὐ βασιλικά.)

CHAPTER 3

Philosophers in Arms

(375–June 371 BC)

At much the same time that George Ledwell Taylor discovered the Lion of Chaeronea, the early nineteenth century was "discovering," or rather, acknowledging, that sexual love was not all of one kind. No word yet existed for men who loved men (or women, women), and no public discussion had taken place. Thanks to Greek texts from the age of the Sacred Band, and thanks to the Band itself, male erôs first became visible to those who did not know it at first hand.

Plato's Symposium *and* Phaedrus, *with their candid discussions of the passions of* erastai *and* erômenoi, *were the primary sources of this revelation, but the tale of the Sacred Band played its part as well. (Since Plato's* Symposium *mentions an army of male lovers similar to the Band, it's often hard to tell which is being referred to.) The Spartans too loomed large in this consciousness-raising, for Greek sources told of state-sponsored love bonds between older and younger soldiers in the Spartan army. It surprised nineteenth-century scholars that, in all three cases—at Athens, Sparta, and Thebes—male erôs was seen as a source of moral virtue and military strength, the opposite of what their biased age expected.*

German classicist K. O. Müller was among the first to confront this seeming paradox. In an 1824 study of the Dorian peoples of Greece, principally focused on the Spartans, Müller considered two Greek reports of lovers fighting side by side in battle. Noting that "feelings" behind such pairings were common to many Greeks, Müller asked, in anguished tones, whether such feelings were ever acted upon. "Let it be well weighed, and let us be careful of casting so black a stain on a large portion of mankind," he warned. His answer was decisively negative. Dorians were "lovers" in only a spiritual sense, he insisted; it was unthinkable that "so horrible a crime [as male-male sexual contact] . . . should really have existed" in such virtuous men.

Müller's Dorian study was published in England in 1830 as The History and Antiquities of the Doric Race, and was widely read there for decades. (Its influence has been detected in Oscar Wilde's choice of name for the gay hero of his 1890 novel, The Picture of Dorian Gray.) It was now safe to admit that Dorians, and Greeks generally, were given to homoerotic "feelings," even if Müller insisted these never led to actions. Among those interested in Müller's work was Benjamin Jowett, an Oxford classicist who also struggled with the meaning of Greek writings on male erôs.

Jowett, himself asexual and homophobic, was nonetheless deeply intrigued by Plato's Symposium and Phaedrus, texts he helped introduce into the Oxford curriculum. He recognized the great humanistic value of these works yet could not accept their (to us) obvious idealization of male erôs. As Müller had done with his Dorians, Jowett found ingenious ways out of the problem. "What Plato says of the loves of men must be transferred to the loves of women, before we can attach any serious meanings to his words," Jowett wrote in the introduction to his Phaedrus translation. Ultimately he decided (as we'll see further on) that Plato's discussions of erôs were merely metaphoric.

A very different encounter with Plato took place at much the same time as Jowett's, on the other side of the Atlantic. The poet Walt Whitman was attracted to Phaedrus precisely because it affirmed his homoerotic passions; his reading notes highlight the most candidly sensual passages. His Leaves of Grass appeared in 1855 (the year that Jowett became Regius Professor of Greek at Oxford) and breathed new life and vigor into the Greek ideal of soldierly male love. Whitman explored that ideal in the so-called Calamus sequence of Leaves of Grass, named after a Greek youth who'd drowned himself out of grief for his drowned lover and was then transformed into a marsh reed.

One of the most intense Calamus poems, number 34, was likely *inspired by Plato's* Symposium *or by the Theban Sacred Band (for Whitman was also a reader of Plutarch's* Lives, *where the Band was most fully described). In its original version, in Whitman's manuscripts, the poem imagines a utopian city defined by male* erôs:

> *I dream'd in a dream of a city where all men were like brothers,*
> *O I saw them tenderly love each other—I often saw them, in num-*
> *bers, walking hand in hand,*
> *I dream'd that was the city of robust friends—Nothing was greater*
> *there than manly love—it led the rest,*
> *It was seen every hour in the actions of men of that city, and in all*
> *their looks and words.*

The poem has been compared to Martin Luther King's "I Have a Dream" speech for its fervor and conviction. But in edits for its published version, in the 1860 edition of Leaves of Grass, *Whitman took out the second line—too candid for his age—and changed the phrase "manly love" in line 3 to "robust love." Other Calamus poems underwent similar toning down.*

Only two years after "I dream'd in a dream" appeared in print, a German jurist, Karl Heinrich Ulrichs, became the first modern man to publicly come out as gay. Ulrichs essentially founded the gay rights movement by speaking and writing, throughout the 1860s, on behalf of those he called Urnings, a term he'd adapted from Plato's Symposium.

The world had come a long way in forty years, since K. O. Müller had first contemplated the "crime" of Dorian soldier-lovers. The Sacred Band of Thebes, along with the writings of Plato, had played a part in that progress. But the world still had a long way to go.

Thebes had fended off the Spartan invasions of 378 and 377, but the sabotage of its crops had taken a toll. Thebes was by now crowded with exiles, democrats who had fled the regimes imposed by Sparta during its subjection of Boeotia. As Agesilaus retreated to his sickbed in Sparta, nursing his swollen leg, the Thebans looked for food imports to fill the gap he'd created. This search led to an episode that intrigued Xenophon, author of *Hellenica*, because it spoke to a problem never far from his mind: the problem of *erôs*.

Thebes had no access to the Black Sea's northern shore (today's Ukraine), the breadbasket that fed much of Athens. It reached out instead toward Pagasae, in Thessaly, the port from which Jason was said to have sailed on the *Argo*. Another Jason had come to power there—Jason of Pherae, whom we'll soon meet more fully—and Thebes had forged an alliance with his regime. Two warships were sent north to Pagasae with ten talents of silver, enough to buy vast stores of grain. But while the purchase was in progress, word of the mission filtered back to Alcetas, commander of a nearby Spartan garrison.

From his post at Oreus, overlooking the narrow straits through which these ships must pass, Alcetas launched a surprise naval attack. He seized the ships as they made their way back to Thebes, impounded the grain, and put the crews—several hundred Boeotians—under guard on the town's acropolis. For a moment, it seemed that Alcetas, an obscure officer in a lonely outpost, had hit Thebes harder than even the great Agesilaus with his army of twenty thousand. But then, *erôs* played its mischievous hand.

Alcetas, according to Xenophon, had struck up a love affair with a male Orean renowned for virtue and beauty. Xenophon calls this beloved a *pais*, a boy, but like the British term *lad*, this need not imply extreme youth; the word was often a synonym for *erômenos*, a male who might well be adult but was younger than his *erastês*.* Alcetas and this *pais* shared a mutual

---

* For this reason *paiderasteia*, the Greeks' term for an erotic bond between males of unequal ages, must be distinguished from our *pederasty*; the Greek word does not imply a child was involved. The Greeks felt that age asymmetry was essential to same-sex relationships, and the term *pais*, like *erômenos*, helped establish that imbalance.

passion, for the *pais* followed his lover through the streets of Oreus, while Alcetas, for his part, went down often into the lower city. There, says Xenophon, he "was about" the younger man—a unique phrase implying, perhaps, infatuation.

The Theban prisoners noted their captor's tendency to disappear from view. Most likely their numbers were greater than those of the garrison troops, for Oreus was a small place, and Sparta had never thought it would be a theater of war. When Alcetas departed for one of his trysts, the Thebans rose up and seized the acropolis, driving out (or killing) the troops of the garrison. It was a small-scale version of the seizure of their own Cadmea, four years before. Oreus was lost to the Spartans and brought over to the Theban side. The supply route between Thebes and Pagasae was reopened, and shipments of grain flowed through.

Xenophon gives only a few sentences to this incident, but no other writer mentions it at all. His interest in the fall of Alcetas is part of his larger concern with male *erôs* generally. He had deep misgivings about sexual love between men, believing it did not enhance but compromised military strength. Those misgivings help explain his egregious bias, in *Hellenica* and other writings, in favor of Sparta and against Thebes—a bias he passed on to modern historians, if only because he deprived them of much of the Theban record.

To understand Xenophon's views on *erôs*, it helps to understand his life, one of the most remarkable lives of all antiquity. Much of that life can be reconstructed from his writings, which survive largely intact. He produced a chronicle of his era, the *Hellenica*; a eulogy of Agesilaus; a romantic, semifictional biography of an early Persian king; essays, how-to manuals, Socratic dialogues—an amazingly large and diverse corpus. Best known today, for its stirring account of survival against all odds, is his *Anabasis*, the story of a Greek mercenary army that fought its way home from deep inside what's now Iraq, under the authority of Xenophon himself.

Authority, in one form or another, is central to all Xenophon's works, for he was no friend of the *dêmos*, despite having grown up in Athens. In every context—an army, a city,
a family home—he stresses the need for strong leaders, men
of supreme moral rigor. Such men would need many virtues,
but above all the virtue that governed all others: what Xenophon called *enkrateia*, "self-mastery." *Enkrateia* was the unique
strength of the Spartans, as Xenophon understood them, and so
he looked to *them* as natural leaders of Greece. He became one
of the foremost Laconists of his time.

It was not from the Spartans, however, but from a middle-
aged, misshapen Athenian, that Xenophon, in his youth,
learned about *enkrateia*. He first met Socrates as the two were
passing in an alley; Socrates blocked Xenophon's way with a
walking stick. "Where does one buy fruits and vegetables?" the
gnomish older man asked, and Xenophon pointed him toward
the market square. "And where are men made virtuous and
good?" asked Socrates, and Xenophon conceded he did not
know. "Then follow me and learn," said Socrates, and Xenophon did so. He joined the coterie of well-bred youths, including Plato, who followed Socrates about the streets of Athens,
listening in on his barbed conversations with city leaders.

Later, Xenophon wrote down memoirs of these conversations, partly in an effort to rescue his teacher's reputation (Socrates had by that time been tried and executed for impiety and
"corrupting the youth"). Xenophon's *Recollections of Socrates*
survive today; so do his *Oeconomicus*, *Apology*, and *Symposium*,
philosophic works featuring Socrates as main or sole speaker.
The latter two of these works overlap, in title and content, with
works by Xenophon's close contemporary Plato; they seem to
have been written in reply or rebuttal (though whose work
came first is not always clear).

Xenophon saw in Socrates a man who had bested hunger
for food and wine, desire for wealth, and passion for younger

men—a model of *enkrateia*. Indeed, in *Recollections* Xenophon quotes Socrates praising *enkrateia* as "the foundation stone of virtue," without which nothing good can be achieved. To make the point, Xenophon's Socrates describes the Choice of Heracles, a moralist's fable. Heracles, Socrates says, one day came to a crossroads and wondered which path he should take. A well-dressed, heavily made-up woman urged him to follow the easy road, where he would find good food, soft beds, sexual pleasure. A plainer, coarser woman then described the other road: rocky and steep, beset by hardship. This second woman bore the unsubtle name of Aretê, "virtue"; the first is called Eudaimonia, "prosperity," or Kakia, "vice." Heracles of course chose the harder road.

The Choice of Heracles was a favorite theme of Early Modern painters. Here, in the treatment by Lucas Cranach the Elder, Heracles prepares to choose the hard road of virtue and reject that of vice.

Xenophon himself was destined to learn a lot about hard roads. At about age thirty, while still in Athens with Socrates, he had a letter from a Boeotian friend, Proxenus. The man had signed on as a paid soldier under Cyrus, a Persian royal, and was off to get rich in the East. Proxenus urged Xenophon to join up too, for Cyrus was hiring broadly, all the Greek soldiers he could get. Xenophon consulted Socrates, who did not support the idea; Cyrus was a friend of the Spartans, and a connection with him, for an Athenian, might not look good. Xenophon went nonetheless. Together with thousands of other mercenaries—the Ten Thousand, they became known—he marched deep into Asia, on a mission whose purpose soon became clear: to unseat Cyrus's brother, the Great King, Artaxerxes, and install Cyrus in his place.

Few Greeks would have volunteered for *that* mission, but by the time they found out, it was too late to turn back. They marched on into Mesopotamia, searching for the army of Artaxerxes, never knowing when they would find it. When at last their foe was spotted, near Babylon—appearing as a huge dark stain on the earth, with flashes of light where bronze weapons caught the sun—the Greeks had scant time to form up ranks. Still, their discipline held firm. They easily bested the troops ranged against them, many of whom fled at the sight of a well-ordered phalanx.

Elsewhere on the field of battle, Cyrus was not so restrained. A rash impulse to kill his brother carried him deep into Artaxerxes' ranks. There, he was unhorsed and slain, allegedly at his own brother's hands. In an instant, the victory of the Ten Thousand turned into a hollow defeat.

Xenophon was only a common soldier then, a hostage to fortune. He watched as his commanders, including Proxenus, cast about for an exit. Trapped in Persian territory, far from a sea route home, the Greeks were in grave peril, yet unassailable so long as they could keep in phalanx formation. The Persians understood this and hatched a plot to undo them. They agreed to a truce with the Greeks and invited the Greek captains to a summit at the tent of a leading Persian. There, they treacherously arrested their guests, then sent out riders to slay the other commanders. A wounded man struggled into the Greek camp, his guts in his hands, to report the betrayal. In one swift blow, the Ten Thousand were rendered leaderless.

No parable of Heracles, no teaching of Socrates, could have prepared Xenophon for that awful night. In the Greek camp, men simply lay down where they stood, not caring what happened next. Yet somehow the gods were watching out for Xenophon and sent him a powerful dream. He dreamed that a thunderbolt fell on his father's house, back in Athens, and set it ablaze. The vision might have seemed to presage disaster, but Xenophon found it hopeful: in the midst of danger, a great light had shone forth from Zeus. Though it was still night, he arose, called together the men he knew best, and started to rough out a plan. The army would need new generals, and Xenophon himself was chosen among these. His cool head and will to survive had fitted him for command.

Winter was approaching, and the Greeks faced an arduous journey. They had to stick to rough terrain, for on open ground, like the plains they had crossed on their way here, the Persians would cut them to pieces. They marched north into forbidding mountains, harassed both by Persians and by tough tribes who hated trespassers. Small numbers were lost here and there, some to the arrows and stones of attackers, others to wind and cold, especially when a blizzard nearly buried the army. Yet Xenophon kept up morale and maintained order. Re-forming the Greeks as needed, now in a hollow square, now in a close-packed column, Xenophon got the men through. One day in eastern Turkey, a scouting party climbed a hill and spotted the Black Sea sparkling in the distance. Wild shouts of *"Thalatta!"*— "The sea!"—echoed back through the ranks.

Xenophon had set out for the East to get rich, and he partly succeeded. By his own orders the Greeks had destroyed much of their plunder, too cumbersome to carry through the mountains. Still, they brought enough back to make for a handsome sum when the whole was sold off and divided. More valuable still was the fame Xenophon won by getting the Ten Thousand home. That fame was now to become his livelihood; for, at some point in the 390s, word came that the Athenians had banished him, stripped him of citizen rights, and confiscated his estate. There was no going home any longer. He lingered in western Asia, with those of the Ten Thousand who chose to stay in arms—a private army of proven strength, available for hire.

Accidents of timing were on Xenophon's side. The Spartans had just then launched their Asian campaign and had plenty of use for seasoned veterans. Xenophon took service with the Spartans as they fought the Persians in Turkey. Soon, Agesilaus arrived to take charge of the campaign and command the Greek coalition—which now included the corps headed by Xenophon. The great mercenary captain attached himself to the great warrior-king, and a powerful bond was formed.

In Agesilaus, Xenophon found his ethical ideal, his model of *enkrateia*. Here was a monarch who, though allotted double portions at meals, gave away both his shares to favored officers; who disdained sleep, wine, and shelter from rough weather; who scorned wealth and luxury goods (though he won a vast haul in his Asian campaign). Here was a Socrates in arms. Xenophon was enthralled. In his later writings, he would lionize Agesilaus, especially in a biographical portrait that defends him at every point and exalts him as a paragon of virtue.

In Xenophon's eyes, the sternest test of Agesilaus, and of all male Spartans, was *erôs*, strongest of appetites. Xenophon knew that the Spartan system encouraged male liaisons, and that Spartan soldiers, even kings, felt desire for other men; but he strangely insisted (as we'll see further on) they never *acted* on that desire. Agesilaus provided him with a model of this restraint. While campaigning in Asia, Agesilaus fell in love with a beautiful youth, Megabates, the son of a Persian ally. It was customary for Persians to bestow a kiss in greeting, yet, notes Xenophon, when Megabates tried to kiss him, the Spartan king drew back. "Many more men can subdue their enemies than can subdue such feelings," Xenophon effuses. He notes that Agesilaus lodged in public places while on campaign, a proof that he had no sexual release.

Here was the leader Sparta needed, and if Agesilaus could lead Sparta, then Sparta could lead Greece—an outcome Xenophon longed for. In Xenophon's harsh worldview, or at least one he ascribed to Socrates, there were only two paths in foreign affairs: rule or be ruled, conquer or be conquered. One could not opt out of the game to pursue wealth or pleasure. The world was made up of masters and slaves, and Spartans were its natural masters. Only they could renew the flagging energies of Hellas. With hopes such as these, Xenophon became an adjutant on Agesilaus's staff and accompanied him out of Asia when the Spartans summoned him home in 395.

Xenophon was by that time nearing forty, a man without a country. As the Spartan army he served made its way back through Greece, Xenophon found himself fighting Athenians, his former countrymen, and Thebans, at Coronea. Agesilaus was badly wounded in that battle, and the Spartan army was blocked. Perhaps it was here that Xenophon formed the dislike of Thebes that pervades all his writings, especially the *Hellenica*, his historical chronicle. Thebes had stood in the way of— and nearly killed—his great hero. These "Boeotian swine" (as others called them), these wearers of wooden clogs, could not, in his eyes, offer leadership to Hellas, yet they *could* prevent Sparta from leading, and for that, he despised them.

At some point Xenophon, married with two young sons, retired from military life. He remained deeply connected to Sparta. At the invitation of Agesilaus, his sons were sent there and brought up in the city's rigorous *agōgē* program. Xenophon and his wife, Philesia, meanwhile, settled in Scillus, in the western Peloponnese, on an estate the Spartans bestowed. The place was well stocked with game and watered by a river with plentiful mussels and fish. Here Xenophon lived as a country gentleman, hunting boars and stags, raising horses, commanding no army but a staff of slaves. With the proceeds from his Asian adventure, he established a shrine to the goddess Artemis, fulfilling a vow he had made while leading the Ten Thousand. In that sacred precinct, he held an annual feast, laying out bread, wine, and game meats for the locals. And, increasingly, he wrote.

His range of topics was huge. Having moved from philosopher to soldier to country squire, from Athenian by birth to adoptive Spartan, Xenophon knew much of the world and wrote about all that he knew. He dealt with the practical—how to run a household, train a cavalry horse, or manage a pack of hunting dogs—as well as the ethical and moral. Looming above all these diverse works is the question of leadership, and the answers that Agesilaus, and Sparta, seemed to offer.

Xenophon was amazed by Sparta's power and tried in a late essay, the *Spartan Constitution*, to analyze its sources. The rules set up by Lycurgus, he decided—Sparta's ancient, semimythic lawgiver—had made Sparta supreme in Greece. These rules kept the Spartans on the hard road of *aretē*. Fine food, indulgence in wine, and private wealth were denied to the Spartans, as were the joys that older men found in *erōs* for their beloveds. Satisfaction of homoerotic desire was forbidden by Lycurgus, says Xenophon, as strictly as though it were incest. No other Greek writer draws such a harsh parallel or speaks of such a law.

At the opposite pole from this chaste Sparta stood the Thebans, who *encouraged* male couples, and their Sacred Band, built on ties of erotic love. Xenophon showed his contempt for Thebes in *Hellenica*, especially by leaving it out of the text when he could. Elsewhere, in his *Symposium*—as we shall see in the next chapter—he tried to prove that the Sacred Band were cowards, not heroes, and that Theban views on *erôs* were deeply corrupt. On this point, he took issue with Plato, his fellow Socratic student and author of a different *Symposium*.

Such was the man who recounted the fall of Oreus, the result of a lapse by a Spartan too much in love. Thebes might have been brought to its knees and forced back into Sparta's orbit had Alcetas not succumbed to the power of *erôs*. Instead the swine of Boeotia got fed, and the wars went on. It would be up to Agesilaus, if his leg ever healed, to bring those wars to a close.

Philosophy and soldiery marched hand in hand among the Greeks, far more than in modern times. Several students of Socrates won glory on the field of battle, as Xenophon did, or led the governments of city-states. Plato, in the *Republic*—a work likely written around the time of the liberation of Thebes— imagined an ideal state in which a warrior caste, the Guardians, would be trained in higher thought as well as in combat arts. But philosophers in arms dwelled not only in Athens, among the students at Plato's Academy. A Boeotian too merits that title: Epaminondas of Thebes, the man who, on the day of the solstice plot, had declined to raise his hand against fellow Thebans.

His story, like that of Xenophon, goes back to an inspirational teacher and, even further back, to the Great One who taught the teachers who taught that teacher.

About seventy-five years before the rise of Thebes, in another corner of Hellas—the sole of the Italian boot, then settled by Greeks—a man named Lysis lived in a city called Croton. He belonged to a strange, cultlike community there, one of the first mystic religious movements on European soil.

Like many modern sects, the group revered a holy man, by then deceased, as its founder and guide. This sage had taught how all things were made of number, and how number, in turn, could translate into music. Music and number, for him, contained the secrets of the cosmos. He showed his followers the power of the *tetraktys*, an equilateral triangle made up of ten dots. In this pattern he saw the perfect ratios of both music and math, indeed the very structure of the universe—since the ten dots stood for ten heavenly bodies (the seven planets seen by the naked eye, plus the sun and moon, and to round out the ten, an unseen "counterearth" hidden behind the sun). Each of these bodies produced a musical note as it moved through space, filling the cosmos with the harmony of the spheres.

This holy man was Pythagoras. Today he is best known for the theorem that bears his name, a formula for finding the length of a side of a right triangle. But to represent him by this equation—which he may only have transmitted, not discovered—is like tagging da Vinci only as the painter of the *Mona Lisa*. Pythagoras applied his scheme of thought to cosmology, theology, ethics, even the minutiae of daily life. He showed his followers practical of ways of achieving purity. Vegetarian diet was key, but even putting on shoes could be a path toward the divine: always begin with the right foot, which is holier than the left. In the community he led, all aspects of life, including sexual life, were subject to such strictures.

Pythagoras claimed to have lived many times before his birth as Pythagoras. He believed in transmigration of souls, a doctrine later adapted (along with other Pythagorean teachings) by Plato. Pythagoras claimed that Hermes, the god who had fathered him first, had given his soul the power to remember past lives. He'd been incarnated as a hero of the Trojan War, a sage, and a fisherman, along with various plants and animals. The idea that he had traveled all of time and could recall what he saw enhanced Pythagoras's reputation as a semidivine being. (Some thought he enhanced it further through quackery: according to one rumor, he built an underground chamber in his home and hid there for a month, then emerged, pale and skeletal, claiming he'd returned from Hades.)

The Pythagoreans formed a closed circle around the Master, and entry into the group was tightly controlled. Their exclusivity created tensions with outsiders. At Croton, a would-be acolyte who'd been turned away led a violent attack on the group's meetinghouse; Pythagoras was driven out. Later, after the Master's death—or as *he* claimed, his translation into another life—the sect returned to Croton and reconstituted itself.

Lysis joined the group here, perhaps in the 460s BC. He was one of the third-generation Pythagoreans, too young to have known the Master in person but taught by those who *had* known him. These heirs to the sacred teachings again held aloof from fellow Crotoniates and again aroused mistrust. One day, when movement leaders were gathering at a member's home, their enemies tried for a knockout blow. They heaped up fuel around the walls and set the house on fire. Only two escaped from that blaze, Lysis and one other man. Lysis fled and disappeared for decades; finally, he landed at Thebes.

One of two known survivors of the Pythagorean holocaust, Lysis, now in advancing age, was taken in by a Theban of modest means, an aristocrat fallen on hard times. The man's two sons, Caphisias and Epaminondas, were young and impressionable. The boys looked up to Lysis with filial admiration and may even have become his legal adoptees. Lysis grew old in that household, apparently living into his nineties. When he died, around 380 BC—the time of the Spartan occupation of the Cadmea— the two boys, now young men, buried him with due Pythagorean rites, as they'd been instructed to do. (It was at this grave, as we've seen, that Epaminondas encountered another Pythagorean, Theanor, on the morning of the solstice revolution.)

What did Epaminondas learn from Lysis, last bearer of the Pythagorean torch? We have no account of their lessons or practices. But to judge by his later behavior, Epaminondas was awed by Lysis's *enkrateia*, the same virtue Xenophon admired in Socrates. Like Socrates, Lysis practiced control of desires, whether for food, sex, wealth, or political power. Pythagoreans were known for such self-mastery: Some would sit down at richly laden banquets, yet not permit themselves to touch a morsel. In sexual matters, they were the first Greeks to practice abstinence (during certain times of the year). In diet, they alone avoided meat.

Under Lysis's guidance, Epaminondas grew up abstemious and strong. He too sat hungry at sumptuous feasts to foster self-control; he even took the exercise one step further, forcing himself to watch as his servants consumed the food. He absented himself from dinners and drinking bouts. Once when a friend invited him to a festive meal, of the sort often made when sacrificing to the gods, Epaminondas arrived to find a table filled with delicacies, and jars of scented oil with which guests might anoint themselves. "I thought this would be a ritual sacrifice, not a display of hubris," he's quoted as saying. That powerful word *hubris*, a kind of arrogance that offends the very gods, reveals a deep level of disgust.

Though cool to the pleasures of food and wine, Epaminondas, according to Plutarch, felt the heat of *erôs* as much as any Theban. Plutarch names two youths who were, at different times, his *erômenoi*, Asopichus and Caphisodorus. Unfortunately the text of Plutarch's essay on love, *Amatorius*, is broken by a textual gap at just the point where we might have learned more. Epaminondas never married, but, again in Plutarch's words, chose a "single" or "solitary" life, in contrast to Pelopidas, who had a wife and children. The word Plutarch uses here, *monotropos*, implies more than mere bachelorhood: an aloofness from society generally.

A moderate temperament made Epaminondas seem harmless during the days of the Spartan occupation. While other Thebans decamped for Athens, Epaminondas remained, confident that his philosophic demeanor, and lack of family wealth, made him a nonthreat in Laconist eyes. He was then perhaps in his late thirties, renowned for a wide array of traits: honesty, generosity, eloquence, athleticism. This last talent he honed in the gymnasia and on the running tracks of Thebes, finding in exercise, especially wrestling, the best training for combat. During the occupation he encouraged his friends to wrestle with Spartans; by such contests, he believed, his countrymen would gain confidence and lose their fear of the troops.

Chief among the virtues of Epaminondas was indifference to wealth, a quality he attributed to the teachings of Lysis. This indifference was to be one of his chief political assets, in an age when rampant bribery made other leaders suspect. Already at this early stage in his career, Plutarch reports, Epaminondas had turned aside a huge bribe offered by a Thessalian tyrant, Jason of Pherae—a "lover [erastês] of monarchy," was Epaminondas's view of Jason, but one who could never corrupt "a man of the people who lives in a free and independent state"— his own self-description.

"Man of the people" he may have been, but Epaminondas was no firebrand. Though he belonged to the circle that sought to liberate Thebes, he felt that the solstice plot, in which violence had to be used, was a mistake. He preferred to wait for the chance to free his city "with justice," though it was not clear when, or whether, that chance would come. Even his brother, Caphisias, could not persuade him. In an argument with that brother, Epaminondas stated his fears: the plot's leaders might strike at only a few, but others of lesser restraint might run rampant and fill the city with corpses. Besides, he reasoned, if the plot should succeed, the new government of Thebes would need men untainted by blood.

Though he abstained from the solstice attacks in part to be ready to lead, Epaminondas did not, initially, seek a leadership role. When day dawned on December 22 and Thebans gathered in their first free assembly in years, Epaminondas came forward to hail the plot's leaders, Pelopidas and Melôn, as the new boeotarchs. The dêmos acceded, acclaiming these two, along with Gorgidas and Charon, with shouts and cheers.

Epaminondas stood off to the side. For the moment, at least, Thebes needed men of action, not students of philosophy.

Though widely respected by his countrymen, Epaminondas was not entirely beloved. Many mistrusted his aloofness, asceticism, and high-mindedness. Plutarch reports that at some point the *dêmos*, to humble his pride, appointed him *telmarch*, in charge of garbage and sewage. Epaminondas did not flinch from the job, but went about it with zeal, saying it was not the post that distinguished the man but the other way around. Plutarch claims that even removal of dung from the streets became a dignified office.

Though he steered clear of drinking parties and feasts, Epaminondas had a passion for music. Thebans excelled at the aulos, a double-reeded pipe, and thrilled to its oboe-like sound. Epaminondas played well himself and also sponsored public performances. He'd never had any money, so he borrowed from Pelopidas to subsidize such events. Epaminondas had remained close friends with this soldier's soldier, beside whom he had fought in the battle near Mantinea. The two made a strange, but complementary, pair: a philosopher, athlete, and musician, who during the solstice plot had refused to shed blood, and a bold man of action who'd killed a Laconist leader that night in single combat. The partnership was destined to endure.

Epaminondas impressed the Greeks, and later the Romans, as a man of impeccable morals. A Roman biographer, Cornelius Nepos, devotes a remarkable paragraph to a list of his qualities: "He was modest, prudent, sober, wise in making use of the moment, expert in war, courageous in action, highly elevated in mind, so devoted to truth that he would not lie even in jest. . . ." The list goes on and on. Among the two dozen surviving profiles of leaders by Nepos, only Epaminondas receives such glowing praise.

In many ways Epaminondas provided a foil to Agesilaus, the other great Greek leader of this era. The first was defined by devotion to justice; the second, by pursuit of power. Agesilaus was a monarch from a centuries-old royal line; Epaminondas, a public official, returned to office by vote year after year, and once at least—as we shall see—*not* returned. These two towering men stood astride mainland Greece in the age of the Sacred Band, on opposite sides of the Isthmus. Their lives would be defined—and in once case ended—by their clashes with each other over a turbulent decade.

The first of those clashes came not on the battlefield, but in the halls of diplomacy, in Sparta. The question at issue, again, was the Boeotian League.

As the King's Peace eroded, new efforts were clearly needed to stabilize Greece. The pact of 387 BC had failed to reduce warfare, despite the vows by its sponsor, Artaxerxes, to intervene against those who broke it. In 375 Artaxerxes sent his royal legates back to the cities of Greece, convening another parley and another attempt at a pact. Again the Great King honored Sparta as conference host. He needed the Greeks to stop fighting one another so that more of them would fight for *him*; his wealthiest province, Egypt, was still in revolt.

The Peace of 375 reaffirmed the King's Peace, but imposed stronger measures, including withdrawal of garrison troops from all across Greece. This clause benefited Thebes, surrounded as it was by garrisoned towns. Athens too made gains under the new treaty, since the pact said nothing that barred its new naval alliance. The terms of the pact showed how much ground Sparta had lost; it had no choice but to make concessions to its two greatest rivals. Even so, Sparta remained the treaty's enforcer, empowered by Artaxerxes to act on his behalf.

Athenians were overjoyed at Sparta's implicit acceptance of its new naval power. Their strategy was working: by avoiding the use of coercion, they stayed on the right side of the autonomy clause. In the year that the pact was signed they commissioned their leading sculptor, Cephisodotus, to create a public statue of

Eirênê or "peace," envisioned as a kind-faced young goddess, holding a smiling baby, Ploutos or "wealth." It was the first image of personified peace the Greeks had produced, and the first time the goddess had been shown as the mother of personified wealth.

The message was clear: the treaty would make Athens rich again, as the hub of Aegean trade and commerce. Athenian naval dominion—retooled now to adhere to the Peace—would revive, after decades asleep.

In fact the treaty was dead before the statue was even completed. An Athenian admiral was recalled from naval duty as soon as the pact was signed, to conform to its terms. But on his way

A Roman copy of the Athenian statue group portraying Eirênê (peace) nurturing baby Ploutos (wealth).

home he made a dubious stop at a port of call. He dropped off on Zacynthus a band of democrats who'd been exiled from that island, and who hoped to reclaim it from ruling Laconists. That drop-off was seen as a violation of the autonomy principle. Sparta ruled that Athens had broken the treaty, and the two cities were soon again at war. The Peace of 375 had lasted a matter of months.

The Thebans meanwhile pursued their own goal, rebuilding the Boeotian League. Sparta still controlled garrisons and puppet regimes in several Boeotian towns. But under the Peace of 375 the Spartans withdrew their troops from these places. When that treaty failed, Thebes saw a chance to also remove their proxies. First on its to-do list was Plataea, a unique political problem—a city that existed only because Sparta had put it there. That tale is as tangled, and tragic, as any in this tangled, tragic age.

From early times, Plataea had rejected the Boeotian League and any coercion by Thebes. The city lay just inside Boeotia's border with Attica and leaned primarily southward, toward Athens. Theban pressure to stay with Boeotia only pushed Plataeans further away. Plataea and Athens became firm friends; the Plataeans alone fought beside Athens at Marathon, in 490 BC, and helped win a glorious victory over the Persians. All this made Plataea a rebuke to the concept of a Theban-led federal state.

At the outbreak of the Peloponnesian War, in 431 BC, Theban commandos, called in by Plataean dissidents, snuck into Plataea at night to install a pro-Theban regime. But that attack failed, as described in grim detail by the historian Thucydides. Dozens of Thebans were cut off inside the town and taken prisoner; the next day, Plataea summarily put them to death. Sparta, at that time allied with Thebes, put Plataea under siege and captured it when a fire destroyed part of the walls. Most Plataeans had by that time fled to Athens, but several hundred were seized by Sparta in the ravaged town.

After a show trial, the men of Plataea were executed and the women sold as slaves, and in a procedure the Greeks called *katalusis*, the buildings and wall were pulled down. The city was wiped from the map. Theban farmers were given ten-year leases to work the land, which was now empty ground, apart from a temple of Hera and a hostel to house the shrine's visitors, built up out of rubble and fill.

Then Thebes and Sparta fell out of alliance, in the 390s, as we've seen. The fate of Plataea was miraculously reversed. In 386, under the King's Peace, Sparta, seeking a check on Thebes, built a new Plataea out of the ruins of the old. It repatriated surviving Plataeans to populate the new town. The gratitude of these returnees made the city a bulwark of Spartan power. Forty years after the fall of Plataea I, Thebes again had an enemy only ten miles away. Plataea II gave the Spartans a secure base in Boeotia from which to do damage to Thebes; on the night of the solstice plot, Plataean and Spartan horsemen had rushed out of the town to quash the revolution then in progress. Thebes had just barely stopped them before they arrived.

When Spartan garrison troops were withdrawn under the Peace of 375, Plataeans knew that retribution was coming. They kept their walls and gates well manned, hoping to stand a siege if attacked. Only on days when the Boeotian assembly met, and Thebans were occupied with politics, could Plataean farmers venture out from those walls and tend to their crops. But a Theban magistrate noted this pattern and told the Boeotians to come armed to the next assembly. The Boeotian army then marched along an unguarded route and arrived while many Plataeans were still in the fields. With these men made prisoners, the city had to submit.

Plataea had fallen a second time, and Thebes imposed a mass sentence of banishment. Plataeans were told to take what they could carry and make their way to Athens, after swearing an oath to never again set foot in Boeotia. Then the buildings and walls were once again leveled, a second *katalusis*. Plataea had ceased to exist, then existed, then ceased once again, in the span of a half century. (This wasn't the end of its changes; Plataea III would emerge forty years further on, after yet another shift in the balance of power.)

As Plataean refugees streamed in toting their valuables, Athens reconsidered its tenuous friendship with Thebes. Isocrates, an Athenian essayist, berated his countrymen on behalf of the Plataeans, in a speech that survives. His speakers decried Theban aggression and urged Athens to act. What good was Athenian leadership, they demanded, or what did Athens stand for, if it could ignore such sufferings? What was the use of making a Common Peace if its clauses were meaningless? The speech sought to rally the Laconist party at Athens, who saw surging Thebes as a threat and sought a détente with the Spartans. For the moment, though, Athens stuck by its Theban alliance.

Shortly after its *katalusis* of Plataea, Thebes pulled down the walls of Thespiae, a less aggressive measure. Thespians* could stay in their homes but, without fortifications, could no longer hold aloof from the rest of the League. Only Orchomenus now remained outside the Boeotian union. That problem still rankled, but in other respects, Thebes had turned back the tide of the last two decades. The League was nearly intact. But could it endure?

Eighteen years had passed since the Theban revolution. Those who'd led the solstice plot and created the Sacred Band were now in their fifties, mature and experienced leaders. They'd fended off the invasions of Agesilaus, now in his seventies, and of his younger colleague, Cleombrotus. But no one in Thebes imagined they'd seen the last of the Spartans. A reckoning was still to come for their take back of the Cadmea, and for earlier sins, going back to Aulis, where they had first incurred Agesilaus's hate. In 371 BC, that reckoning came.

• • •

---

* Not connected to the modern term for "actors," which derives instead from an early Athenian dramaturge named Thespis.

A Spartan army was then in Phocis, just north of Boeotia, led by Cleombrotus, the junior of Sparta's kings. Ostensibly he'd been sent to protect the Phocians from attacks by Thebes, but a larger plan may also have been at work. Sparta was about to host another treaty conference, a further attempt by the Greeks to arrive at a Common Peace. The Thebans would wield new strength at that parley, and a forceful new leader—Epaminondas—would represent them. Agesilaus, the conference host, could anticipate that the Boeotian League would once again be on the table. To have an army in Phocis, only days from the walls of Thebes, was much to the advantage of Sparta's diplomats.

This conference was the first arranged by the Greeks themselves, not by Artaxerxes, the Great King of Persia. Athens, according to sources, had gotten the peace talks rolling by first approaching Thebes, its nominal ally. Both cities then sent delegations to Sparta, still regarded as leader of Greece. Though Thebes and Athens arrived together, their interests did not coincide. Indeed, some in Athens, shaken by the fate of Plataea, by now regarded Thebes as a threat and hoped for a rapprochement with the Spartans.

The Athenians spoke first at the conference. Xenophon records three speeches they delivered, revealing, with this triad, their conflicted position. The first speech appealed to Sparta for fellowship and disparaged Thebes; the second supported Thebes and questioned the motives of Sparta. This second speech, Xenophon says, discomfited all the delegates in the hall. "You Spartans appear to delight more in tyrannies than constitutional rule," said the Athenian speaker, Autocles. "You seized the Cadmea and did not allow the Thebans to be autonomous." A tense silence fell as Autocles finished. A third speaker tried gamely to reconcile the words of these first two.

Among the Theban delegation, Epaminondas listened intently to these Athenian speeches, especially Autocles' callout of Spartan aggressions. Epaminondas too had bold words to deliver, perhaps

86

prepared beforehand, perhaps inspired by those of Autocles.* He'd watched in disgust as the attendees at the conference, intimidated by Spartan power, groveled before Agesilaus. Rising to speak in the conference hall, Epaminondas accused Sparta of starting endless wars from which it alone benefited, while all the rest paid the price. "If we are to have peace," he declared, "it must be on the basis of equality and justice. If we aren't all equal, then peace won't endure."

Agesilaus took his first measure of Epaminondas during this speech, a man he would soon see more of—to his woe. To be challenged by an Athenian was bad enough, but a scolding from an upstart Theban—*that* was galling. "As for 'justice' and 'equality,'" Agesilaus sneered, "don't you think the cities of *Boeotia* would have these, if they stayed free?"

Epaminondas, unfazed, returned the volley: "Don't *you* think it just that *Laconia* go free?" This astonished the "allies" of Sparta in the room. They'd accepted their servitude, but now it seemed *someone* cared about their plight. Agesilaus grew angrier than ever, stung by this public attack. He sprang from his seat, enraged. *"Will you grant independence to Boeotia?"* he shouted, to which the Theban again countered, "If *you'll* do the same for Laconia."

What happened next is unclear. According to Plutarch, Agesilaus, nearly apoplectic, ordered the Thebans removed from the new peace charter. Xenophon puts this exclusion at a later stage of the conference, when the treaty was being signed. He says that the Thebans signed for their own city, but returned the next morning with changed minds, demanding to sign instead for all Boeotia. This demand, says Xenophon—a repeat of one the Thebans had made long before—enraged Agesilaus. He promptly ordered the name "Thebans" struck out of the treaty. Whichever version we follow, the outcome ends up

---

* Or perhaps, as some scholars suspect, the speech Xenophon gives to Autocles in *Hellenica* was in fact delivered by Epaminondas—stolen from the Theban by Xenophon and given to an Athenian instead.

the same. Agesilaus pronounced the Thebans *ekspondoi*, outside the protection of the new Peace. It was in effect a declaration of war.

Epaminondas and his countrymen left the conference and hurried back to Thebes to prepare for a Spartan invasion. The army of Cleombrotus, just across Boeotia's northern border, could attack at any time, and with massive force—fully two-thirds of Sparta's manpower. Most Greeks expected this army to make short work of the Thebans. The Athenians—excused by the new Peace from aiding either side—thought that Thebes would soon be "tithed," that is, utterly destroyed, with a tenth of the spoils taken out to offer to Delphic Apollo. Others, according to Diodorus, expected the entire population of Thebes to soon be made slaves.

Xenophon says the Thebans went home "entirely despondent," but nothing reveals his bias more than moments such as this, when he tries to intuit the Theban state of mind. Epami-

The "signatures" of city-states on a Greek treaty of the 370s BC. The name "Thebans" (ΘΗΒΑΙΟΙ) can be seen at center right.

nondas had not acted impulsively or without popular support. Everything he'd done suggests confidence and planning. Though not well schooled in generalship—he had never, as Plutarch points out, led troops in battle—he had seen what had happened at Tegyra four years earlier; the Sacred Band, outnumbered two to one, had proved its mettle. If Sparta would not relent, then *now* was the time for a showdown.

Agesilaus too wanted no delay, though his phlebitic leg had not healed. He kept up pressure for war despite efforts to slow the momentum. The new Peace required action by coalition; a Spartan named Prothoös urged that Sparta heed that clause, since to ignore it might offend both the gods and Sparta's allies. But the Spartan assembly, swayed by Agesilaus, derided Prothoös's words as nonsense. "It seems that *to daimonion* was leading them on," comments Xenophon, using a layered Greek word that can connote fate, luck, or the gods, or all three at once.

Orders went out to King Cleombrotus in Phocis to give Thebes one last chance to dissolve its League. When that ultimatum was spurned, Cleombrotus marched. He led his troops south by a rough mountain track, thus avoiding the Theban advance guard sent to block him. Within just three weeks of the conference at Sparta, he'd reached the plain of Leuctra, about ten miles southwest of Thebes. It was now late July or early August 371 BC.

Meanwhile, in the other cities of Greece, diplomats were returning from Sparta and giving reports to assemblies and councils of state. They told of a new Theban leader who'd attended the conference at Sparta. This man had spoken up for the rights of Sparta's neighbors, peoples too cowed by Agesilaus to speak up for themselves. He'd described a new order in Greece, shaped not by balance-of-power wars but by ideals of equality and justice.

The news must have been met with much surprise. Somehow, the Greeks now knew, a philosopher had emerged among the Boeotian swine.

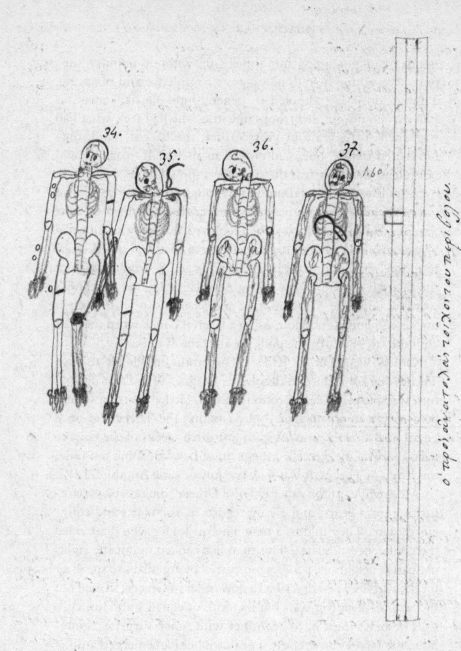

CHAPTER 4

Otototoi!

(July 371–370 BC)

The two years preceding the Battle of Leuctra had seen many omens in Hellas. First, a fiery column appeared in the night sky, shaped not like a comet but a sort of wooden beam (Greeks called it the "flaming plank"). Then, an earthquake destroyed two cities in the north of the Peloponnese, Helicê and Bura. The quake hit at night and therefore had a high mortality rate, since residents were indoors, asleep, when their houses collapsed. In Helicê, survivors emerged from the rubble at dawn, only to be drowned by a tsunami that swept in from the sea. After the twin disasters, Helicê remained underwater, and tourists taken across the site in boats would gape at the sunken ruins for centuries afterward.

The same earthquake had a more disturbing impact at Delphi. The temple of Apollo there—the seat of the Pythia who delivered the god's oracles—was destroyed, perhaps by a rockslide shaken loose by the tremors. That temple, built at huge expense, had been the pride of the collective Greek world; within it sat an omphalos stone marking the "navel" of the earth. That the gods would destroy such a holy structure—for Poseidon was thought responsible for earthquakes—made no sense, and seemed to portend a tear in the cosmic fabric. The puzzled Greeks began collecting funds for a new, more magnificent temple, a project that would take decades to complete.

At Leuctra, where the armies led by the Spartans and the

Thebans were camped on opposing hilltops, such omens were thickly clustered. Some seemed to presage victory for Sparta; others, for Thebes. Among the latter were those that concerned the "Leuctridae," two daughters of a long-ago Boeotian farmer named Scedasus. Victims of a legendary rape, their bodies supposedly lay buried in the plain below the two camps.

The story of the Leuctridae is found in several ancient versions. Here is one: The girls lived with their father, Scedasus, on a humble Leuctra farm. Two Spartans happened by and spent the night, on their way to Delphi; they praised the girls' beauty in a menacing way, but, for the sake of the father, made no attempt to go further. On their return journey the Spartans found the two girls home alone. They raped them and killed them, then threw the bodies down a well to conceal the crime. Scedasus found the bodies the next day with the help of the family dog, then heard from his neighbors that Spartans had been seen leaving his house.

Scedasus went to Sparta to seek justice. He spoke to the magistrates, to the kings, and to any citizen he met, but everyone turned a deaf ear. Finally he fell upon the ground and beat the earth with his fists, asking the Furies—underworld deities who avenged crimes of blood—to rise and take his part. Then, he hanged himself. From that time on, it was said, oracles had warned the Spartans to "beware the wrath of Leuctra."

The ghosts of the Leuctridae were thought, by all who wrote about this era, to have hovered over events on those fateful days. Xenophon says that the Thebans found the girls' tomb and adorned it with offerings just before the battle. Plutarch tells a more elaborate story, about a dream that came to Pelopidas, the man of *thumos* who led the Sacred Band, as he slept in his tent at Leuctra. He dreamed that the Leuctridae were weeping over their own graves and cursing the Spartans; Scedasus, their father, was there too, bidding the Thebans sacrifice a fair-haired virgin to feed the Furies. That command seemed unthinkable, but, as Pelopidas related the dream to his senior officers, a mare with a white mane suddenly bolted through camp. "There's your 'fair-haired virgin'!" exclaimed a priest, and the horse was offered in sacrifice to the ghosts of the raped women.

Epaminondas, head of the boeotarchs who commanded the Theban army, did not put much credence in portents. When he heard reports of such signs, he was known to say, quoting Homer, "Only one omen is best—to fight for one's country." The pious and superstitious were sometimes appalled at this indifference. On one occasion, in the army camp, a messenger rode up with a communiqué, holding a ceremonial spear topped with a ribbon. A sudden breeze tore off the streamer and blew it such that it wrapped around a Spartan gravestone— the marker of a tomb set up by Agesilaus on one of his invasions. Awestruck bystanders urged an immediate end to the campaign, but Epaminondas ignored them.

All the same, Epaminondas knew that omens improved an army's morale. He himself, according to rumor, spread reports of two apparitions "seen" in the temples of Thebes. First, the rusty weapons heaped up in a temple of Heracles were found newly polished and laid out in order. Then, a statue of Athena on the Cadmea was found to be holding, in battle-ready position, a shield that had formerly lain on the ground before her. Epaminondas reportedly told the troops that Athena herself, patroness of justice and friend to democracies, had taken up arms in the Theban cause. (Other sources accuse the Theban himself of contriving the "omens.")

There was need of such confidence building in the Boeotian camp at Leuctra, even among the board of boeotarchs. Three of the seven thought the army should not be there at all. During earlier Spartan invasions, seven and eight years before, the Thebans had largely stayed behind walls; they could do so again, it was argued, even if that meant standing a siege. The women and children could be sent to Attica, in part to get them out of harm's way, in part to reduce the pressure on food supplies. Spartans were notoriously poor at siegecraft; the Thebans might well outlast them. In a battle *outside* the walls, where the Thebans were outnumbered three to two, their chances were slimmer.

Epaminondas disagreed. A passive defense would not solve anything; the Spartans might withdraw from Boeotia this year, but they'd be back. The time to settle this fight was *now*, he thought, and two of his colleagues agreed. That made an even split of the boeotarchs, three against three; a seventh member, Bacchylidas, was still out on maneuvers, guarding the Cithaeron passes against a second invasion. And so the Thebans waited, their high command deadlocked.

Across the plain of Leuctra, a half hour's walk to the south, the Spartans were in waiting mode as well. Their general, King Cleombrotus, had not made a move toward Thebes even

One of few surviving objects that bears the "stamp" of Epaminondas: a Boeotian two-drachma coin with the first four letters of his name. Dozens of names are found stamped on Boeotian coins in shortened form; perhaps they are the names of officials in charge of the mint.

at times when it had been undefended. His soldiers became restive, recalling his past campaigns: on his first invasion of Boeotia, just after the solstice plot, Cleombrotus had marched around a good deal but accomplished little; on a second foray, he'd turned back from the slopes of Cithaeron. It was widely suspected he was in cahoots with Thebes or, at least, lacked the anger that drove Agesilaus. His advisers had to warn him, at his Leuctra camp, that he risked banishment, or worse, if he failed to act.

If our sources told us more about Cleombrotus, we might discern his thinking at this moment, but they're nearly a blank. Plutarch, who loved to record the clever sayings of Spartans—he collected them into an anthology—gives but a single remark to Cleombrotus, and a rather flat one at that.* In the *Stratagems* compiled by Polyaenus, which lists the tactical feats of more than two dozen Spartans, the name of Cleombrotus is conspicuously absent. Alone among Spartan leaders, this monarch seems not to have said or done anything memorable, beyond what he did—or failed to do—at Leuctra.

He was now in his thirties, with a wife and young sons; he'd been on the throne nine years, replacing an older brother who'd died of disease. Throughout those nine years he'd stood in the shadow of Agesilaus, a man perhaps four decades older who'd ruled almost two decades longer. Cleombrotus had fought the Theban wars on behalf of his awesome partner, despite his own sense—discernible from the record—that Athens, not Thebes, was Sparta's real enemy. If it was indeed he (as many suspect) who arranged Sphodrias's raid on Piraeus, then he did so in an attempt to replace the war against Thebes with one against Athens. But it seemed that nothing he undertook was destined for success.

---

* As a child, Cleombrotus reportedly told a man who belittled his father, "My father's greater than you, until you too become a father."

Normally Sparta did well with one weak king and one strong one, since two strong monarchs tended to fight each other. But in this case, their strongman was out of action, still nursing a phlebitic leg, and more than seventy years old. Cleombrotus served as his agent, enacting a program crafted by other hands and aimed at others' goals. Cleombrotus had played this role from the first, when Agesilaus—healthy as yet, but somehow unwilling to march—had sent him to avenge the fall of the Cadmea. He'd dithered then, and he was dithering now. When the moment for action came, he may have fortified himself by getting drunk.

On the Theban side of the field, the seventh boeotarch, Bacchylidas, returned to camp from his post on Mt. Cithaeron and cast his vote for fighting then and there. The tie was broken; Epaminondas, the head of the board of seven, had won. Thebans and Spartans began to prepare for the highly formal event that was a Greek infantry battle.

At some point, perhaps the morning of that day, Epaminondas stood in front of his army, holding up a live snake. As his soldiers watched, he crushed the creature's head, causing the whole body to go limp. Then he drew the lesson: "You see how the body is useless once the head is gone. So it is with the heads of armies. If we smash the Spartans"—the seven hundred Spartiates in the vast coalition—"the 'body' of their allies will be useless." His strategy is still known today as "cutting off the snake's head."

What Epaminondas had glimpsed, as few others had done, was how much distance there was between Sparta and its so-called allies. Most of the troops Sparta led—Achaeans, Arcadians, Eleans, and other Peloponnesian Greeks—were forced to follow its orders, by oaths it had demanded and governments it had installed. *They* had no vendetta with Thebes; they'd marched on Boeotia unwillingly, for the fourth time now in eight years. Epaminondas would not fight these troops unless he had to. He'd hit the Spartans first and hit them hard.

The Sacred Band was key to this plan. At Tegyra, four years before, the Band had been badly outnumbered but had still prevailed. It had charged the strongest point of the Spartan line, where the polemarchs were stationed, and smashed it apart on contact. The Band's small numbers and tight cohesion made it more like a projectile than a phalanx; it struck its target head-on, with hurtling force. And its commander, Pelopidas, had shown he had expert aim.

The Theban plan included another innovation as well. In nearly all infantry battles, both sides put their strongest units on the right wing, weaker ones on the left. Both sides often won on their right while losing the left; victorious right wings then swung toward the center to fight each other. The Thebans and Spartans had done this at Coronea in 394, their last major clash. But Epaminondas broke with long-standing conventions. He loaded his *left* wing with strength: the Sacred Band and a phalanx arranged *fifty* deep, more than triple the norm. That weakened his right, but he didn't intend that wing to enter the fight. Facing Sparta's allies but no Spartans, this wing would hang back or even withdraw as their foes advanced, so as not to make contact at all.

Even on the Spartan right, where Cleombrotus was stationed, the Thebans saw weaknesses and shaky loyalties. Full Spartan citizens, Spartiates as they were called, made up only a tenth of the army at Leuctra and were not even in the majority in their own wing. An unrelenting erosion, the causes of which are debated to this day, had sapped Sparta's strength for decades, accelerating over time. The Greeks gave this affliction the six-syllable name *oliganthrôpia*: population shortfall.

All the central Greek cities were in demographic decline in the age of the Sacred Band. But at Sparta the falloff had become an out-and-out crash. The roll call of Spartiates had fallen to perhaps an eighth of what it had been a century earlier. This potent warrior caste was fast becoming an endangered species. The seven hundred Spartiates serving at Leuctra represented fully two-thirds of the total that Sparta could muster, scattered among a much larger aggregate force the Greeks called the Lacedaemonians.

Among those who filled out these ranks were the *hypomeiones*, or "inferiors," former Spartiates who could no longer afford the food contributions imposed on that class. This group had swelled as land and wealth became concentrated in fewer hands. Alongside these stood the *perioikoi*, residents of the towns and villages surrounding Sparta, attracted into Spartan service by gravitational pull. And somewhere in the lists could also be found the *mothakes*, "stepbrothers," illegitimate sons of Spartiate fathers, brought up in the famous *agôgê* training but lacking a citizen's rights.

Most puzzling of all were the *neodamôdeis*, "new men from the masses," former helot slaves, now freed in exchange for military service. Remarkably, Sparta, because of its steep population decline, was willing to arm its helots, and more remarkably, these abused slaves were willing to fight. By the time of Leuctra, the helots, originally freeborn Greeks from the region west of Sparta, had spent almost three centuries filling the Spartans' larder while suffering random attacks, beatings, mistreatments of every kind. Despite all this, helots continued to join Spartan ranks and fight to defend their masters.

These Lacedaemonian forces—subcitizen classes and non-Spartans—by now so outnumbered the Spartiates as to pose a security threat. In the early 390s an aggrieved *hypomeiôn*, Cinadon, recruited others like himself to overthrow the Spartan state. He took one recruit to the market square of Sparta and, to demonstrate his chance of success, reckoned up the crowd he saw there. Out of four thousand milling about on that random day, only *forty* wore the dress and gear of the Spartiate elite. The rest, claimed Cinadon, had so much rage against Sparta that, given the chance, they'd gladly devour raw that 1 percent. (Ultimately his conspiracy was exposed by an informer and crushed before it could act.)

Such was the army the Spartans fielded that morning in Leuctra. The Spartiates formed a skeleton crew, with one or two at the head of each file of the phalanx (at its assumed depth of twelve men per file), plus a special corps of three hundred "knights" who surrounded the king. Just one or two Spartiates led ten or eleven others when orders came to advance, to turn right or left, or to make the complex maneuvers for which their lifelong training had prepared them. These front-edge troops also absorbed the first shock of phalanx collision, a jolt they were trained to withstand.

On this day, however, Cleombrotus posted his *cavalry* troops in front of these file leaders, rather than at the phalanx's sides where generals usually deployed them. Xenophon, who describes the battle in his *Hellenica*, gives no reason why Cleombrotus would do this, and to this day, no one has quite figured it out. Whatever his reasons, his bizarre decision would help make this the most disastrous day in Spartan history.

The sun had already passed noon. As the Boeotians took their places, in full sight of the Spartans, one contingent began moving off and leaving the field. The men from Thespiae, who had recently had their walls pulled down by Thebes, were unwilling to fight, and Epaminondas agreed to dismiss them, along with other reluctant troops. His move sent a message to those on the other side: Thebes, in contrast to Sparta, would not bully its neighbors to serve. The Mantineans on the Spartan left, who had lost their walls as well, no doubt found this departure noteworthy.

The Spartans commenced the fight by advancing in time to the music of flutes. The sun was behind them and shining in the eyes of the Thebans—a small advantage. Visibility counted for much in the opening phase of a battle; each side scrutinized the other's formations as they drew closer. If the enemy did not break into a run, there would be enough time to make final adjustments to counter what one saw.

What Cleombrotus saw, in this case, shocked him deeply. As he got close enough to perceive depth of line, he realized the Theban left wing, facing his own position, was deeper and stronger than he had ever imagined. What was more, it was moving to his right as it advanced, as though to get around his rightmost flank. With numbers on his side, *he* had planned to outflank and encircle, but the thickness of the approaching wing would make that impossible. He had to move troops to the right, and fast. To gain more time, he ordered his cavalry forward.

These horsemen were an unimpressive group, for Spartans had little esteem for cavalry warfare. They simply assigned horses, on the day of battle, to those chosen to ride them— often the worst of their troops, demoted from infantry ranks. Thebes by contrast had a long tradition of proud horsemanship. Its cavalry had shone in many recent contests, including during the campaign for Boeotia. When Epaminondas saw the Spartan riders in motion, he brought his own cavalry forward and sent them to meet the foe.

The gap between phalanxes was closing. The Spartans advanced at their usual leisurely pace, pausing midfield to sacrifice to the gods, while the Theban left wing moved more quickly. The cavalry action between the two lines raised dust clouds and obscured their view of each other, exactly as Cleombrotus intended: he did not want the Thebans to see his rightward maneuver until it was complete.

A phalanx entering combat could not simply turn and

march right, for exposing its flank could draw an immediate charge. The Spartans had a more complex method for shifting troops rightward. One by one, files of men would peel off from the left, march around the rear of the formation, and re-form on the rightmost side. If that peel-and-reel movement was used at Leuctra, then each file had to traverse behind hundreds of others to reach its new position. This took time, and time was in short supply; the gap was still closing.

Cleombrotus expected the cavalry skirmish would buy him the time he needed. But Thebes's horsemen proved their mettle and quickly routed the Spartans. Some defeated riders, fleeing pell-mell from the rout, careened in disorder into the Spartan lines. Cohesion was briefly lost as this shock was absorbed. That was what the Thebans were waiting for.

Pelopidas and the Sacred Band charged forward on the run, seizing this moment of Spartan disarray. They hit the Spartans head-on while many were still in midcrossing, behind their own lines. Cleombrotus fell, wounded, and was carried off the field by the "knights," who struggled to defend him. High officers were killed where they stood: Sphodrias, who had earlier led the raid on Piraeus, with his son, Cleonymus, and Deinon, a polemarch. Meanwhile the rest of the advancing Thebans, led by Epaminondas, slammed into the Spartan ranks. Sparta's allies on its left, not yet engaged in combat, took fright at what they saw to their right and fled from the field. The Spartan line began to collapse.

Greek battles were decided by a "turning," or *tropê*, by one side or the other, and a "trophy," *tropaion*, was later set up by the victor to mark the point of the turn. Spartans had not been turned in an open-field battle in the past three centuries, but they turned now, leaderless, and ran for high ground. A ditch that stood in the way slowed them down, and many were slain by the Thebans as they tried to cross it. The rout became total.

A thousand of Cleombrotus's troops lay strewn across the plain, including an astonishing four hundred Spartiates.

The Spartan survivors reached their camp and assessed their situation. Their king was dead by this time, the first Spartan monarch slain in battle in generations, and surviving polemarchs had taken over command. These men convened an emergency council. Many Spartans wanted to reengage, before the Thebans could set up a trophy. But the allies, fighting under duress, had no heart for a new effort, and some even seemed pleased at the Spartan disaster. They had borne for eight years now the burden of war on Thebes, a war not their own.

With grim resignation, the polemarchs dispatched a herald to the Thebans, seeking a truce to recover their dead. In the conventions of Greek warfare, this was a formal admission of defeat. Epaminondas granted the truce but imposed a unique condition: the Spartans must first allow their allies, city by city, to collect their own countrymen's corpses. He knew that Sparta had in the past concealed its casualty numbers by mingling its dead with those of its partners. This time, Sparta's appalling losses would be plain to see.

Meanwhile the Thebans set up their trophy at Leuctra: a set of captured weapons mounted, scarecrow-like, on a pillar or tree stump, marking the spot where the Sacred Band had smashed the Spartan right. At some later date they replaced this ephemeral structure with a version cast in bronze, set atop a marble pedestal—a monument built to endure.

The pedestal, reassembled but lacking its trophy, stands in an open plain at Leuctra today, a simple stone cylinder ornamented with bas-relief carvings of shields.

The Thebans celebrated that night, and for once Epaminondas joined the festivities. The next day, however, he regretted his indulgence. When his troops saw him looking sullen and unkempt, they asked what was wrong. His answer was such as few, perhaps, understood: "Yesterday I found my thoughts

A reconstruction of the monument erected by Thebes on the Leuctra battlefield. The rebuilt pedestal still stands there; the trophy itself, depicting captured Spartan arms, is patterned on an image the Boeotians later stamped on their coins.

were soaring higher than was good for me. So today I'm chastising myself for immoderate joy."

Word of the Spartan defeat spread to the rest of Hellas, bringing astonishment in its wake. Riders and runners carried it from Leuctra, traveling as fast as fifty miles a day. One of these arrived in Sparta probably three days after the battle.

In their plays and historical writings, the Greeks often dramatized the arrival of disastrous news. A century before Leuctra, Aeschylus, in the tragedy *Persians*, staged the moment at which the Persian people, in the royal city of Susa, learned of their navy's defeat two thousand miles away. In that scene, a breathless messenger describes the catastrophe, causing the chorus, made up of Persian elders, to unleash an anguished cry: *Otototoi!* That word (if it can be called a word) went on to serve, in other tragic plays, as a way to express extremity of pain—the pain of a nation suddenly glimpsing ruin.

As their own turn arrived to look into the abyss, the Spartans showed how different they were from Aeschylus's Persians, and indeed from every other race on earth. Their response prompted Plutarch, a great student of national character, to meditate on the link between virtue and adversity. Just as strong wine shows the greatness of people, says Plutarch (citing Xenophon), so violent grief shows the greatness of nations. In drink, or in shock, *enkrateia*, self-restraint, meets its ultimate test.

Word of Leuctra arrived at Sparta on the last day of the Gymnopaidiai, a local religious festival. The event for which the fest was named, a dance of naked young men, was then being performed. The five ephors, the city's head magistrates, were told the news first, but did not announce it or interrupt the performance. Foreigners attending the dance, they knew, would depart for home the next morning; Sparta would have privacy in which to nurse its wound. Couriers were sent to the families of the fallen, bidding them keep silent until the Gymnopaidiai concluded.

The next day saw bizarre scenes in the streets of Sparta: fathers of the slain greeted one another with smiles, while the kin of those who'd survived wore solemn garb and dour expressions. The same inversion was seen among mothers: the bereft paid each other cheerful visits, chatting merrily about their lost sons, while those who would soon see their sons again grieved as though in mourning. Xenophon, who may well have been in Sparta that day, reports this admiringly, praising a feat of citywide self-control. Plutarch gives a different perspective: many in the city, he says, were furious with Agesilaus, and fearful that Sparta's enemies might soon invade.

Resent him though they might, the Spartans needed Agesilaus. Cleombrotus was dead, and his successor, his son Agesipolis, was perhaps ten years old. The city was facing a manpower shortage unlike any other it had known. A huge number of Spartiates—perhaps a third of the total—had died at Leuctra, and nearly all who survived were now, officially, "tremblers" (*tresantes*). Under Spartan law, tremblers who fled from a fight were unable to wed or to borrow fire from neighbors and were forced to wear ragged cloaks and shave off only half their beards. Anyone might freely kick or punch tremblers they encountered in the streets. Under Sparta's ancient code, hundreds of young men—potentially, a rebel army—would be condemned to this cruel humiliation.

Only a man of Agesilaus's stature could deal with this social crisis. The ephors awarded the king the temporary title Nomothete, "lawgiver," empowering him to do as he thought best. Agesilaus addressed the public, assuring them he intended no change to the city's laws. "It's good for our present laws to stay in force—*starting tomorrow*," said the septuagenarian king. The penalty for tremblers could "sleep" for one day, he proclaimed. The survivors of Leuctra would receive amnesty—but any who ran from danger would, in future, once again be shamed.

Agesilaus focused on getting back at Thebes and, if possible, getting Thebes back. Cleombrotus's army was still in Boeotia, beaten, but able to fight again. Agesilaus moved to reinforce and support them, recruiting troops from the allies: Tegea, Mantinea, Corinth, Sicyon, Phlius. He put his own son, Archidamus—serving here in his first known command—in charge of the composite force and sent them north, over Cithaeron and past Boeotia's borders. Perhaps it was not too late to retrieve his city's fortunes. While he still had the throne, and a tiny remnant of the Spartiate corps, Agesilaus would not give up on the war against Thebes.

At Leuctra meanwhile, the defeated Spartan army was still in its camp. Some soldiers were unwilling to leave without fighting a second battle; others were afraid of what might await a retreat. They were safe on their fortified hill, but descent into the plain would expose them to fresh attacks. Nearby, the Thebans stood ready to mount those attacks, especially the Sacred Band, now no doubt being talked of across the Greek world.

For its part, Thebes wanted to close the net and destroy these defeated Spartans. It sent an envoy to Athens—still officially its ally, though cool to the current war. This messenger arrived wearing a garland of celebration, expecting a warm welcome. But the Athenians omitted a customary state dinner in his honor; then, when he made his request for aid, they gave no reply. Their silence spoke volumes. They were already wary of Theban power, and the outcome of Leuctra had made them much warier. They had taken one more step away from the Boeotian League.

Rebuffed at Athens, the Thebans sent an envoy to another ally, Jason of Pherae. Jason had taken power in Pherae, in eastern Thessaly, some years before and by now aimed at controlling all Thessaly as *tagus*, commander in chief. His ascent had been as sudden as that of the Thebans, though fueled by different resources: family wealth, limitless ambition, and a strength that inspired awe in tough, professional soldiers. He was among the first of a new breed arising in Hellas—charismatic warlords whose only cause was their own. For that reason, he deserves a closer look.

Jason had been born into a wealthy Thessalian family and learned early on how to shake down his kin. Our sources tell amusing stories of how he fleeced cash from his mother by ransoming her favorite servants, or sacked the house of his brother, or staged a fake sacrifice to the gods, collecting gold and silver offerings from the pious. He'd seen the new truth of Greece's balance of power: the land was awash in veteran soldiers uprooted from homes and cities; those who could pay them could quickly amass a huge army. By the time of Leuctra, he'd collected more than six thousand troops.

Xenophon has preserved a portrait of Jason's character and methods. In a speech he attributes to Jason, as reported by another Thessalian, we hear Jason brag about his hired military muscle: "I don't think any city could easily fight against such a force. In every city, only a few do lots of physical training; but in *my* force, no one draws pay who does not equal *me* in endurance." The Thessalian who quotes this speech confirms it with observation: Jason, he says, has been leading his men in daily full-armor drills, weeding out the weak, rewarding the strong with double, triple, or quadruple pay. With honors for the brave and lavish burials for the fallen, he was building a martial cult among his men.

In only a few years in power, Jason became "the greatest man of his time," said Xenophon, "in that no one could look down on him." Everything seemed to go right for this man, nicknamed Prometheus for his gift of foresight (since Prometheus had knowledge of the future). When a swelling tumor threatened to end his life, and the doctors despaired of a cure, Jason went into battle nonetheless; a thrust by an enemy swordsman lanced the boil, and Jason quickly regained health.

The story was told long afterward to show how the gods look after extraordinary men.

Should he become *tagus*, with the right to mobilize Thessaly's forces, Jason's might would more than double. With such a vast army, what could he not accomplish? According to Xenophon, he believed himself able to unite northern Greece—Macedonia, Thessaly, and the hill tribes of the Balkans—into a land empire; deprive the Athenians of ships' timber and build a navy of his own; make allies, then subjects, of all Greeks willing to align against the Spartans; cross the Aegean and attack the Persians, as Agesilaus had done; control both land and sea, Europe and Asia, money and military force. Forty years before Alexander the Great, he aimed at doing what that man later did, if we believe Xenophon's quoted speeches.

Jason considered Thebes an ally and potential partner. He'd married a Theban woman, and he'd named their first child, a daughter, Thebe—an obvious gesture of friendship toward the regional superpower. It was not a natural friendship, for Thebes was a democracy, while Thessaly, under Jason, was something close to an armed dictatorship. The two states had little in common beyond their hatred of Sparta, but that was enough, thus far, to sustain an alliance.

Like many strongmen, Jason was loved by some of his people but feared and hated by others. His home city, Pherae, stood firmly behind him, but other Thessalians regarded him as a bully or tyrant and longed to be rid of his rule. The city of Pharsalus appealed to the Spartans, asking them to send an army to Thessaly—not just freed helots, they pleaded, but Spartiates, quality troops. The Spartans deliberated over that request and seemed to want to respond, but when they counted up their other commitments, they found they had too few men. Pharsalus laid down its arms, and Jason's takeover of Thessaly was complete.

In the aftermath of Leuctra, Thebes asked for help from this

extraordinary man. Jason arrived on the double with a body of
elite troops, moving so fast through the lands in between that
no one knew he was coming until he was past. He took stock
of the situation at Leuctra and of his own increase in stature: no
longer a mere Thessalian upstart, he stood between two of the
three great powers of Greece, holding in his hands the scales of
their destinies. Assessing his own advantage, he chose to leave
those scales in balance. He shuttled between the two armies
and convinced them to stand down and come to a truce. No
doubt he hoped they'd continue to counterweight one another,
thus strengthening *him*.

Even after the truce was arranged, the Spartans at Leuctra were wary. Their polemarchs told the troops to pack for
a predawn departure, but suddenly, as the evening meal concluded, gave the order to strike camp and march. In this way,
any leak of their plans would keep their pursuers at rest a few
hours longer. The Spartans traveled at night along a circuitous
route, then struggled across Cithaeron, sleepless, in the dark.
En route they encountered the force led by Archidamus, sent
to reinforce them. It had come just a day too late. Both armies
then marched south, through the Isthmus, and returned to the
Peloponnese.

Thus ended the fifth, and last, Spartan attack on Thebes, the
catastrophic result of one man's simmering hatred. A quarter
century had passed since the episode at Aulis, when the Thebans had aborted Agesilaus's sacrifice. Sparta had controlled
events for much of that time, but then, on the night of the
solstice plot, the tide had turned. The Sacred Band had been
formed in the wake of that night; now, the Band had dealt the
Spartans their first open-field defeat in centuries. The "gigantic bluff" by which Sparta had intimidated all of Hellas, with
only a thousand or so full citizens, had been called. Leadership
of Greece was suddenly in Thebes's grasp.

• • •

"If by some contrivance a city, or an army, of lovers and their young loves could come into being . . . then, fighting alongside one another, such men, though few in number, could defeat practically all humankind. For a man in love would rather have *anyone* other than his lover see him leave his place in the line or toss away his weapons, and often would rather die on behalf of the one he loves."

Those words, according to Plato, were spoken on a spring evening in 416 BC, in Athens, at the house of Agathon, a young tragic playwright. In fact Plato composed them himself decades after that time and put them in the mouth of Phaedrus, a participant in *Symposium*—a dialogue on the theme of *erôs*, sexual love, and Eros, the god who embodied it. The words appear to refer to the Sacred Band of Thebes, or else to imagine a corps just like it.

No one can say just when *Symposium* was written. Around 380 BC seems a likely date—very near the time Thebes was liberated and the Sacred Band was created. One prominent scholar, K. J. Dover, dated *Symposium* to just before the creation of the Band, on grounds that the work speaks only hypothetically of a corps of lovers. If the Band had already existed, Dover reasoned, Plato's language would be more concrete. But this argument collapses when one takes account of the work's fictive setting. The dinner party it dramatizes supposedly took place in 416, so Plato could not refer to the Band without anachronism.

Plato had two Thebans in his circle, Simmias and Cebes, both of whom had followed Socrates in his life and were present at his death. Simmias was also a leader of the Theban revolution and a member of the solstice plot; it was at his house, we recall, that the plotters had met, as they awaited the exiles arriving from Athens. The events at Thebes, and the victories over Sparta, must have intrigued Plato, just at the time he was contemplating the power of *erôs*. In the thesis he gives to Phaedrus—that male *erôs*, harnessed on the battlefield, might conquer any foe—Plato seems to acknowledge what Thebes, and the Sacred Band, had achieved.

Plato was no stranger to the political power of *erôs*. In the early 380s, in his forties, he had formed a close bond with a young man named Dion, in the western Greek city of Syracuse, on Sicily. Dion, brother-in-law of the city's ruler, was then in his twenties, energetic and idealistic, filled with hope for what Syracuse could be if ruled wisely. Plato's arrival inspired Dion with fervor, and his ardor in turn inspired Plato. The bond between the two men would extend over decades, enriching the lives of both and altering the course of Syracusan history.

Dion ultimately overthrew the regime and governed Syracuse himself, but was assassinated by his enemies. Plato, by then in his seventies, wrote a verse elegy that proclaimed his love for his friend. It's the most direct evidence we have for Plato's emotional life, and its authenticity is doubted by some, since other poems that masquerade as Plato's work are clearly forgeries. The Dion ode, however, seems genuine. In its final line, Plato addresses Dion as one "who drove my spirit mad with *erôs*," a sign of the intense and possibly sexual nature of their bond.

It's noteworthy, then, that in *Symposium*, written after he'd first met Dion, Plato not only speaks of an invincible army of lovers, but also paints an admiring portrait of a long-term same-sex union. Pausanias, another guest at the fictional dinner party, was, in real life, widely known as the *erastês* of the party's host, Agathon. So when Pausanias delivers a speech in praise of *erôs*, we're meant to see that he knows whereof he speaks. His theme is the bliss of lifelong commitment between lovers, as compared with the briefer pleasures of a "fling." This lasting *erôs* is described as "Uranian," belonging to the heavens, while the briefer version is said to be earthly and common. Pausanias and Agathon, as Plato's readers knew, stayed together, in an exclusive bond, for good—a new kind of lifestyle for Athens, but, as we have seen, one customary at Thebes.

Both Phaedrus and Pausanias, the first two speakers in *Symposium*, cite legendary examples for their views on *erôs*. Phaedrus speaks of Achilles, the warrior whose love for Patroclus—a love here assumed, without challenge, to be erotic in nature—roused Achilles to turn the tide of the Trojan War. Pausanias, for his part, invokes a historical couple, the Tyrant Slayers of early Athens. These lovers had risen up against Hippias, then tyrant of Athens, when the tyrant's brother threatened to come between them. To protect their bond they'd armed themselves with daggers and set out to assassinate Hippias and his brother. Their plot miscarried and they killed only the brother; the tyrant survived, but was ousted two years later, in part thanks to a popular uprising. The Tyrant Slayers, who died for their act, were celebrated long afterward, especially in a pair of memorial statues in Athens.

Several more speeches follow in *Symposium*, including that of Socrates, containing Plato's main doctrine: the highest form of *erôs* is not sexual at all, but brings both *erastês* and *erômenos* toward higher, nonphysical truths. This *Platonic love*—the term has been much reduced in scope since it was coined in the Renaissance—can turn us into philosophers, once we see that bodily pleasures pale next to those of the mind. Much can be said on this point, but our concern here lies with Phaedrus and Pausanias—not sages like Socrates, but worldly men, involved with political change. The principal change in Greece, at the time *Symposium* was written, was the rise of Thebes, propelled by the Sacred Band—an army of male couples, in a city where men could be "wed."

Did Plato intend to refer to the Band in the words he gave Phaedrus? On balance, that seems a likely conclusion, though proof can never be had. It's possible too his encounter with Dion, in the years before he wrote *Symposium*, prompted his thoughts on "Uranian" *erôs*. If the Dion funeral ode is truly by Plato, then he too felt a long-lasting commitment to an *erômenos*.*

Erôs was also of deep concern to Xenophon, as we've seen—the man who'd started off as a fellow student of Plato's, in the circle of Socrates, but ended up on a very different path. Xenophon too composed a *Symposium*, probably soon after Plato's work was published. In that work he looks at male *erôs*, and the Sacred Band of Thebes, in a very different light.

As Plato had done, Xenophon contrasts two types of male *erôs*, heavenly and earthly. The distinction he draws, though, is based not on longevity, but on whether sex is involved; spiritual love between men is celestial, while physical love is base. In general Xenophon's Socrates is far more sex-negative than Plato's: on several occasions, he forbids male lovers to have any physical contact. (Late in life, in his last work, the *Laws*, Plato too advocates banning sex between men, but his earlier works are far less censorious.)

This "Socrates," in Xenophon's work, cites Achilles and Patroclus as examples of erotic love, just as Plato's Phaedrus had done, but insists these heroes were mere "comrades" and not bedmates. So too Orestes and Pylades, Theseus and Perithous, and other mythic pairs. Then, moving forward in time, "Socrates" deals with the *erastai* and *erômenoi* of his own day. He extols "those willing to suffer and endure danger for the sake of praise"—that is, the chaste—but reproaches "those who make a habit of preferring pleasure to glory." It's the old hard-road, soft-road opposition from his parable of Heracles, this time applied to male couples. When these submit to "pleasure," that is to desire, they become weak and contemptible, while abstainers ascend to the heights.

---

* Unusually for Athenians of his time, Plato never married.

Finally, with the air of one wading into a running debate, "Socrates" turns to the idea that older men and their younger lovers could fight as a unit—a Sacred Band, though he doesn't give it a name. Referring directly to Plato, but getting his names crossed, he says this idea had been advanced by Pausanias, *erastês* of the poet Agathon. In fact it was Phaedrus, not Pausanias, who had spoken of a band of lovers in Plato's work. Xenophon's slip is perhaps deliberate: Pausanias and Agathon had a well-known "Uranian" union, so Pausanias, one might assume, was biased toward bonds like his own. Xenophon seems to hint at such bias when he describes Pausanias's thesis as an "apology," a tendentious speech, like one written by a defendant in a trial.

"Socrates" takes up the cudgels against the "love's warriors" thesis. He attacks the hypothetical lover-soldiers as "those wallowing in *akrasia*"—lack of self-control. In Xenophon's moral scheme, inspired by the actual Socrates, *akrasia* stands at the opposite pole from *enkrateia*, self-mastery, the foundation of all virtue. Acratics, that is, are those who follow the soft road of the Heracles parable—the path of indolence and self-indulgence.

"Socrates" then launches his harshest assault on warriors of love. "Pausanias thinks these men feel shame at deserting one another," he says (again using the wrong name), "but what he says is incredible—if men who . . . act shamelessly toward one another are ashamed to play the coward." Since their sex lives (in his view) are "shameless," there can be no question of noble motives in battle. "Socrates" turns to the Thebans (and another state said to use couples in battle, the Eleans) as his case in point. Where *erastês* and *erômenos* stand beside each other in war, as at Thebes, they do not spur each other toward courage, but merely keep an eye on each other to guard against desertion.

After thus besmirching the Thebans for accepting "disgraceful" couplings, and dismissing the notion that *erôs* inspires virtue, "Socrates" goes on to exalt the Spartans. These soldiers, he claims, avoid all sex between men: "They believe that if someone even yearns for the body, he will get no part of goodness or grace." These chaste Spartans, "Socrates" concedes, do form pairs of *erômenoi* and *erastai,* but their love remains pure of any physical taint. In battle, Spartan *erômenoi* are brave without need of watchdogs, and thus Spartan generals do not place *erastai* beside them. The courage of soldier-lovers, unlike at Thebes, does not diminish with distance from their beloveds.

The bitterness of this attack is startling, especially since in his other writings Xenophon shows full awareness that Spartan soldiers were not immune to homoerotic desire. But here he juxtaposes a chaste and virtuous army, that of Sparta, with the "shamelessness" of Thebes. Like all he wrote, his *Symposium* is tainted by anti-Theban, pro-Spartan bias, this time channeled into his examination of *erôs.*

How it must have galled Xenophon to see the results of Leuctra—a battle in which the Sacred Band, despite their "shamelessness," had defeated his very models of *enkrateia* and moral strength. His one consolation was that his great hero, Agesilaus, had not been in charge, but a man of lesser morals, Cleombrotus. To drive that point home, he mentions a rumor—not heard of elsewhere—that Cleombrotus and his officers had had too much wine in the hours before the battle. A swerve into *akrasia,* Xenophon hints, had brought the Spartans down.

Hellas was again in disorder after the Battle of Leuctra. The Peace signed at Sparta, by all but Thebes, had become a dead letter. A new conference was convened, this time at Athens, to draft a new treaty.

Not all states agreed to join in. The Thebans held aloof, perhaps regarding this Peace as one more attempt, led by

Athens this time, to break up its Boeotian League. If so, their suspicions were likely well founded. Athens was now more concerned about Thebes than about Sparta, and Athenian Laconists increasingly argued that their city should make common cause with the Spartans and keep the Boeotians down.

The more of Boeotia it encompassed, the more serious a threat the League presented. Soon after Leuctra, the Thebans added Orchomenus, the last remaining holdout, to the Boeotian ranks. The Thebans had to use force to achieve this, though not as much force as they might have: once Orchomenus was taken, sober-minded Epaminondas convinced the assembly not to give rein to its anger and enslave the whole city. "For those who aim at leadership of the Greeks," he told the assembly, "it's crucial to preserve with *generosity* what's been won by courage." The word he used here, *philanthrôpia*—literally, "love for one's fellow man"—was a new one in foreign relations, which had too often known only machtpolitik, the use of raw power.

The Greeks perceived a new order arising, based neither on Spartan militarism nor Athenian mercantilism. Allies flocked to the side of Thebes, including much of northern Greece and even Euboea, traditionally loyal to Athens. South of the Isthmus, the Peloponnese too was rocked by the outcome of Leuctra. The blow Thebes had dealt to the master of that region, without harming the servants, had roused a yearning for self-determination. The Spartan bloc there began to shift and fragment.

The fracture began in Arcadia—the mountainous center of the peninsula, where early Greek peoples, who'd arrived before even the Spartans, still held to ancient dialects and customs. The isolation of Arcadia set it apart from its neighbors. Its legendary tranquility made it a dreamy literary landscape for later Roman poets and, eventually, also for early modern

Europe. Renaissance painters depicted this land as a pastoral idyll, making the name Arcadia synonymous with rustic peace. But in the years following Leuctra, Arcadia was to be anything but peaceful.

The region's largest city, Mantinea, had long held democratic and anti-Spartan views. Fifteen years earlier, it had suffered a *dioikismos* at Sparta's hands, its walls pulled down, its people dispersed. Now the Mantineans wanted to reverse this with a *synoikismos*—a rebuilding of walls and reaggregation. And more than that, it sought to unite with other Arcadians, those in neighboring Tegea and points west—an Arcadian League, an ethnic federal state. It was just what Thebes had achieved in Boeotia with stunning success. A Mantinean statesman, Lycomedes, working hand in glove with the Thebans, began to beat the drum of Arcadian pride.

In Sparta, Agesilaus tried his best to stop this movement. But his hands were tied by the autonomy clause he'd sworn, in both of the Peaces he'd signed in the previous year. He went in person to Mantinea—his leg now healing at last—and offered to pay for the city's rebuilding with Spartan funds, if the process only might wait a few years. Attempting to bribe hostile neighbors was a humbling role for the king, and even more humbling when the bribe was refused. The Mantineans set about raising their walls in spite of Agesilaus.

Next, Tegea, some twelve miles south of Mantinea, was likewise swept up in anti-Spartanism. But Tegea stood closer to Sparta than Mantinea did, both in geography and politics. The *beltistoi*, or "best men," there still stood behind Sparta and guarded their own control of the city's *dêmos*. In a meeting of the governing council, this power elite blocked a set of proposed reforms, and the *dêmos*, enraged, took up arms. An anguished condition the Greeks called *stasis*—violent strife between classes—suddenly took hold in Tegea. As the streets began to run with blood, troops from Mantinea arrived to support the democrats. The oligarchs fled out Tegea's southern gate, into a temple of Artemis beyond the walls.

Stasis in Greek cities tended to spiral out of control, as Thucydides pointed out in a now-famous study of events on Corcyra (modern Corfu). Under pressures of *stasis*, Thucydides wrote, humanity itself becomes mistrustful and mean, losing "the ancient simplicity that is the greatest part of a noble nature." Events at Tegea proceeded along just these lines. The democrats ignored the sanctity of Artemis's temple and broke through the roof from above, then hurled heavy tiles down onto their enemies' heads. The Tegeans trapped in the temple surrendered under this barrage. Their opponents bound them and carted them back to Tegea, where a show trial, assisted by the Mantineans, produced convictions and mass executions. Out of this bloodshed, Tegea was reborn as an anti-Spartan, pro-Arcadian state.

Winds of change were blowing elsewhere in the Peloponnese, some with hurricane force. In the region's northeast corner lay Argos, a city already democratic but, in the eyes of some Argives, not democratic enough. An uprising there produced the bloodiest *stasis* in all Greek history, in the judgment of its sole chronicler, Diodorus. He gives it the name *skutalismos*, or Affair of the Clubs—a name that resembles Germany's Night of the Long Knives in evoking a spasm of riotous violence.

Like the Arcadian revolution, the *skutalismos* began with fiery rhetoric. Assembly speakers stirred up the masses' anger at the *beltistoi*. The fear this provoked in the rich prompted a group of them to attempt a rightist coup. When the plot was uncovered, those caught were tortured for information; most killed themselves rather than name names, but one man broke and denounced thirty of the leading citizens. The democrats put those thirty to death and confiscated their estates, but the mob had become fearful now of the entire upper class. Wielding clubs, rather than the swords they were too poor to own, they beat to death no fewer than twelve hundred *beltistoi.*

Finally the revolution devoured its own children: the speakers who had first stirred up the mob became victims themselves when they tried to halt the carnage. Stripped of its oligarchs, Argos was more democratic than ever. It allied with the new Arcadian League, and with the city of Elis in the far west, to form a coalition of anti-Spartan states stretching nearly from coast to coast.

Could this cordon hold, Sparta would be forever cut off, unable to march north out of its region. Agesilaus watched with dismay the closing of the net. Well past seventy, with one lame leg and another barely healed, he donned armor for the first time in years and prepared to lead his battered, diminished army into battle. He'd had to give up on Boeotia, but he'd fight for the Peloponnese, no matter how few resources he had left.

As southern Greece came alive with ferment and revolt, a different shock struck in the north, in Thessaly. Jason of Pherae, employer of Greece's largest private army, had gone from strength to strength in his rise to power. After his statesmanlike role at Leuctra, he had finally been chosen as *tagus*, commander in chief of all Thessaly, with the right to levy its highly skilled cavalrymen. Now, though, he faced a reckoning with those who hated or feared him.

Jason had glimpsed that leadership of Hellas—"a prize of virtue, for those willing to compete for it," says one ancient writer, perhaps quoting Jason's own words—was up for grabs. The Spartans, he reasoned, had been dealt a fatal blow at Leuctra, and Athens was only concerned with control of the *sea.* The Thebans—again the words may be Jason's own—"were unworthy of first rank." Greece was a power vacuum he thought he himself could fill.

After leaving the Leuctra truce parley, Jason had used his hired troops to destroy Heracleia, a stronghold that guarded the north end of Thermopylae. This legendary pass gave Jason access to central Greece, and he resolved to keep it in his control. Then, as the Pythian Games approached—a festival held every four years at Delphi—Jason arranged for magnificent sacrifices and offered a gold crown to the city that sent the finest bull. He seemed to be looking to play the presiding role at the games, an honor that conferred enormous stature.

As Delphi prepared for the quadrennial festival, Jason told his army to mobilize for a march. It occurred to some that he might seize Delphi itself, with its heaps of gold and silver—sacred objects the Greeks had brought to Apollo over the centuries. The Delphians consulted the oracle as to what they should do if that happened. Apollo reportedly told them, through the words of the Pythian priestess, that he could look after himself. Since the god's own temple lay in ruins at this moment, there was room for doubt on that score.

No one knew what Jason intended or where he would go—and no one would ever find out. As Jason reviewed his cavalry forces in Pherae, then sat to hear petitions from his people, a group of seven young men approached, seeming to quarrel among themselves. At a signal they drew their daggers and stabbed Jason to death. The number of the attackers helped ensure their success: Jason's bodyguards killed one of the youths as he struck and a second as he fled, but the other five escaped, finding refuge in various places. "Prometheus," the man who'd foreseen many dangers, had in the end been blindsided by his foes.

Thessaly was thrown into turmoil, at just the moment that *stasis* and war were sweeping the Peloponnese. Between the two regions stood Thebes, "unworthy of first rank" in some eyes, "Boeotian swine" to others, clog-wearing men who fed on round loaves of coarse bread. Rustics though they might be, the Thebans had Greece's best army, its most revered leader, and its most potent infantry corps, the Sacred Band. These assets gave them the power, perhaps even the duty, to keep Greece from falling apart.

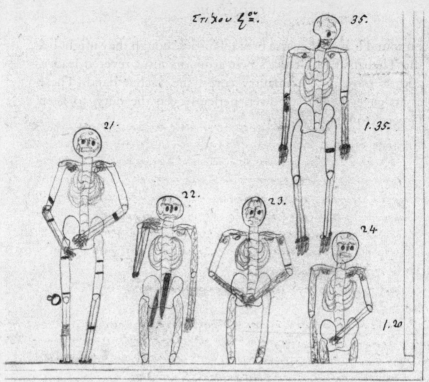

Στίχου ζ^{ου}.

35.

1. 35.

21.

22.   23.   24.

1. 20

Μεσημβρινὸς τοῖχος τοῦ περιβόλου.

CHAPTER 5

The Three Free Cities

(370–367 BC)

*"It should here be noted that the military aspect of Greek love . . .
was nowhere more distinguished than at Thebes." Those words were
penned by the eminent British Hellenist John Addington Symonds,
in 1873, just before the remains of the Sacred Band were uncovered at
Chaeronea. Symonds could not yet admit to the world his own erotic
passion for other men, so he instead explored the history of such passion in the Greek world. Even then, he printed only ten copies of the
pamphlet he produced, "A Problem in Greek Ethics." In that work he
included a glowing tribute to the Sacred Band, the "pith and flower" of
a city—Thebes—that formed "the last stronghold of Greek freedom."*

The word homosexual *had been coined a few years earlier but
was not yet in wide use. To his fellow Britons, Symonds was a Uranian, a term derived from Plato's* Symposium—*where it denotes the
"heavenly" passion that binds (male) lovers together throughout life. It
was through a chance encounter with* Symposium *and Plato's other
exploration of erôs,* Phaedrus, *that Symonds, at age seventeen, discovered "the revelation I had long been waiting for." Male erôs, Plato
taught him, "had its virtue as well as its vice" and could be connected
to heroism and valor, as it was at Thebes.*

*Symonds went on to study Plato at Oxford with Benjamin Jowett,
and the two remained friends throughout their lives despite Jowett's
homophobia. But the friendship came under strain when the two men,
in 1888, collaborated on a translation of* Symposium. *Symonds was
appalled to learn that Jowett had come to consider Plato's erôs to be*

123

"*mainly a figure of speech.*" *Symonds wrote an impassioned letter to Jowett to dissuade him from that view, a missive so deeply personal that he later included it, verbatim and entire, in his memoirs.*

"*Many forms of passion between males are matters of fact*" *in England, he wrote to Jowett. For those who feel such passion, "the reveries of Plato . . . ha[ve] the force of a revelation. They discover that what they had been blindly groping after was once an admitted possibility. . . . Greek history confirms, by a multitude of legends and of actual episodes, what Plato puts forth as a splendid vision." Among these "actual episodes" Symonds no doubt had in mind the Sacred Band.*

In later life Symonds became fascinated with Walt Whitman, a fellow reader of Plato's erotic dialogues, and especially with the Calamus sequence of Leaves of Grass. *Symonds sensed a fellow spirit expressing itself in these poems and, in an intense correspondence with Whitman, tried to get the poet to avow their homoerotic meaning. Whitman humored him for a while but finally slammed the door on the inquiries. He told Symonds, in a claim now judged to be false, that he'd fathered half a dozen illegitimate children, testament to a long string of adventures with women.*

"*About the questions on 'Calamus,' etc., they quite daze me,*" *Whitman wrote to Symonds. "I am quite fain to hope that the pages themselves are not to be even mentioned for such gratuitous and . . . undreamed and unwished possibility of morbid inferences—which are disavowed by me and seem damnable." The time had not yet come when a poet who had written of "manly love" could admit his intended meaning, even when writing to a fellow closeted gay man.*

Symonds was often in mind of the Sacred Band when he read Leaves of Grass, *especially later editions with poems based on Whitman's experience of the Civil War. Some of these later poems dealt with love between fellow soldiers, a theme that resonated deeply with Symonds. His notes to his copy of the 1884 edition relate this theme to the Greek world and to the Sacred Band in particular. He found the following lines, where Whitman again seems in mind of the Band, especially meaningful:*

But when I hear of the brotherhood of lovers, how it was
    with them,
How together through life, through dangers . . .
. . . how unfaltering and affectionate and faithful they were,
Then I am pensive—I hastily walk away filled with the bit-
    terest envy.

*As a gay man in Victorian England, Symonds too suffered "bitterest
envy" when he pondered the world of the Greeks. He became an expatri-
ate and suffered bouts of crippling depression, made worse by the tuberculo-
sis that finally killed him in 1893. His closeted life and sham marriage had
been unhappy in the extreme. To Jowett, Symonds wrote, "The contest in
the soul is terrible," describing, in part, his struggle between identity and
the need for acceptance. Amid that struggle, Symonds gained a measure of
peace from Plato, from Whitman, and from the tale of the Sacred Band.*

In the wake of the Battle of Leuctra, stonecutters and masons
were busy across the Greek world. Walls and towers were going
up everywhere.

At Mantinea, an elegant, state-of-the-art wall was underway, far finer than what the Spartans had torn down fifteen
years before. That older wall had been of mud brick; it had
melted away when the Spartans diverted a river to flow around
its base. The new rampart was made of stone to a height of six
feet, with mud bricks extending it farther, and a thickness of
fourteen feet (including the rubble that filled it). The river that
formerly destroyed it now formed its moat. At every eighty or
ninety feet stood a horseshoe-shaped tower, over a hundred
towers in all, with wooden staircases for the guards to climb
up on their watches. They watched for the Spartans, only two
days' march to the south.

Farther west, a long day's walk from Mantinea, another
city was being laid out, Arcadia's new capital. Megalopolis, the
"great city," was planned on a vast scale, as vast as the new

Arcadian democracy: its assembly was termed the Murioi, a word that means "ten thousand" but also connotes a numberless multitude. An Arcadian federal army, the Eparitoi or "chosen (i.e., best) men," is said to have numbered five thousand, an astonishing size for a standing, state-sponsored force. Megalopolis would need houses, shops, and gymnasia for all these (and funds to pay their salaries), plus a gathering place for the assembly, as well as a constitution to guide its deliberations. Plato's help was supposedly sought for this last task.

The Thebans, too, were building at this time, at the oracular shrine of Delphi. Apollo's temple there was in ruins, the result of an earthquake two years before, but smaller treasury houses, erected by leading cities to hold their gifts to the god, were still standing. Thebes now added its own treasury, larger than all the others, positioned so that many visitors would encounter it first. Inside, no doubt, the Thebans placed rich dedications tithed from the spoils of Leuctra. Builders used chunks of the old temple's rubble for a platform, to elevate the Theban structure above those nearby. Intentionally or not, they created a metaphor: Thebes was attempting to build a new Hellas on the ruins of the old.

Elsewhere in Greece, the Thebans were putting up forts, using sturdy, neat-dressed ashlar blocks so closely fitted that some are still partly intact. At Eleutherae, where Boeotia borders Attica, stand the remains of one such fort, almost certainly built by Thebes in the years after Leuctra. Its walls, seven feet thick and over fourteen feet high, were punctuated by two-story towers every thirty feet; intact portions of both can be seen today, far away from tourist pathways. The fort, called Gyphtokastro (Gypsy Castle) by modern Greeks, allowed the Thebans to guard the pass over Cithaeron, an invasion route Sparta had often used in the past. Now, it seemed, Thebes might need to guard against Athens using it too.

The Thebans of the age of the Sacred Band were pioneering

The expert stonework of the fort at Eleutherae, most likely a Theban defensive post from the age of the Sacred Band.

wall builders. Where standard methods called for two courses of stone—an outer and an inner face—with loose rubble fill in between, Thebes devised a technique of binding the two together with crosspieces. That made their walls sturdy and strong, a potent symbol of their defiance of Sparta—a city that had no walls of its own and despised those of others. (Once Agesilaus, when shown a well-built city wall, was asked if it wasn't a great thing. "Yes, for women, not men, to live in," he replied.)

Epaminondas dispatched Theban masons to other cities in the same way a modern leader sends military advisers. Such assistance firmed up alliances and spread influence. He sent Pammenes, one of the strategists behind the Sacred Band, with a contingent of a thousand Thebans to build Megalopolis's walls. He meant to bind the Arcadian League to his new Theban-led coalition, as firmly as if with mortar.

But the greatest feat of Theban wall building was yet to come. No one in 370 BC could yet foresee that, within the

year, another new city would rise, even larger and more consequential than Megalopolis. Epaminondas would build it himself, on a site revealed by a dream. It would be his greatest,
most lasting riposte to his nemesis, Agesilaus.

Arcadia was asking for help. With its League now a target of
Spartan wrath and Agesilaus on the move, the newly formed
federation needed allies. Its diplomats went first to Athens, but
were rebuffed; Athens was more inclined now to support the
Spartans than those who opposed them. So the Arcadians went
to Thebes, lead city of the league that had inspired their own.

The arrival of these envoys presented Thebans with a stark
choice. They had seldom ventured outside Boeotia's borders,
and never into the Peloponnese, a Spartan preserve. But they'd
heeded Epaminondas once already when he'd urged them past
their limits. *"Give me one step more,"* the great commander reportedly shouted at Leuctra, at a moment when the shield-on-
shield clash had become a stalemate. Now too he must have
asked the Thebans to take one step more, this time a giant one.
The assembly agreed to send troops into Sparta's backyard.

Epaminondas led his army south as winter was setting in.
Such off-season marches were rare, and this one presented a
problem. A boeotarch's term of office expired at the winter
solstice; it was death to exceed this term. Epaminondas set out
when the expiration date was fast approaching. He perhaps
meant only to drive the Spartans back from Mantinea, a task of
just a few weeks. But by the time he arrived, the Spartans had
already left Mantinea, and his new Arcadian allies urged him
to chase them. Sparta was weak, they insisted; its mirage of
strength was maintained by tricks and smoke screens. With the
forces Epaminondas now led—over seventy thousand, including the Sacred Band—an assault on Sparta itself, unattempted
in five hundred years, could succeed.

As the boeotarchs debated this move, the problem of the

calendar weighed heavily. The dilemma they faced, on the march as the solstice approached, had never before arisen. Most of them sought to obey the charter and return to Thebes, but Epaminondas insisted on going onward. He stood at what the Greeks called a *kairos*, a decisive and opportune moment, the importance of which, he felt, outweighed written laws. He argued it would be a greater offense to let such a moment slip by.

Informed that Sparta's neighbors, the *perioikoi*, stood ready to revolt from their masters, Epaminondas led the coalition forward, dividing it into four columns for four invasion routes. The passes leading into Laconia were narrow, and Spartan units could hold any one or two against greater numbers. But defending all four at once was beyond the reach of Sparta's dwindling manpower. Some columns at least would get through. In the end, all four did. The Theban contingent, perhaps six thousand strong, took the most direct route, a straight shot south through the village of Caryae. The Caryans, exultant at Sparta's discomfort, served as guides through the mountains, terrain that few non-Spartans had before seen.

The four invading columns rendezvoused at Sellasia, only ten miles from Sparta, forming what Plutarch called a *kludôn*, a billowing wave, of might. This host of seventy thousand was, in Greek terms, a tsunami. The armies of two great leagues, the Boeotian and the Arcadian, had joined forces, together with Argives, Eleans, *perioikoi*, and many others who had cause to hate Sparta or fear it. The juggernaut paused to plunder the countryside, then moved to the banks of the river Eurotas— less than an hour's walk from its target.

In Sparta meanwhile, King Agesilaus was ruing a boast he had often made, that Laconian women had never seen the smoke of an enemy's campfires. Spires of smoke were now clearly visible to the north and east. The women of Sparta were panicking, while older men, veterans of earlier wars, raged at the king for squandering all they had won. Even the leadership felt the grip of fear: Antalcidas, the diplomat who had brokered the King's Peace, spirited his children out of the city and landed them on Cythera, an island off the coast.

Less than a thousand Spartiates could be called on for defense. With them stood four thousand recruits from Corinth and six thousand helots who'd answered a call for volunteers. This latter group was so numerous that the Spartans feared to arm them. Some of the slaves chose to liberate themselves, sneaking away in the night to join the opposing side. Those who deserted left their heavy shields behind, and in the morning the sight of abandoned gear had a chilling effect on morale; Agesilaus appointed a detail to make predawn sweeps of the camps and remove the shields. The Spartan mirage had to be preserved at all costs.

With so few Spartiates, Agesilaus could not risk an open-field battle, but he hoped he would not have to. The Eurotas was in full spate, fed by recent snowfalls, and ran cold and turbid through the whole length of Laconia. By posting units up and down its bank, he could deter any crossing. This passive defense was the best plan he had.

The Spartans stationed on the Eurotas could clearly see a huge host on the opposite bank, including Epaminondas himself, leading the phalanx forward. Agesilaus glimpsed his adversary and, after watching him in silence, exclaimed, *"Ô megalopragmonos anthrôpou!"*—"O man of great deeds!" Plutarch records the remark without hint of a sneer; it expressed genuine respect. For their part, the Thebans shouted across the roar of the river, calling on Agesilaus by name to offer battle, reminding all who heard it was *he* who had started the war.

As the Thebans ravaged their fields and farms in plain view, the Spartans became seditious. A group of two hundred, mostly disaffected non-Spartiates, gathered in a fort called Issorion, planning to link up with the invaders and overthrow the state. Agesilaus got wind of the plot and went to Issorion with a single servant by his side, pretending nothing was amiss. He told the rebels they had mistakenly taken up the wrong post and needed to move. The rebels shifted ground to avoid suspicion, abandoning their stronghold. Then Agesilaus closed the trap, ordering a night attack that killed fifteen of their leaders. Seldom before had Sparta put citizens to death without trial, but "war is a savage teacher," as Thucydides famously wrote. With survival on the line, civil rights were annulled.

Even then the danger of collapse was not past. A second plot took shape, forcing Agesilaus to resort again to extrajudicial measures. But the Spartans' greatest fear, a helot revolt, never happened. Of all our meager glimpses into the world of the helots, none is more puzzling than this: when their masters were desperate, when a small push would have toppled those who had beaten and flogged them, the long-abused slaves did not deliver that push.

As Agesilaus worked to hold his city together, Epaminondas crossed the Eurotas, unopposed, at a point far to the south. He made his way back northward toward Sparta. He had no obstacle before him any longer, not even a curtain wall, for the Spartans had never built one. But time was working against him. His army of seventy thousand was rapidly consuming all the food the region could yield; it would soon run out of supplies. And Sparta had gotten fresh help in the days the river delayed him. A new combatant—Athens—had entered the fray, sending its best general and thousands of troops to Sparta's rescue.

Xenophon dramatizes the assembly debate that finally tipped the scales in wavering Athens. Five Spartan ambassadors addressed the Athenian *dêmos*, one by one; they invoked the glorious teamwork of Athens and Sparta in the wars against Persia, now more than a century past, and promised the utter destruction, and plunder, of Thebes. Even so the Athenians held back, memories of the Peloponnesian War still fresh in their minds. "So they say *now*, but while they were thriving, they made war on us" was the murmur that passed through the crowd.

Finally Procles of Phlius, close friend to Agesilaus, came before the Athenians, describing the debt they'd be owed if they saved Sparta. Security, in the end, argued for laconizing. The *dêmos* made up its mind. Reversing the policy of the last six decades, Athens cast its lot with the Spartans and decisively turned against Thebes. It dispatched an army into the Peloponnese, headed by the swashbuckling Chabrias.

With these troops en route and food supplies running short, with his term of office already officially over, Epaminondas found himself in a difficult spot. To force his way into Sparta, through narrow streets where women and slaves would pelt him with roof tiles and stones, held little appeal. He opted not to advance, but could not leave Sparta unvanquished, after breaking the law in order to come this far. He still had tens of thousands at his command, even if (as Xenophon snidely reports) some had slipped away from the fight to return to their homes. With so many hands to assist, he might accomplish wonders—even create a city ex nihilo on a rocky mountainside.

Off to the west, across the rugged Taygetus range, stood a peak, Mt. Ithomê, watered on one face by a gushing spring called Clepsydra. Thanks to this plentiful water supply, Ithomê had long offered refuge to those fleeing Spartan oppression. A century before this, after an earthquake left Sparta reeling, a band of helots entrenched themselves on this mountain, so securely that Sparta needed a decade to dislodge them. Since then, the peak had loomed large in Greek minds as a symbol of liberation. Epaminondas marched there with his army, trailed by a long line of helots escaping from Sparta.

Elsewhere, across the Greek world, former helots were on the move, making their way toward Ithomê. Epaminondas had sent word to all corners of Greece: those who had fled Messenia to avoid Spartan dominion there, or who had escaped helotage one way or another, could return to their homeland, a place some families had not seen in generations. The summons reached distant places, since runaway slaves—as Spartans deemed the Messenian refugees—had traveled far. A large group had landed in Libya (North Africa), where recent Greek settlers needed any and all, even fugitives, to help fight nearby tribes.

The leader of those Libyan Messenians, Comon, had foreseen, in a dream, that he'd soon return home. He had dreamed of sleeping with his dead mother, then seeing her come back to life. It was not a fantasy of necrophiliac incest, but a promise of restoration. His motherland, Messenia, was reviving from political death and preparing to embrace him.

Meanwhile in the Peloponnese, other dreams were telling the Thebans to build a city at Ithomê, even pointing them toward the spot it should be sited. An officer in the Theban-led army, Epiteles, dreamed of an old man dressed as a priest of Demeter. The man told Epiteles to look for a yew and a myrtle growing close together, then dig at the spot in between. "Rescue the old woman, for she is weary and cramped in her bronze bedroom," the old man said. At the foretold spot Epiteles unearthed a bronze urn and brought it to Epaminondas. Inside were mystic writings inscribed on a scroll of tin.

Tens of thousands went to work on the site where that urn was found, raising up walls to the spirited music of flutes. Epaminondas himself laid the plans: a wall more than five miles in circumference and eight feet thick, rising two dozen feet or more, with thirty adjacent towers. Through openings in these towers, defenders could shoot at approaching foes, then close wooden shutters against incoming arrows. A gate allowed guards to admit travelers to a circular enclosure, then examine them before letting them inside the wall. A modern-day road passes through this circle, still partly intact, as it reaches the city: Messene.*

---

* Pronounced "mess-EE-nee," with three syllables. It was apparently founded under the name Ithomê but soon after renamed.

The carefully dressed, tightly aligned stones of the wall, many still standing today, give no sign of haste, yet Messene was built in a hurry. The chief architect's term of office had elapsed well before it was started. The Thebans had stayed long in the field, in winter no less, living off plundered supplies. Their farms needed tending, but they could not leave until all was complete, for the Spartans would quickly exploit any weak points.

In the plains surrounding Ithomê, surveyors got busy marking out boundaries in fields once tilled for the Spartans. Freed helots were given small plots they could work for themselves, rather than feeding a faraway master race. Inside the walls, public buildings arose: halls of state, a theater, gymnasia, stoas, and shrines. The water of Clepsydra was channeled into a market square where all could fill their vessels.

The circular gate at one entrance to Messene, with Mt. Ithomê rising in the background.

The entire city was built, according to Diodorus, in *eighty-five days*.

Epaminondas marched homeward through a transformed Peloponnese. Three walled cities, completed or in progress, now cut a diagonal swath through its center, like *O*'s on a winning tic-tac-toe board. Mantinea, Megalopolis, and Messene formed a palisade of democracies that hedged Sparta off from its foes. The Spartan lion would be locked within its den—provided that cordon could hold.

The army's return to Boeotia was surprisingly uneventful. An Athenian force that might have blocked its route home failed to do so, thus earning the contempt of Xenophon. The Athenian commander, Iphicrates, was otherwise talented, Xenophon wrote, "but what he did on this occasion was entirely useless and incompetent." He sealed off one road but left the best one unguarded. Xenophon failed to consider this might have been deliberate. Though obliged to support the Spartans, Athens had little stomach for fighting the victors of Leuctra.

Back in Thebes, Epaminondas was put on trial by the state for exceeding his term of office, a capital charge. When called on to speak, he urged the jurors, if they executed him, to write this on his grave monument: "Epaminondas forced the unwilling Thebans to ravage Laconia, unharmed for five hundred years, and to resettle Messene after three hundred twenty years, and to bring the Arcadians in as allies for that task, and to restore to the Greeks their autonomy"—that is, by dispelling the threat of Spartan power. The case against him was instantly dismissed.

Beyond Boeotia's northern frontier, in the broad plains of Thessaly, new leaders arose to replace the murdered Jason of Pherae, and to take command of his six thousand well-trained, well-paid troops.

Jason's sons were too young to rule, so two brothers, Polydorus and Polyphron, tried to share the title of *tagus*. But in only a few months Polyphron was dead, almost certainly killed by his brother. Then, in a family drama worthy of Greek tragedy, Polyphron's son killed Polydorus, avenging his father and seizing the *tageia* for himself. That son, Jason's nephew, was a cruel and callous youth named Alexander—Alexander of Pherae, we'll call him, to keep him distinct from "the Great." Deploying his uncle's mercenaries, he began cracking down hard on Thessaly, making clear he intended to rule with an iron hand.

In describing the nature of Alexander of Pherae, our sources employ extreme language, in particular the Greek word *ômos*, "savage." Even Xenophon, who often admires authoritarians, castigates him as "an unjust pirate on both land and sea." Plutarch expresses outright disgust, comparing Alexander's moral condition to that of a wild beast. Like the later Caligula, Alexander seems to have lived by the motto *oderint dum metuant*, "Let them hate me, so long as they fear."

Alexander made a god of the spear with which he had stabbed Polydorus to death and gained sole power. He named this weapon Tychon, suggesting good fortune, and set it upright in a homemade shrine, where he crowned it with garlands and offered it sacrifices. The message to Thessalians was clear: armed force was this man's deity. And thanks to the family wealth he controlled, he could hire plenty of it.

Opponents of Alexander met terrible deaths. Some he buried alive; others he hunted as prey, forcing them to don animal skins and then loosing his hounds to tear them apart. He joined the "hunt" himself by hurling javelins at the "game," enjoying high sport. He seemed devoid of human feeling—yet tragic dramas could move him. He once rushed out of a theater during Euripides' *Trojan Women*, a portrayal of the suffering of captives; later he explained that he had left out of shame because he could cry for Hecuba and Andromache, but not for those who died at his hands. ("What's Hecuba to him?" asks Hamlet after watching an actor weep, perhaps an adaptation by Shakespeare of this story.)

The rise of this amoral man, close to the northern border of Boeotia, presented a new test to the leaders of Thebes. The hard-pressed cities of Thessaly reached out to Thebes for help (before, when beset by Jason, they'd reached out to Sparta). Again Thebans faced the question of how far to extend their commitments. Epaminondas had already taken them farther and done more than they'd expected or planned. The Peloponnese was unsettled, requiring more interventions; Epaminondas had already set out there again, or perhaps was preparing to leave, at the moment the Thessalian envoys arrived. Could the Boeotian League muster a second army to open a second front?

Fortunately the League had a second great commander. Pelopidas was then at Thebes and had not headed south with Epaminondas. Perhaps that year's term-of-office trial, in which Pelopidas reportedly testified against his old friend, had driven a wedge between the two men. Or perhaps rivalry had eroded their friendship, which had up to that point stayed uniquely close. Whatever the cause, their paths had begun to diverge.

A new theater of war was just what Pelopidas needed. If Epaminondas had won fame by marching south, Pelopidas could do so by marching north, to tame the tyrant of Pherae. A notorious sadist with an army of hired thugs was just the right challenge for a man of *thumos*—a warrior driven by honor and righteous anger—and the right sort of cause for the democratic League. Though councils at Thebes were divided—one faction preferred a policy of "Boeotia first"—Pelopidas staked himself to the struggle against Alexander. He took a squad of troops and headed for Thessaly.

Since Jason had been a Theban ally, and his nephew was still one in theory, Pelopidas arranged a parley to try for a peaceful accord. Thebes would recognize Alexander as *tagus* if he agreed to treat his fellow Thessalians well and respect their rights. The meeting was set in the city of Larissa, now partly held by Macedonian troops; the king of Macedon had also inserted himself in Thessalian affairs. Pelopidas chased out these occupiers and made ready to meet the fearsome tyrant of Pherae.

Alexander arrived with an armed retinue, and a tense negotiation began. Alexander sought recognition and thought he deserved it, while Pelopidas insisted on better behavior first. Finally Pelopidas lost his temper and spoke too frankly about Alexander's abuses. Alexander stalked out of the room, trailed by his armed guard. The summit broke up in discord. It seemed that armed force would have to resolve the matter.

Pelopidas proceeded north to Macedon, where rival claimants to the throne had both asked for Theban support. He settled their dispute and sealed an alliance with the reigning king (also, to our dismay, named Alexander). To guarantee the pact, he accepted hostages, the standard means by which such treaties were enforced. Macedonians of noble and royal blood were sent to live at Thebes, insurance against any treachery by their kin back home.

Among this group was the king's own brother, a teenager named Philip. This youth—Philip of Macedon—was destined to change the fate of Hellas. He and some thirty others marched south with Pelopidas, through the storied pass of Thermopylae, toward Thebes.

On his homeward march Pelopidas took more steps to contain Alexander of Pherae. Following the pattern of his own region and the one emerging in Arcadia, he organized Thessaly into a league, with a federal army, treasury, and assembly. But in Pherae, Alexander remained entrenched and able to do much harm. The Thessalian League would need Theban help to survive, much like the Arcadian League in the Peloponnese. Pelopidas returned home only to be sent back, within the year, to further stabilize Thessaly against Alexander.

This time he did not have an army. Trusting in his diplomatic skills, his countrymen voted to send him as an envoy, together with a comrade named Ismenias.* The two tried to hire mercenaries to back them up, but these troops deserted when offered better pay by another employer. The pair were defenseless then when Alexander of Pherae appeared on the scene, at the head of his troops.

Pelopidas and Ismenias went forward to greet Alexander, believing perhaps the tyrant had come to mend his ways, or else that their diplomatic status would protect them. "Pelopidas put a reckless, foolhardy trust in the very last person he ought to have trusted," comments the historian Polybius, who regarded this episode as a huge black mark on the Theban's record. "He knew very well that tyrants always regard the champions of freedom as their worst foes." Hewing to this age-old pattern, Alexander ordered the two Thebans seized and taken prisoner. Pelopidas had walked straight into a trap.

By now Epaminondas had made a second march into the Peloponnese, close on the heels of the one that had built Messene. He'd been called in by Thebes's new friends, the Arcadians and Argives, to lend Theban support to their anti-Spartan alliance. But Sparta had new friends too, the Athenians, as well as a wealthy magnifico who ruled in far-off Sicily and who owed the Spartans a favor. This man, Dionysius of Syracuse, now the leading potentate in the Greek West, had started to extend himself into mainland Greece, hoping to awe the cities there as he'd astonished his own.

Dionysius† had held sole power in Syracuse for almost four decades and had purged away all remnants of its former democracy. He packed off those who opposed him to the *lato-*

---

* Most likely the son or grandson of the famous Ismenias, the man who had first set Thebes on an anti-Spartan course.

† The name is derived from that of the god Dionysus, but the extra i in the final syllable gives the s a "sh" sound in English.

A coin struck by Dionysius of Syracuse reveals
the grandness of that ruler's ambitions. At ten
drachmas' weight, it was the largest denomina-
tion of its day, and the superbly engraved image
attests to the regime's magnificence.

miae, limestone quarries north of Syracuse, to be imprisoned
in clammy hollows carved out when the city was built. Some
prisoners grew old in these caverns and even married and raised
families; their children, brought up in a wilderness of rock,
were said to run screaming in terror when later they came to
Syracuse and glimpsed yoked horses and carts. Today the deepest of these caverns is called l'Orecchio di Dionisio, "the Ear of
Dionysius"; a seventeenth-century visitor, the painter Caravaggio, imagined the tyrant had used its echoing walls to listen in
on prisoners' whispers.

But Dionysius was far more than a dictator. He also fancied himself a talented poet and playwright (a few lines of his

verse have survived). He gadded about Syracuse in the purple robes of a king from the tragic stage, deliberately blurring the lines between myth and life. Backed by wealthy supporters, he spent lavishly on improvements to the city, especially to "the Island," a peninsula that stuck out into the harbor of Syracuse from a narrow isthmus. The palaces and temples he built there, including a shrine of Athena (the core of the modern city's duomo), made the Island a glittering gem, and also an impregnable fortress. The storerooms there held shields and weapons for 140,000, an arsenal of autocracy.

Like many a Greek tyrant, Dionysius collected thinkers and writers from all over Greece to improve his cultural standing. Plato paid a visit there in the 380s, finding a decadent place "where life is spent in gorging oneself twice a day, and never sleeping alone at night" (Plato's own description, if the *Seventh Letter* is his work). Plato's teachings displeased Dionysius, who reportedly ordered the sage to be taken away and sold into slavery. Another intellectual who crossed swords with the tyrant was the poet Philoxenus, once a court favorite, but sent to the quarries after giving Dionysius too frank an opinion of his poems. Dionysius regretted his rage the next day and had Philoxenus recalled. But at a state dinner, the tyrant once more recited from his work and once more asked Philoxenus what he thought. The hapless poet merely turned to the guards and said, "Take me back to the quarries."

Another member of the Syracusan court, Damocles, became legendary in a tale of the perils of power. Damocles kept praising Dionysius's wealth and magnificence, until finally the tyrant offered to trade places for a day. He furnished Damocles with fine food and wine, a dining couch wrought with gold and embroidery, scented wreaths, handsome attendants. Then Dionysius arranged for a glistening sword to be suspended from a single horsehair directly above the man's head. Damocles quickly renounced the swap, having learned that a tyrant's fear negates all his pleasures. The story, later recounted by Cicero, conferred immortality on "the sword of Damocles."

Along with thinkers and writers from central Greece, Dionysius also imported the finest engineers. His shipwrights designed bigger and faster warships, *pentêreis*, or quinquiremes, rowed by a hundred more oars than the standard Greek trireme. His team of inventors devised, around 400 BC, the first Greek artillery weapons: small, spring-driven crossbows called *gastraphetae* or "belly bows" (since one braced them against the stomach to load them). These greatly surpassed the range an archer could shoot, proving so effective that within thirty years they had spread throughout Greece.

All this largesse was expensive, as were the troops Dionysius hired from the Italian mainland, Celts and Gauls who had recently sacked a small town called Rome. Like Jason of Pherae, Dionysius devised ingenious schemes to raise cash. He collected gold and silver vessels for offerings to the gods, then melted them down into coin for his treasury or else simply plundered the temples, stripping the gods' statues of their gold and ivory "clothes." When those gains ran out, he issued coins made of tin, then forced the assembly to rule these were just as valuable as the old kind. His rise gave yet more support to a thesis emerging in Greece: cash, in an age of surplus military labor, could make kings.

The cities of mainland Greece looked askance at this western grandee. At an Olympic festival in the 380s, an Athenian orator denounced "the tyrant of Syracuse" as a clear and present danger. Within sight of his speech were gold and purple pavilions set up by the Syracusans; inflamed by his words, the crowds rampaged and tore down these resplendent tents. But not all opinion ran against Dionysius. Another Athenian, the essayist Isocrates, published an open letter, probably just after Leuctra, in which he tried to recruit Dionysius to be the savior of Greece. "Who should I more justly address than the leader of our race,

the holder of greatest power?" fawned Isocrates in that letter—
the first of many such he would write in the next three decades.

Of all the mainland Greeks, the Spartans had the most affection for Dionysius, as he did for them. They'd supported his
rule by allowing his agents to hire soldiers from the Peloponnese, the best-trained fighters around. In turn he'd helped *them*
on two occasions, by sending warships to aid them in fights
against Athens. Now, after Leuctra, the Spartans stood much
more in need of his help. Dionysius did not ignore them. He
loaded a rescue fleet with horses and troops, blue-eyed Celts
and Iberians, who, thanks to a strange device called a saddle—
as yet unknown to the Greeks—made excellent cavalrymen.
Two thousand of these auxiliaries made ready to cross the Adri-
atic, the newest entrants in the Theban-Spartan wars.

Athens was now on the Spartan side in those wars, so it too
reached out a hand to Dionysius. Two inscribed stones record
Athenian decrees, passed in two successive years—probably
369 and 368—making Dionysius and his sons honorary citizens and firm allies. Then in the following year, Athens bestowed on Dionysius a prize that surpassed these, in his own
eyes, at least. A tragedy he'd composed, *The Ransoming of Hector*, was chosen by an Athenian jury as best play of the year, the
Greek world's most distinguished literary honor.

As the ships of Syracuse sailed to Sparta's defense, the Athenians too sent their forces: six thousand troops, and, as their
general, Chabrias. The man who'd defended Thebes from
Sparta, a decade before, now made ready to defend Sparta from
Thebes, following the wavering foreign policy of his city. He
rendezvoused at Corinth with the Spartans and their allies
and began to dig. With trenches and palisades he sought to
barricade the Isthmus, just as he'd earlier barricaded Boeotia.
Working flat out as the Thebans advanced, he got the passage-
ways blocked, just in time.

Epaminondas arrived and took stock of this barrier. Its

weakest spot was guarded by Spartan troops. The Thebans carefully measured the distance from their own camp, then set off for the place at night, timing their march to arrive at dawn when the Spartans changed shifts. The scheme worked perfectly. The Spartans were busy with morning tasks when the Thebans arrived and attacked. Within a few minutes, the Thebans were through and the Spartans were scrambling onto a nearby hilltop.

A standoff ensued, for the Spartans could easily descend and attack the Thebans as they passed by, but their hill could also be cut off from food and supplies. Not wanting to waste time on such a blockade, Epaminondas forged a truce with the Spartans, allowing both sides to move past each other in peace. This pact would later be held against both commanders by those who found their solution too amicable.

Now joined with his Peloponnesian allies, Epaminondas again swept through the region, firming up his anti-Spartan cordon. Sparta and Athens did not confront him, preserving their strength to defend a more vital objective, the city of Corinth. As guard post of the Isthmus, Corinth was an essential Spartan asset, or, in the eyes of the Thebans, a tempting target. As the Thebans marched homeward, they passed close to this city and dared to attack it—showing, as Xenophon tartly observes, an utter disdain for their foes. He was likely an eyewitness to what followed, for the previous Theban invasion had chased him off his Scillus estate; still banned from his native Athens, he'd taken refuge in Corinth.

Xenophon describes how the Sacred Band—whom he calls "the picked men of the Thebans"—charged at a run toward Corinth's western gate, hoping to find it open or not yet barred. A desperate fight ensued only four hundred feet from the wall, as light-armed Corinthian troops rushed out to engage. They climbed atop monuments erected along the road there—mausoleums and tombs—and hurled anything

they could find, spears if they had them, or rocks, finally forcing the Band to turn back toward the rest of their army. The
Corinthians pursued and killed a few, then dragged their bodies back to the wall, where the Thebans could not retrieve
them except under truce. Epaminondas made a formal request
to get back the corpses, and Corinth set up a trophy. The Band
had suffered its first official defeat.

Epaminondas still controlled the field and held the advantage, but then Dionysius's Celts arrived on the scene. Their
cavalrymen, aided by pommels and stirrups, attacked at will,
then nimbly turned and escaped whenever a Theban gave
chase. The javelins they cast from horseback took an enormous
toll, forcing the Theban army to shift ground each day to find
safety. A few days of that was enough for Epaminondas. He
disbanded the army and led the Boeotians home.

Back in Thebes, Epaminondas once again felt the sting of his
city's displeasure. Not only had he lost a few of the Band, he'd
given safe passage to a Spartan force he might have annihilated.
An old rival, Menecleidas, attacked him for this leniency. When
yearly elections came around again, the Thebans did not return
Epaminondas to the boeotarchy. The architect of the Theban
state, the victor of Leuctra and builder of Messene, the man
who had penned the Spartans within a small tract of ground,
became just another clog-wearing Boeotian, a private citizen.

In Pherae, as weeks stretched into months, Pelopidas's confine-
ment grew steadily worse. At first Alexander permitted Thessalian sympathizers to talk with the Theban. But Pelopidas
used these visits to muster opposition, assuring Thessalians that
Thebes would soon teach their tyrant a lesson. After that, all
visits were barred. Somewhere in that fetid stronghold, unseen
by Pelopidas (and by our sources), Ismenias, a second Theban
captive, moldered in his own isolation.

Through his guards, Pelopidas carried on a dialogue with

his captor. He asked why Alexander was keeping him alive while showing no hesitation to kill his own people. A reply was delivered: "Why is Pelopidas so determined to die?"

"So that you may perish the sooner, being more hateful to the gods," Pelopidas wrote back.

Alexander's wife was half-Theban—Thebe, the daughter of Jason. She went to visit Pelopidas in prison, intrigued by reports of his proud bearing. Thebe too was a prisoner of a sort, forced into a dynastic marriage, subjected to cruelty and humiliation (our sources mention that Alexander had raped her brother). At first sight of ragged, filthy Pelopidas, Thebe burst into tears. "I'm amazed you can keep your spirits up while chained," she said, to which Pelopidas replied, "And I'm amazed *you* can endure Alexander while *not* chained." That visit began a series of parleys between the two, a conspiracy of hatred of the tyrant.

In Thebes, the Boeotian army mobilized and prepared for a rescue mission. They would not leave Pelopidas, the hero of the solstice revolution, to rot in a stinking cell. When the call-up was complete, eight thousand men were ready for the march.

Alexander of Pherae, in only his second year in power, now faced all-out war with Thebes, the city that had beaten Sparta. A more prudent man would have cut a deal and released his prisoners, but Alexander instead reached out for allies. He sent to Athens, by now an open enemy of Thebes. Incredibly, that famously liberal city, where the Turannoktonoi, the Tyrant Slayers, were revered as champions of freedom, dispatched a fleet to back Alexander, among the most depraved tyrants the Greek world had seen (he reportedly promised to sell to Athens the flesh of their mutual foes by the pound). In those ships they sent a thousand troops and a crack Athenian commander. From Sicily, Dionysius of Syracuse too joined Alexander's side, dispatching a new contingent of Celts—though these were commandeered by the Spartans, who felt they needed them more.

The Theban army, poorly led by inexperienced generals,

marched into Thessaly, hoping to force Alexander to yield. But their Thessalian allies deserted them, and with too few cavalry, they could not defend their foraging crews from attack. Provisions began to run short. Then the Athenians arrived, creating even more troubles for the beleaguered troops. The Thebans began a dismal retreat, hungry and thirsty, with nothing to show, harassed from the rear by the tyrant's arrows, slings, and spears.

With faith in their generals lost, the soldiers turned to one in their ranks who they knew had the power to save them. Epaminondas, fighting now as a common soldier, was suddenly called out and given command. The Thebans clearly regretted their ire; they'd recklessly turned their most talented man out of office. In a moment, all that was reversed. Epaminondas reorganized the rear guard and led it in person, fending off Alexander's attacks, protecting the retreat until all were home safe in Thebes.

At the next election, Epaminondas was returned to the boeotarchy and soon thereafter led his own rescue mission into Thessaly. This time, Alexander quickly released his prisoners, in exchange for merely cosmetic gains. Pelopidas and Ismenias were free. Epaminondas was back in charge of the Boeotian League.

Agesilaus of Sparta, in his late seventies, had seen the world of his youth turned upside down. He'd spent half his life warring against Athens, but Athens was now his best ally on the Greek mainland, a bulwark against further invasions by Thebes. The states of the Peloponnese, long proud to march behind him, were now his sworn enemies, harassing his troops from behind their new-built walls. In Messene, farther west, the helots he'd once beaten and flogged now mocked and defied him. And by the side of his few remaining troops fought strangers from Italy, shaggy-haired, blue-eyed Celts, the gifts of his despot friend in Syracuse.

Another arrival from Syracuse was causing further disruptions, though it seems Agesilaus's son, Archidamus, was quicker to spot its importance. A new class of weapons devised by Dionysius, *katapaltai*, or "down-hurlers," had made their appearance in Hellas. These spring-driven devices hurled metal bolts at attackers, farther and more fearsomely than *gastraphetae*, which only shot arrows. "Man's virtue is done for," remarked Archidamus when he first beheld the machines—a sentiment echoed often in modern times, at first encounters with new kinds of armaments.

The one constant for Agesilaus, prevailing for the past two decades, was the support of Artaxerxes, Great King of Persia. This friendship, founded on mutual interests, had endured through twenty years, as other alliances changed. Yet even Artaxerxes was showing less favor, withdrawing from Sparta the right to host his peace parleys. The previous one had been held in Athens, not Sparta, and now, in 368, Artaxerxes convened a new synod, this time at Delphi—essentially, neutral ground.

Philiscus, the Great King's Greek agent, convened the conference and proposed its terms. At issue was Messene, a city now burgeoning with former helots, Sparta's ex-slaves. The Spartans insisted they still held rights to Messene and its population—the farmlands that had fed their soldiers and the slaves who had tilled them. Thebes, for its part, demanded autonomy for Messene and recognition of its statehood. Neither side could compromise on these points, so the synod broke up in discord, without drafting a Peace. Before departing, Philiscus gave his two thousand mercenaries to Sparta—a last-ditch Persian attempt to help a fallen friend.

Sparta's network of alliances was collapsing—but so too might that of its foes, and in this lay its hopes. Only two years after its formation, with its capital city, Megalopolis, barely begun, the Arcadian League was beginning to chafe at its principal ally, Thebes.

Lycomedes of Mantinea, the architect of the League, had come to power on a wave of anti-Spartan feeling. But now he thrilled the Ten Thousand, the Arcadians' assembly, with attacks on *Thebes* instead. "If you follow the Thebans blindly," he told the Ten Thousand (according to Xenophon), "and if you don't demand an equal share of the lead, perhaps you'll soon find you're following *other Spartans*." Such nationalism made Lycomedes the darling of the *dêmos*. The coalition that Thebes had built in the region was starting to fray.

Maintaining that coalition required constant effort, but the Thebans stayed out of the Peloponnese in 368. Their resolve to lead Greece was wavering as the costs of the role became clear. Thessaly had become a complex second front; the rescue of Pelopidas there had required *two* invasions, one of which had nearly ended in disaster. Meanwhile at Corinth, the Thebans had lost a portion of their precious Sacred Band. Their ouster of Epaminondas following that campaign showed how their mood was changing. The Spartans, noting this change, made haste to show their neighbors who was boss in the Peloponnese.

Too old now for generalship—or so it seemed at the time— Agesilaus put his son, Archidamus, in charge of the Spartan army. This prince took the troops on a raid of Caryae, a village that had betrayed Sparta two years earlier and joined with Thebes. After slaughtering everyone he could catch there, he invaded Arcadia and began ravaging its farmlands. He meant to destroy the Arcadian League, a vital part of the cordon that kept Sparta down. Accompanying him were more Celts, on loan from his western friend, Dionysius of Syracuse.

The term of this loan, however, expired in midcampaign. The Celts left the field and headed for the coast, where their transport fleet rode at anchor. En route, they suddenly found themselves trapped by Arcadian troops and called for help. Archidamus came to their aid but soon he too was surrounded. With Messenians camped on one side, Arcadians on the other, he was forced to fight a pitched battle, with his very survival at stake.

Zeus himself seemed to encourage the Spartans, with thunder and lightning from a clear blue sky. They advanced on their foes with a courage born of needing to win or die. The Arcadians, facing Spartans for the first time without Theban support, broke and ran before even striking a blow. Many were slaughtered by Celts pursuing on horseback, or by Spartans on foot. Thousands of Arcadians lay dead by the day's end, while, according to sources, not a single man fell on Archidamus's side.

This clash was dubbed the Tearless Battle because it saw no Spartan losses, yet it *did* evoke tears. When the results were reported in Sparta, Agesilaus, a man not given to emotion, began to weep tears of relief. After him, say our sources, the ephors wept, then the senators, then the elders, and finally the entire city burst into shared sobs, a communal catharsis. After three years in which their fate hung in the balance, in which their citizen numbers had been reduced nearly by half, in which (Plutarch says) men had been ashamed to look their own wives in the face, the Spartans had at last won a battle. Despite all that Thebes and the Sacred Band had dealt them, they had not lost control of their destiny.

In Thessaly, Alexander of Pherae, though constrained now by treaties forced on him by Thebes, went back to his old bad behavior. Money, as always, was his most pressing concern; his mercenaries were costing him dearly. And so he undertook the grimmest, ugliest fundraising effort the Greeks had ever seen, in the town of Scotussa, a center of resistance to his regime.

The men of Scotussa held their assemblies in the open-air theater of town—unarmed, for civilized Greeks did not carry weapons to councils. Alexander's archers surrounded the theater and, standing on the heights of the semicircular bowl, shot into the crowd until all were dead or wounded. The troops then massacred men they found in the town and rounded up women and children for the slave mart. They hurled the corpses into a mass grave outside the walls and ransacked the empty homes for valuables. The entire town, and its people, had been monetized.

This mass shooting must have disconcerted the Thebans, Pelopidas most of all. He'd sought twice now to civilize Alexander, but the man was more savage than ever. His next reckoning with the tyrant of Pherae was not far off. But first Pelopidas had a mission of greater urgency—an embassy to the Persian city of Susa. It's there we'll next meet him, at the court of the Great King, Artaxerxes.

Meanwhile, in Syracuse, the city of Dionysius, the Celts who had helped save Sparta from ruin returned to their barracks. Around that same time, a messenger arrived from Athens, hurrying to be first with happy news: *The Ransoming of Hector*, Dionysius's play, had won first prize at an annual festival. The tyrant was overjoyed. He heaped rewards on the messenger, then staged a lavish banquet for the court. As the wine flowed freely, Dionysius drank deep. Too deep, it seems, for the next day he fell ill, and within a few months he was dead.

An oracle had told Dionysius that he'd die "when he had overcome his betters." He'd assumed this referred to a victory in war and was wary of defeating a stronger foe. Now, as his body was magnificently buried beside the city gates, the wags of Syracuse claimed that the prophecy had come true. Dionysius had beaten the "better" poets of Athens, but was still just a hack for all that.

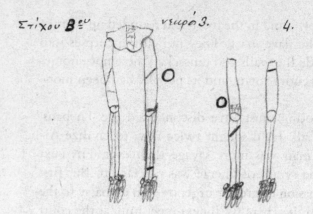

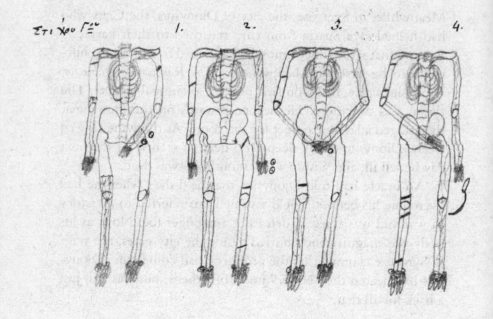

CHAPTER 6

A Death in Thessaly

(367–364 BC)

The Spartan-Theban wars had raged for fifteen years by the time of the Tearless Battle, in nearly symmetrical segments. In the first phase, Sparta had occupied Thebes and thrice invaded Boeotia; then, the Thebans had twice invaded the Peloponnese and nearly captured Sparta. The reversal was mirrored by changes elsewhere in Greece. Athens had aided Thebes when Sparta was winning, then allied with weakened Sparta against Thebes. Arcadia, led by Lycomedes, had eagerly partnered with Thebes against Sparta, but then, as Theban victories mounted, had grown mistrustful and wary and sought its own course.

On the fringes of Hellas, ambitious warlords—Dionysius in Syracuse, in Thessaly Jason of Pherae, followed by his deranged nephew, Alexander—had stepped into the contest for power, backed by enormous wealth and hired armies. The regime of the first was closely allied with the Spartans, the second, with Athens; and both were opposing Thebes.

Farther away from the theater of war, in the heart of the Persian Empire, Artaxerxes Mnêmon, the aging Great King, watched these events with concern. Two decades ago he had favored the Spartans, enshrining them in the King's Peace as his enforcement arm. But he too was thinking of switching sides. The Spartans could no longer help him in Greece, by keeping the peace and freeing up soldiers to fight on his western front. His need for Greek recruits was pressing: Egypt was still unconquered, despite an army of two hundred thousand he'd sent against it.

The Spartans made one more attempt, in the wake of the Tearless Battle, to strike a pact with Artaxerxes for mutual benefit. They sent an ambassador, Euthycles, to Susa, in the heart of what's now Iran, to negotiate a new Common Peace. (Their champion diplomat, Antalcidas, seems to have already been in residence there.) With more idle soldiers to help him, Artaxerxes could regain control of his western marches, perhaps Egypt as well, while Sparta, with Persian funds, might conquer Messene, the symbol of their broken power. Persian aid could, as it had done before, make Sparta master of Greece.

The Thebans got wind of Euthycles' mission, as did the other powers of Hellas. Each sent its own envoys eastward to court the Great King. The Thebans sent Pelopidas and Ismenias, just recently sprung from the dungeons of Alexander of Pherae. Leaving the Sacred Band behind with Epaminondas, this stalwart pair set off down the long Royal Road to Susa.

Artaxerxes had by now been on the throne nearly four decades. He'd survived many upheavals, not least within his own family. Early on in his reign, he'd had to fight his brother Cyrus, who'd led an army against him (a force that included the mercenaries later led homeward by Xenophon). He'd reportedly killed the charging Cyrus with his own hands. Then, his domineering mother, Parysatis, killed his wife Stateira, to remove a rival for her son's allegiance. Parysatis had used a special knife, with poison on only one side, to carve the bird on which the two were dining; Stateira went into convulsions and died a lingering, painful death. Artaxerxes forgave his mother, but Gigis, the servant who'd helped her deliver the poison, paid a terrible price: her head was placed on one flat stone, then crushed to pulp with another.

Mashing of skulls was a cruel punishment, but the royal

A relief carving depicting Artaxerxes Mnêmon, from the facade of the rock-cut tomb in Iran where he was buried.

court at Susa was often cruel, beset by purges and executions. Another courtier who made the King's blacklist, Mithridates, died even more horribly than Gigis. In his cups, Mithridates had boasted that *he* had killed Cyrus in battle, a feat Artaxerxes claimed as his own. (According to Greek sources, Mithridates had in fact dealt Cyrus a serious, but not fatal, wound near the eye.) A eunuch reported the boast to Parysatis. After Mithridates' arrest, two small "boats," or troughs, were fitted around him to form a hollow chamber, with his head sticking out of the top. A mixture of milk and honey was force-fed to him, to promote excretion, and also smeared on his face. Flies settled on him and fed on his excrement inside the troughs, until, after seventeen days, the maggots they laid consumed enough of his body to kill him. The Persians called this grotesque torture "getting troughed."

The Persian court held many forms of death, but also many varieties of love. Artaxerxes kept 360 concubines, who bore him over 100 sons (and an untallied number of daughters). To replace the poisoned Stateira, he married his own daughter by her, Atossa. Persian kings had long been accustomed to marry their sisters, but filial marriage was a new frontier in incest. The breaking of this greater taboo was endorsed by Parysatis, as a way to demonstrate her son's absolute power. But Artaxerxes also seems to have loved Atossa; he cared for her tenderly when she later became a leper.

Susa was a place of luxury and splendor in the age of Artaxerxes, according to a Greek doctor named Ctesias, who served for seventeen years as the royal family's physician. Among its wonders was a vast *paradeisos* (the Greek version of an Iranian word), a walled game park for the king's private use, watered by an elaborate irrigation system. Ctesias told of a team of counting cows that drew water to fill its canals. Each cow would draw precisely a hundred buckets a day, no more and no less; their minders could not force them to draw one pail above this total, even by beating them. The lushness of this and other walled parks impressed the Jews living in Persia; they patterned the Garden of Eden after them and called it, in Hebrew, a *pardesh*. This word and its Greek sibling, *paradeisos*, stand at the root of English *paradise*.

Ctesias told of other marvels in Artaxerxes' realm and other examples of the King's enormous power. A miraculous sword the King possessed, Ctesias said, could drive off hailstorms and hurricane winds when struck into the ground. The sword was forged from iron taken from the bottom of a wondrous spring, which also produced liquid gold in great quantities. This gold was collected by royal servants in clay jars; it then solidified and the clay was smashed, leaving jar-shaped ingots, each weighing as much as a full-grown man. A hundred such ingots were harvested every year for the King's treasuries in Susa.

Jewish writers recorded impressions of Susa in the biblical Book of Esther, a text read aloud in synagogues to this day at the spring festival of Purim. The story of Esther begins with a banquet thrown by King Ahasuerus—perhaps Artaxerxes, though more likely one of two previous monarchs named Xerxes—for Susa's entire population. The feast was held in a palace courtyard, a place paved with a mosaic of alabaster, turquoise, and white and black marble. Linen curtains surrounded the space, hung from silver curtain rods and tied with purple cords. The guests drank from thousands of gold goblets, no two alike. This display of magnificence went on for seven days and ended unhappily when the drunken King banished his queen—here called Vashti—for refusing to display herself, pageant-style, before the crowds.

Such was the city and the court to which a stream of Greek envoys was heading. Pelopidas and Ismenias were hindmost, straining to close with the Spartans in front, a gap of several weeks. Between the two were representatives of Athens, Elis, and the Arcadian League, and perhaps other places as well. All had cases to make before the Great King. Artaxerxes held the scales of the Greek balance of power as never before.

Before they entered Artaxerxes' presence, Greek envoys were prepped by a royal chamberlain. Protocol differed widely between the King's world and their own. Persian subjects greeted their monarch by making a solemn bow, the depth of which reflected their rank; those less wellborn would prostrate themselves on the ground. To the Greeks, such a bow was distasteful, even impious, and some envoys refused to perform it, even at risk to their lives. When the Thebans arrived, they found a way to gratify the King but still save dignity. Upon entering the throne room, Ismenias stealthily dropped a ring, then stooped to the ground to pick it up. In Artaxerxes' eyes, he'd performed his salaam.

The royal court at Susa began to bustle with Greek diplomacy, conducted both in open speeches and conspiratorial whispers. To gain an edge with Artaxerxes, some of the envoys secretly sought his ear and informed on others. An Athenian named Timagoras sent a note to the king divulging privileged information of some kind. Artaxerxes awarded the man a huge gift of cash, a herd of eighty dairy cows (to supply the milk he took for a stomach condition), plus a silver-footed couch with exotic coverlets, and a slave to spread these in elegant Persian arrangements. Timagoras joked to his staff that Athens, instead of electing magistrates, should choose new envoys to the King, each year, from among the poorer classes. Over time this would enrich the whole population.

The Persians at Susa waited eagerly to hear from Pelopidas. The rise of Thebes had won their admiration, and courtiers whispered that *this* was the man who'd hemmed the Spartans in between the river Eurotas and the mountains, their tiny stretch of home ground. Artaxerxes sensed the buzz and basked in reflected glory. He showed by his gifts and attentions that he leaned toward Pelopidas and no longer favored the Spartans.

Xenophon, in his *Hellenica*, uses this embassy to Susa as the first of only two times to speak of Pelopidas. Xenophon ignores the man's earlier ventures, including the leadership of the solstice plot (a role he assigned to Melôn instead). He never mentions the Battle of Tegyra, the charge of the Sacred Band at Leuctra, or the confrontations with Alexander of Pherae. He chooses *this* moment to spotlight Pelopidas, and to put in his mouth a speech containing prominent mention of Theban collusion with Persia, against other Greeks, 150 years earlier. With a heavy authorial hand, he erases the man's nobler deeds and depicts him as a scheming Medizer, heir to the shame of Thebes's distant past.

For Artaxerxes, ancient allegiances were of less concern than the present moment. Troubles were brewing in the west. His satraps there had grown seditious, and one among them, Datames, was already in revolt. In the waters off his western coast, the eastern Aegean, Athenian ships had grown bolder, threatening once again to pry away his Greek holdings. He needed an ally that could counterweight that fleet and help him keep the coast under control. Thebes, he knew, was not a naval power, but huge outlays of cash could make it one; and Persia had *that* much money. If Thebes had won at Leuctra, despite all odds, what might it achieve on the sea, in Chios, Rhodes, and Byzantium?

At last Artaxerxes announced the terms of the Peace. Thebes would be his new enforcement arm, displacing Sparta from its place of honor. Messene, the freedom city founded by Epaminondas, would remain free—a body blow to Sparta's hopes. Athens would forgo its naval adventurism and draw its ships onto the land. Pelopidas had gotten everything he asked for; indeed, according to Xenophon, he had helped write the document. Persia had entirely switched sides.

The diplomats left Susa and made for their home cities. Timagoras the Athenian received a lavish escort: bearers to carry him to the coast (no doubt on his silver-footed couch), and money to pay them. He'd done some sort of backroom deal that sold out Athenian interests and advantaged Thebes. A Persian royal joked that Timagoras "would have to pay a price"—

by further forms of collusion—for all that he'd received. The jest took on a grim double meaning when Timagoras reached home. Denounced by his fellow envoys as a secret supporter of Thebes, he was indicted and put to death by the Athenians.

His was not the only life that ended as a result of the Peace of Thebes. Antalcidas, formerly the darling of Artaxerxes, was another casualty. He'd negotiated the King's Peace twenty years before, a boost to Spartan fortunes, and thought he could pull off a similar feat this time. Instead he'd watched as a treaty was framed that recognized Messene, the clause that Sparta most dreaded. His enemies at Sparta blamed him for this disaster. Disgraced and disillusioned, he starved himself to death.

Pelopidas returned to Thebes, accompanied by a Persian officer who carried the writ of the Great King. Possession of this scroll gave Thebes the right to host the next interstate treaty conference and, by extension, to claim leadership of the Greeks. It was a challenging role for clog-wearing Boeotians who had little experience on the international stage. Many were eager to see them fail, and fail they did, spectacularly.

Xenophon recounts the episode in *Hellenica*, and his schadenfreude is unmistakable. The envoys of Hellas heard the new Peace read aloud, and the Thebans asked them to swear to its terms. Not a single one did. They claimed they were empowered only to *hear* the Peace, not sign it; Thebes would have to send to each city in turn for commitments. Then Lycomedes, the firebrand orator who led the Arcadian League, asked why the conference was taking place at *Thebes*, rather than where peace was needed (meaning, the Peloponnese). This infuriated the Thebans; they accused Lycomedes of undermining the bond between their two Leagues. Lycomedes stormed out of the hall, and the conference broke up in disorder.

There was more to this walkout than a mere dispute over venue. Arcadia had held a grudge against Thebes and its Peace ever since that document was drafted. In laying down treaty terms, Pelopidas had resolved a territorial dispute between the Arcadians and their neighbor, Elis, in favor of Elis. He seems not to have held the requisite parleys to soothe hurt feelings, and these had festered. Thebes was finding the role of leader of Greece meant arbitrating its quarrels, invariably angering one of the parties, or both. For this role too the Thebans had no practice.

Thebes began the laborious task of approaching each city in turn to sign the new Peace. First on its list was Corinth, a pro-Spartan state; to gain traction there would mean truly rising in stature. But Corinth rejected the Peace, and then all the Greek states followed suit. The envoys went home to Thebes empty-handed. "Thus the cloak of leadership, of Pelopidas and the Thebans, was removed," crows Xenophon in *Hellenica*—his last mention of the great Theban hero. His metaphor from clothing suggests that, as a diplomat, Pelopidas had been wearing a kind of costume.

Military affairs were getting as sticky for Thebes as diplomacy. Epaminondas marched a third time into the Peloponnese, where his influence was strong, to shore up the Theban-Arcadian alliance, but only embroiled himself in new disputes. His plan was to lead more states away from Sparta and into the new arc of democracies. He stormed several cities that were still in the hands of *beltistoi*, landed nobles who'd always toed the Spartan line. These men promised they'd switch sides and ally with Thebes, but only if allowed to stay in their homes and in office. Though Epaminondas stood for the *dêmos* and government by assembly, he also stood for *philanthrôpia*, political moderation. He let these *beltistoi* retain power and keep their states oligarchic. That only made the Arcadians more mistrustful.

Thebes was finding it could do no right in Arcadians' eyes. It tried to appease them by reversing course and booting out the *beltistoi*; but these men raised armies, regained control of their cities, revoked their alliance with Thebes, and re-bonded, even more firmly, with Sparta. Arcadians, their fears fed by Lycomedes, wondered if this was all some covert Theban plan to take over the Peloponnese. If it was not malfeasance, then it was lack of competence, which was almost as bad.

Though he'd risen to power with Theban assistance, Lycomedes, ever the opportunist, had glimpsed the advantage of leaving the orbit of Thebes. He looked for alternative allies abroad and found a willing partner—the city of Athens. He went there in person to propose a friendship pact, despite the fact that Athens was already allied with his worst foe, the Spartans. This triangulation required all the subtlety that diplomacy could muster, but somehow Lycomedes pulled it off. He left with a pact of mutual Athenian-Arcadian defense, a rebuke to Epaminondas and to Thebes.

But Lycomedes had made many enemies in his rise to power. Throughout his career, he'd stoked the rage of the *dêmos* by playing on its resentment of *beltistoi*; he'd helped get the rich and powerful ousted from Arcadia and banished to the coast of the Peloponnese. As he set sail from Athens for home, Lycomedes was wary of meeting up with embittered exiles, so he had his steersman follow the route he himself had laid out. But somehow that route landed him precisely where his foes were gathered. They seized him and cut him down, and so, comments Xenophon, despiser of rabble-rousers, the will of heaven was done.

Thebes could now plainly see it would soon have to deal with the problem of Arcadia. But just as this bond was fraying, another was formed, quite unexpectedly. Corinth had up to now been a firm friend of Sparta's, unshaken in an assault by the Sacred Band, unmoved by invitations to join the Peace of Thebes. Suddenly, though, the Corinthians sent an envoy to Thebes, to sign that very document. The circumstances, as told by Xenophon, are vague (and contradicted by another account), but it seems the tectonic plates of Hellas were shifting again, creating bizarre realignments. Corinthians had learned of a plot, hatched at Athens, to take over their city. Since Athens was now linked to Sparta, Corinth reached out instead to Thebes.

To sign the Peace of Thebes meant recognizing Messene as an autonomous state, a dagger to Spartan hearts. Corinth moved carefully before taking this perilous step. It sent first to Sparta, to ask if the Spartans would join it in signing the Peace. There was no real hope they'd say yes and agree to give up on Messene, but the gesture helped soften the blow. The Spartans made clear that Corinth, or indeed any ally, was free to chart its own course. As for the Spartans, in words Xenophon gives them in *Hellenica*, "they'd fight on and take whatever the gods saw fit to give them and would never accept being stripped of Messene, a place handed down by their fathers." (The words make no sense in that work, since Xenophon, eager to soothe Spartan pride, has pretended up to this point that Messene did not exist.)

A remarkable speech survives from the time of this Sparta-Corinth parley. It assumes the voice of the Spartan prince Archidamus, son of Agesilaus, though its author was in fact Isocrates, the Athenian essayist. For much of his long life—he was already seventy, with nearly three decades more ahead of him—Isocrates had sought a leader to unify Greece. He'd reached out first to Dionysius of Syracuse, as we've seen. Now, like his fellow conservative Xenophon, Isocrates took up the banner of wounded Sparta and the house of Agesilaus. In the speech he put in Archidamus's mouth—perhaps even meant him to deliver at the parley—he envisions a hard road back toward Spartan power. To read this speech today is to see how bleak the world looked, in the eyes of Greek Laconists, in 366 BC.

Reconquest of Messene is the central theme of the speech. "Archidamus," the fictive speaker, produces a mash-up of obscure myths to prove that Sparta's control of the helots was ordained by the gods. Sparta's moral rigor could still win back that prize, the speech maintains, despite all the reverses of recent years. But the difficulties will be huge. "Archidamus" concludes with a grim proposal: the Spartiates still in service should take to the hills and fight a guerrilla war.

> I say we must send our parents, our wives, and our children out of Sparta, some to Sicily, others to Cyrene, others to the Asian coast. . . . We who are left, those willing and able to fight, must abandon our city and all our possessions, except what we can carry with us, and seize the strongest and most strategic place we can find, and harass and raid our enemies by land and by sea, until they stop laying claim to what is ours. . . . What peoples would not be disturbed and frightened if an army assembled that had done such things?

It's a nightmarish vision of the future, yet still, to "Archidamus," preferable to accepting the loss of the helots.

The Corinthian envoys left Sparta and headed north, to sign the Peace of Thebes. The Thebans hoped they'd do more—ally with Thebes and break their ties with Sparta—but what they *had* done was enormous. Epaminondas could breathe a sigh of relief: Whatever else was slipping away in the Peloponnese, his greatest achievement there seemed secure. And with Corinth officially neutral, the door of the Isthmus stood open, should Thebes need to use it again, as now seemed almost certain.

Meanwhile in Susa, in the heartland of Persia, the royal court of Artaxerxes was roiled once again, and once again by a woman. She was one of the most enthralling Greek women since Helen of Troy, if we believe even half of what was recorded by Plutarch and another Greek writer, Aelian, a collector of anecdotes and legends. Her story demands to be told here, if only because it is otherwise barely told at all.

She came from Phocaea on the Turkish coast, a Greek city subject to Persian control. Her countrymen called her Milto, "ocher," for her ruddy complexion, but she became known as Aspasia—a nickname borrowed from the famous mistress of Pericles, who lived half a century earlier. Like her namesake, she was famed not only for beauty but intelligence, pride, self-possession. It was this, as much as her looks, that drew the attention of powerful men, who found they enjoyed female pushback—a rare thrill in their patriarchal age.

Aspasia grew up poor and motherless, but to judge by a tale told of her childhood, the goddess Aphrodite was watching over her. A growth had appeared on her chin, threatening to spoil her appearance, but one night she dreamed of a dove—the bird of Aphrodite—that suddenly transformed into a woman. "Take the roses from Aphrodite's shrine, crush them up, and sprinkle them on your chin," the dream vision told her. The growth promptly vanished, and Aspasia's loveliness increased from then on.

Aspasia came to the notice of Cyrus, brother of Artaxerxes, who was then (before his rebellion) a satrap in Persia's western reaches. One day a procurer, charged with stocking Cyrus's harem, brought her to the palace, but she refused to put on the fine clothes and makeup he gave her or to take his lessons on returning the satrap's kisses. She wore plain Greek dress when she was brought before him, at his banquet table; stolid and defiant, she refused to take her seat there. When Cyrus's men tried to drag her, she cried out, "Whoever lays hands on me will rue the day!" Cyrus was intrigued. "This is the only free and unspoiled girl you have brought me," he said to the procurer. "The others are mere merchandise."

Cyrus set out to win Aspasia's affection, and—so we are told—a bond of love and respect grew up between the two. Cyrus treated Aspasia with great deference and addressed her as Sophê, "wise one." It was even said that he had no lovers but her (though another source speaks of a second Greek woman, unnamed, as part of his retinue). Aspasia, remembering her childhood dream, gave thanks to Aphrodite for her romantic triumph: she placed a golden statue within the goddess's shrine, along with a jeweled image of a dove.

Politics and war disrupted this love affair. Cyrus began hiring Greek mercenaries—Xenophon's Ten Thousand—and launched a rebellion against his brother, marching eastward with Aspasia by his side. In a battle at Cunaxa, near Babylon, he fought Artaxerxes for the throne and lost his life (as we've seen). Pursuing the fleeing rebels, Artaxerxes and his men captured Cyrus's baggage train, an enclosure guarded by Greek troops. Xenophon, who was on the scene, watched as Artaxerxes sought for and found "the Phocaean woman, said to be wise and beautiful," among the spoils of Cyrus's camp. The Great King had heard of her fame and wanted her for his own—but not as a slave. When his officers brought Aspasia to him in chains, he had them thrown into prison; he unbound her, then offered her a sumptuous robe.

Aspasia now joined the royal court at Susa and the family of Artaxerxes, a perilous place for a woman. She already understood the power of Parysatis, the jealous, scheming queen mother; when Cyrus had once offered to Aspasia a beautiful necklace, she'd insisted he send it to Parysatis instead. What she made of Atossa and Amestris, Artaxerxes' two daughter-wives, is anyone's guess, not to mention the hundreds of harem girls who shared the King's bed. She was given an honored place among this crowded household and, after long grief for Cyrus, developed a kind regard for Artaxerxes too. At least that is the impression left by Aelian, in the strangest chapter of all in the saga of Aspasia.

Along with his concubines and wives, Artaxerxes had at least one male lover: his eunuch Tiridates, reportedly the handsomest man in the empire. But Tiridates died in youth, leaving the King prostrate with grief. Aspasia, says Aelian, was the only one who could cheer him after this loss. She put on mourning garb and placed herself in a part of the palace where the King would happen upon her. When Artaxerxes asked what she was doing there, she said she had come to comfort him, if comfort could be had. Artaxerxes bid her await him in the bedroom, but when he came in, he was holding a garment Tiridates had worn. He asked her to put it on and found that the eunuch's garb brought out her beauty more fully. Thereafter he always asked her to wear Tiridates' clothing before they made love. "She cured the suffering of his grief," concludes Aelian, who lacked our modern terms for gender fluidity but seems aware of the complexities here.

As Artaxerxes grew older and weaker, Aspasia got caught up in the court's most complex maneuver, selection of a successor. It seems she looked out for herself by forming a bond with the likely heir to the throne, the Great King's eldest, Darius. This led to a grave dispute between father and son. Persian tradition held that, on the day the King's heir was proclaimed, the one so chosen could ask for any favor. Artaxerxes proclaimed Darius his successor, and Darius immediately asked him for Aspasia. The law said Artaxerxes could not refuse, but he insisted Darius could have Aspasia only if she *preferred* him. So Aspasia was brought into the throne room and, in a scene straight out of a fairy tale, was asked to choose between kings. Much to Artaxerxes' dismay, she chose Darius.

By all accounts, the Persians were fiercely possessive of women, and Artaxerxes was more possessive than most. He simply could not let go of this wise Phocaean, the darling of Aphrodite. He broke the naming-day rules and denied his son's request, appointing Aspasia instead a priestess of Anahita—a Persian goddess linked to fertility and flowing water. She was sent to Ecbatana (modern Hamadan), to Anahita's temple, one of the most lavish and beautiful shrines in the empire. Her sacred office there required her chastity, but we may guess that Artaxerxes could break that rule too, when he wished.

That is where the saga of Aspasia must end, for none of the Greek writers who tell it follow it further. Possibly Aspasia lived out her life in the temple of Anahita, amid the splendors of Ecbatana, one of several Persian imperial capitals. Had Darius assumed the throne after his father, as planned, she might have become chief consort of yet a third Persian royal. But the rivalry over her favor had opened a rift between father and son, disturbing the plans for succession. For Artaxerxes, the cost would be high—as told in a further chapter of *his* story.

Epaminondas of Thebes, like Pericles of Athens before him, held no monarchic or executive office. He was returned to the boeotarchy, a board of seven, at this time, year after year, in democratic elections; at least once, he was voted out (after his return from the battle of Corinth). Also like Pericles, he declined to court the *dêmos* or deceive them with false hopes. Each time he was again chosen, he warned the Boeotians, "Think over your decision, for if I'm your general, you'll have to go on the march." To preserve your power, he told them, you must keep your hand upon your *porpax*—the handle by which the infantry soldier held aloft his heavy shield.

But Theban hands, Epaminondas now saw, might need to grip not only shields but oar handles, sheet ropes, and rudders. Thebes had never before run a sizable navy; it had few overseas interests, and Boeotia's poor harbors did not lend themselves to a fleet. But in 366, the year of the Peace of Thebes, Epaminondas convinced the assembly to build a hundred triremes, enough to contest with Athens for the Aegean. Though he'd never fought a naval battle before or even captained a ship, he prepared to become chief admiral and lead the clog-wearing Boeotians onto the sea.

The goals for this unlikely move are unclear, and still less clear is how Thebes could afford it. Triremes cost money to build and even more money to staff; with a crew of two hundred per ship, the new Theban navy required twenty thousand men, each drawing a daily wage on active duty. Almost certainly Artaxerxes footed the bill, with funds he provided as part of the Peace of Thebes. It was he who most needed an ally in the Aegean, to counterweight Athens, increasingly his foe, and force his western satraps into line. These ambitious regional rulers, sensing weakness in Susa, had banded together and launched the Great Satraps' Revolt.

It started with Ariobarzanes, who governed a Persian province on the west coast of Turkey. For years this man had built friendships with leading Greek states, including Athens and Sparta, and recruited mercenaries. Now he felt ready to defy the crown. He refused to hand over his post when a new royal appointee, the Great King's grandson, arrived to take his place. Allies and supporters rushed to join his cause: Datames, another satrap, already in partial revolt in Cappadocia; Orontes, governor of Mysia; and Nectanebo, rebel pharaoh of Egypt, now coruling with a son the Greeks called Tachos or Teos. And from Sparta, gasping Sparta, came Agesilaus, the lame-legged king, now nearly eighty and bowed by a dozen defeats, yet still trying to save his city—in this case, by bringing home cash the wealthy satraps would pay him.

When his fleet was completed, Epaminondas sailed into a theater of war as complex as any known to the Greek world. Up and down the Turkish coast, Greek cities and islands were variously controlled by Athens, by Artaxerxes, or by the rebel satraps, and these last were often at odds with one another. On land, a Spartan king was directing operations, with troops lent by an Egyptian pharaoh; on the sea, the Athenian fleet vied with that of a Persian satrap, Mausolus, loyal to Artaxerxes for the moment but destined soon to switch sides. (After his death, this man's wife would build him a splendid tomb, the original "mausoleum").

To advance Theban goals in this region required Byzantine maneuvering, and it was in fact at Byzantium, as yet a minor Greek city on the Straits of Dardanelles, that Epaminondas first dropped anchor. He found a friendly welcome there and made diplomatic gains, as he also did later at Chios and at Rhodes. Diodorus even says Thebes made these places "its own," though this seems both vague and overstated. Plutarch, though elsewhere a champion of Epaminondas, concedes he "fell short of virtue and expectation" in the Aegean, but gives him a noble excuse. He eventually cut short the mission and brought the fleet home, Plutarch says, lest Boeotians turn into decadent mariners rather than stalwart hoplites.

What did Thebans hope for from this naval venture? No one has ever been sure. In later years, an Athenian orator would claim Epaminondas had aimed at a takedown of Athens and had even sworn to move the Propylaea—the grand marble gateway to the Acropolis, built in the heyday of Athenian naval power—to the gates of Thebes. That phrasing is no doubt hyperbolic, but beneath it lies a kernel of truth. To lead the Greeks required dominion over both land and sea, as the earlier wars between Athens and Sparta had proved; Sparta could not prevail until it could master both. The Sacred Band had given Thebes control of the land; now the sea too lay within its grasp, thanks to subsidies flowing (no doubt) from imperial Persia.

While the Theban fleet was still near Byzantium, a summons came from an unlikely source farther east. A Greek city rent by civil strife, Heraclea on the Black Sea, called on Epaminondas to help with a growing crisis. Its upper and lower classes, the *beltistoi* and *dêmos*, were at one another's throats; Epaminondas, renowned by now for moderation and justice, was one of few whom both sides could trust. The fleet sailed through the Bosporus, site of the mythic Clashing Rocks, but found the clashing factions of Heraclea were beyond its help. Epaminondas left Heraclea to its fate—which soon was to take strange and cruel turns.

The fleet spent only one sailing season at sea; thereafter, it disappears from the record. Perhaps Artaxerxes, underwhelmed by its performance, cut off the money required to pay its crews. Or perhaps the wind was knocked out of Theban sails—quite literally—by events that took place on land while the fleet was abroad. New troubles had reared their heads in both Thessaly and the Peloponnese, resulting in new damage to the Theban order; and even Boeotia itself had been roiled by strife. With so much maintenance still required at home, the Aegean quickly slipped out of Thebes's reach. The Great King would have to reclaim his western coast without Boeotian help.

The year of this naval excursion was, in the Greek calendrical system, the start of the 104th Olympiad. The Greeks prepared to celebrate the quadrennial festival at Olympia, in the Peloponnese, as they had done 103 times before, over 412 years. A sacred truce called the Ekêcheiria, "staying of hands," announced by runners to all the cities and posted on a bronze discus at Olympia itself, had prevented warfare from disrupting the games. Even amid the most grievous conflicts—the Peloponnesian War—the festival had gone on, for such was the will of Zeus, the god worshipped in a magnificent temple at Olympia and in whose honor the competitions were held.

But this year, the passions unleashed in the Peloponnese were threatening to overwhelm the Ekêcheiria. A chain that linked the Greeks to their past, stretching back more than four centuries, was about to be broken.

Some talented athletes were heading to Olympia that year. A young pancratiast (in modern terms, "extreme fighter"), Sostratus of Sicyon, dubbed Akrochersitês, or "the Fingertipper,"

171

was competing in his first Panhellenic games, though he'd go on to fight in many more. He earned his nickname by bending back his opponent's fingers until the pain forced a surrender. Also attending those games was Eubotas of Cyrene, a champion *stadion* (200-yard) runner. He'd won his first Olympic race forty-four years earlier, a victory foretold to him by an oracle. Too old now to race but unwilling to retire, he was competing vicariously by fielding a chariot team.

Not only runners and martial artists had their eyes on the games. This was the second Olympiad held since the Arcadian League was founded, and the first since the League had charted its own foreign policy course. Part of that course was its conflict with Elis, a neighbor to the northwest. Both states had been in the anti-Spartan camp after Leuctra, but Elis had since changed governments in an oligarchic coup. Arcadia invaded, in an effort to reinstall a democracy, but the Eleans called in the Spartans and forced a retreat. Now clearly leaning toward Sparta, Elis had become a thorn in Arcadia's side.

As the summer of 364 approached, the Arcadians sought to gain the upper hand. For centuries Elis, a neighbor to Olympia, had presided over the games, a role that brought the Eleans pride and prestige. This time, though, the Arcadians moved to usurp that role from Elis. Using their allies the Pisans as a surrogate—a people who had an old claim to headship of the games—they moved in troops and occupied the festival site, along with allies and four hundred horsemen from Athens. They gambled that Elis would be deterred by such a force, if not by the Ekêcheiria, the armistice sacred to Zeus.

They gambled wrong. The Olympian athletes had just completed the horse races and were midway into the events of the pentathlon when the troops of Elis appeared on a nearby road, fully armed and arrayed for war. They halted at the bank of the Cladeus, the stream that bordered the sacred precinct, and sacrificed there as though to begin combat. The Arcadians and their allies marched forth to the river to meet them. As the assembled spectators, wearing festive garlands atop their heads, looked on in amazement, a full-scale infantry battle broke out in the sanctuary of Zeus.

At first the Eleans had the best of the fighting. They pushed the Arcadians back toward the Council House and the altar of Zeus, with festivalgoers cheering for kills and woundings as though for wrestling matches. But then the Arcadians started to turn the tide. They climbed atop precinct buildings, even the roof of the temple of Zeus, to hurl down tiles and stones on Eleans below. An Elean commander, Stratolas—one of the leaders of the oligarchic coup—was killed in the barrage. As night fell, the troops of Elis retreated to camp.

The sacred site had now been profaned in multiple ways, and the Arcadians added one more violation that night, breaking apart its elegant lodging houses and using the wood for a fort. On the next day the Eleans found this fort impassable, and with Arcadians once again atop the roofs, the Eleans withdrew in frustration. The Arcadians had won the Battle of Olympia.

The games went on, and Sostratus the Fingertipper took the prize in pancratium, the first of his illustrious career. He won at the next two Olympiads as well, and at sixteen other Panhellenic contests, as we know from an inscribed stone recovered from Delphi, the base of his now-lost statue. His finger-bending trick worked so well that, according to the inscription, all his opponents went down without fighting back.

The Eleans, embittered, declared the games of that year an Anolympiad, employing a prefix that translates to "non-." If *they* had not presided, the word implied, the festival did not count. But their clash with Arcadia that summer was hardly a nonevent. It was soon to have repercussions that traveled far beyond their own borders, beyond even the Peloponnese, to arrive at the gateways of Thebes.

• • •

In his account of the Battle of Olympia, Xenophon mentions a squad called the Three Hundred among the Elean troops, in a way that suggests it was known to his readers. No other notice of this squad has survived, but it seems to have been an offspring of the Theban Sacred Band. Elis, it bears noting, is often said by Greek writers to resemble Thebes in its attitude toward male *erôs*. And Xenophon states in *Symposium* that *both* Thebans and Eleans stationed male lovers side by side in battle. If the Three Hundred were organized on that principle, then Elis had followed the model established by Thebes.*

The number three hundred held a talismanic charge for the Greeks. When Sparta and Argos had been at war, around 550 BC, both sides chose a team of three hundred to represent them in battle. Next came a more famous three hundred, the Spartans led by Leonidas, who died at the hands of the Persians in the pass of Thermopylae. (In fact not all were killed; two members of the troop were absent from the battle, on other missions, and survived. The Spartans labeled them "tremblers" and shamed them mercilessly.) That episode has been dramatized in recent mass entertainment, under titles that draw on the same numerical power.

Groups of three hundred, in the Greek mind, at least, possessed a special cohesion and mutual strength. So it was distressing to Thebans when, while Epaminondas was gone on his naval excursion, a band of three hundred arose in their own backyard, dedicated to overthrowing democracy and installing a pro-Spartan regime.

The plot was hatched at Thebes but drew members from Orchomenus, a city that had been at odds with Thebes since mythic times. Recently, Orchomenus had willingly served as a Spartan base, and the Thebans had pulled down its walls to end its defi-

---

* The Carthaginians too are said to have deployed a unit they called the Sacred Band, though nothing is known of its makeup beyond its large number (more than two thousand).

ance. Three hundred wealthy Orchomenians now saw a way to get revenge and also flip Thebes back to the Spartan side. They joined the Theban rightist plot, and a date was set for action.

Before that date arrived, the Theban conspirators, for unknown reasons, lost their nerve. They confessed their plans to the boeotarchs and named their Orchomenian allies. Those three hundred were arrested and hauled to Thebes for a trial. Their guilt was clear, but the Boeotian assembly voted to act more broadly and harshly. The *entire male citizen body* of Orchomenus was put to the sword, women and children were sold, and the city itself suffered *katalusis*, destruction of all standing structures. In the blink of an eye, Orchomenus was no more.

Thebes had done just as Athens had done, fifty years earlier, when it mass murdered the island of Melos—an act that, as dramatized by Thucydides, embodied its arrogance. That atrocity had forever stained the Athenian record, and now the record of Thebes was similarly stained. Upon his return from the Aegean, Epaminondas was horrified and declared that the Thebans would never have gone so far had *he* been on the scene. It was he who had spared Orchomenus before, by urging his doctrine of *philanthrôpia* on the Boeotian assembly.

Plutarch says that Pelopidas too would have deterred the Thebans, had he been present. "Epaminondas and Pelopidas never killed anyone after a victory or enslaved any cities," the moralist observes. But Pelopidas was also off the scene at the critical moment, driven by his high spirit to pursue Alexander of Pherae—the butcher of Scotussa, the thug of Thessaly, the sadist who worshipped his own homicidal spear. That twisted warlord had been misbehaving again, emboldened this time by his new alliance with Athens. It was time for Thebes to settle things once and for all.

The Boeotian assembly assigned Pelopidas an army of seven thousand. That was enough force to bring the tyrant to heel.

But on the eve of departure, in mid-July, an eclipse of the sun was seen at midday. The city's seers called a halt to the march; the army would have to stay home. Pelopidas, though—his *thumos* leading him on—set off without it, accompanied by a small force of cavalry volunteers.

Only one omen is best—to fight for one's country, Epaminondas had once declared, quoting Homer. In this case Pelopidas fought not for his own land but for the free Thessalians. They'd asked for him by name when requesting help from Thebes, regarding him as a champion of their cause.

Pelopidas recruited Thessalian troops as he moved toward his foe, gradually assembling a rough, untrained infantry phalanx. Far stronger was his cavalry, three hundred from Thebes augmented by Thessaly's horsemen. Still, he was outnumbered by Alexander, perhaps two to one.

The two armies sighted each other at Cynoscephalae, "dogs' heads," so named for low hills that protrude from the plain. Both made a dash to seize this high ground, and Alexander got there first. Pelopidas sent his Thessalian infantry up the slope to attack, but the untrained troops could make little headway against hardened veterans. On level ground below, the Theban-led cavalry, with Pelopidas in command, fared better against Alexander's horsemen. They soon put these to flight and cleared the plain.

Pelopidas pulled his cavalry back from pursuit and ordered them to advance up the ridge. By ascending its south side, they might strike Alexander's infantry in its flank. Parting from them, Pelopidas rode up to the rear of his beleaguered phalanx. There he dismounted, donned hoplite gear, and pushed his way to the front, where he began pressing the infantry attack.

With sheer force of will, Pelopidas moved the Thessalian line forward. Alexander, seeing this advance, and watching the Theban cavalry approach from the side, began a controlled retreat. He shouted orders to his men as they stepped slowly backward, down the slope, with spears still leveled at the Thessalians.

What happened next was of deep interest to Plutarch, biographer and ethicist. The character of Pelopidas, as Plutarch read it, was *parathermon*, "overheated," and ruled by *thumos*, the quality of soul that seeks victory, honor, and justice. *Thumos* gave power to warriors, but only, in the Platonic system to which Plutarch subscribed, if ruled by *logos*, the rational mind. Now, as Pelopidas spied Alexander in the retreating host, he yielded to *thumos* and abandoned *logos*. Unsupported by other troops, he ran straight at the tyrant.

In the heroic world to which this act belonged, a duel between two leaders would have ensued, but Alexander came from a different world. He slipped behind the curtain of his bodyguard, safely disengaged. His guards came to grips with Pelopidas, who slew several. But the spearmen jabbed at him from beyond his striking range, piercing his armor and inflicting wound after merciless wound.

The Thessalians dashed forward, but Pelopidas had fallen before they reached him. The Theban cavalry meanwhile arrived on the ridge and laid into Alexander's troops. These turned and fled in disorder. Three thousand were killed, according to Plutarch, as the plain filled with corpses.

Back on the ridge, the Thessalians, clad in armor and bleeding from many wounds, laid a ring of captured weapons around the lifeless Pelopidas. This was trophy reconceived as memorial bier, an honor never before seen on a Greek battlefield. They cut their hair and sheared their horses' manes as offerings of grief, as in the days of Achilles, and stood in silent dejection. Their victory at Cynoscephalae—for the day was indeed theirs—was ruined by this desperate loss.

As word of the disaster spread, magistrates arrived from nearby towns, bearing rich grave goods to bury Pelopidas. Thessaly had sought, and won, the right to inter him, regard-

The base of Pelopidas's commemorative statue at Delphi. Pelopidas's name (ΠΕΛΟΠΙΔΑΝ) is clearly legible in the third line from the bottom, that of the commissioning Thessalians (ΘΕΣΣΑΛΟΙ) just below it.

ing his death as a greater loss to their land than to Thebes. "You have only lost a good leader, but we have lost that, and freedom too," their envoys declared. They saw little chance of further Theban efforts on their behalf. But in this they were mistaken; Thebes was already preparing a punitive expedition.

The Thessalians gave Pelopidas a funeral that Plutarch praises as modest but *truly* splendid, in contrast to merely sumptuous rites, such as those of Dionysius in Syracuse. They awarded grants of land to his children and cast a bronze statue to honor him. The base of this statue survives, uncovered in the 1930s. Only a few words are legible there, the left side of its verse inscription: "Sparta . . . ," "Pelopidas . . . ," "the Thessalians . . .". Amazingly, the final line begins "Lysippus . . . ," identifying the lost statue as the earliest known work of the era's foremost sculptor.

Pelopidas died as he'd lived, a freedom fighter who rushed

fearlessly into the fray. He had headed the exiles who stole into Thebes on solstice day 379 to begin the overthrow of Sparta; he had dashed into the bedroom of Leontiades, the Spartan puppet, and killed him in sole combat; he had led the Sacred Band in its two great charges, first at Tegyra, then at Leuctra; he had rushed to Susa to head off a Spartan envoy and brought home a sovereign Peace. Thebes had elected him boeotarch thirteen times in fifteen years and also made him commander of the Sacred Band, the Thebans' chief tactical weapon. The Band must have mourned him bitterly, as they prepared to vent their rage on Alexander.

Hardest hit by the loss was Epaminondas, who'd relied on Pelopidas as a staunch ally. The two men had jointly led the great freedom march to Messene and built a city there; the trial that followed seems to have set them at odds, yet their partnership had endured. Epaminondas had, by personal effort, freed Pelopidas from Alexander's clutches, three years before. Now there could be no rescue, nor, for Epaminondas, any partner of comparable stature. The success of the Theban project would rest on him alone.

The army that had been detained in Thebes made haste to attack Alexander, whose forces had been weakened at the Battle of Dogs' Heads. Rather than risk another loss, the tyrant came to terms. He agreed to restrict his rule to Pherae and its harbor, and to become an ally of the Boeotian League. He'd been contained for the moment but had not learned his lesson or changed his ways. He had more woes to inflict on Thessaly, and Hellas, in the years ahead.

Warlordism was contagious in the age of the Sacred Band. The success of one strongman instructed others around the Greek world as to how to build power with money, forts, and paid professional troops. Dionysius of Syracuse had first shown the way, followed next by the Pherae regime. Soon a third Greek tyrant arose, the most cunning and ruthless yet, in the city of Heraclea on the shore of the Black Sea.

This city, we recall, had reached out to Epaminondas while he was sailing the Aegean, hoping he'd heal its bitter class-based strife. When the Theban proved unable to help, the Heracleans sent for one of their own. Clearchus was a native son who'd gone to Athens to train in philosophy, first with Plato, then with Isocrates. It was not just a stretch of "study abroad" but an exile. His fellow citizens had banished him, suspicious of his nature. Now their need for a guiding hand was so great, they agreed to bring him back home.

Clearchus had studied with deep political thinkers, but his real teachers were the warlords who'd come before. He'd watched the ascent of Dionysius in Syracuse and Alexander in Pherae; he'd seen these men build cults around themselves by acting so lofty, or cruel, as to seem something more than human. He especially admired Dionysius, after whom he named one of his sons. His opening moves at Heraclea were nearly the same as his model's. With demagogic skill he enflamed the people against the *beltistoi*, then got the assembly to grant him dictatorial powers. Using these, he had the wealthy seized and imprisoned, then released to their kin in return for huge ransoms.

With the money he raised by this extortion scheme, he hired professional troops, hardened thugs who would do any bidding. He sent these men out in the streets, at night and disguised in plain clothes, to rob and attack Heracleans. The citizens came to him to beg for protection. Concealing his part in their troubles, he convinced them to build a walled fort on the city's high ground, then occupied it himself with his troops and locked the citizens out. Now that he had an impregnable base—like Dionysius's "Island"—he could do whatever he pleased.

Just as Dionysius had done in Syracuse, Clearchus went about town wearing the elaborate purple robes and high boots of a tragic actor. But he carried these theatrics even further than Dionysius, perhaps believing himself truly semidivine. He began painting his face red and applying glistening oils for fearsome effect. He called himself a son of Zeus, and named one of his sons Keraunos, "thunderbolt." When Clearchus moved through the streets, a golden effigy of an eagle, the bird of Zeus, was grandly carried before him. A golden crown—another property of the tragic stage—adorned his head.

Opponents of the tyrant fled from Heraclea and organized a resistance, forcing Clearchus to raise fresh troops. His recruitment method relied on a new form of social mobility: he freed the city's slaves, then, to elevate their status and secure their backing, allowed them to marry their masters' wives and daughters. This was another trick he'd learned from Dionysius, for one source reports that the Syracusan had done just the same. Heraclean noblewomen were forced to submit to these matches on pain of death, though many, we're told, took their own lives before their wedding nights. With his newly emboldened recruits, Clearchus won a battle against the exiles, then dragged his captives before the *dêmos* for torture or threw them into dank prisons.

The scale of the abuses became disturbing, especially to those who had taught Clearchus in Athens. Isocrates, the essayist and political thinker with whom Clearchus had studied, was careful to disclaim responsibility for a pupil gone wrong. "When Clearchus was at my school, all who met him agree he was the most liberal, gentle, and humane of my students," he wrote in a letter to one of Clearchus's sons. "When he took power, all who knew him before"—principally, Isocrates himself—"were astonished at the magnitude of his change." Both Isocrates and Plato—the latter of whom, we recall, had tried and failed to advise Dionysius of Syracuse—were suspected, by their contemporaries, of supporting authoritarian rulers. Modern scholars have often shared that suspicion.

Two of Plato's students, Chion and Leonides, had joined the court at Heraclea, brought in by Clearchus as philosophic trimming. These men gathered fifty supporters and set out to end the city's nightmare. Chion was related to Clearchus and so was able to get close to the tyrant. At a public sacrifice, he and Leonides drew daggers and struck, dealing a blow that proved fatal to Clearchus two days later. But they did not live to see the success of their scheme. Their fifty supporters failed to arrive in time and they were killed on the spot by palace guards. Clearchus's brother, Satyrus, took power as regent for the tyrant's young sons and soon proved an even harsher despot than Clearchus.

When Clearchus's sons came of age and took the reins from their uncle, it seemed Heraclea would go the way of so many Greek cities: tyranny descending from bad to worse in the second generation. Yet strangely enough, Timotheus, the elder son, proved an enlightened and generous ruler—perhaps because all opponents had been purged. However, a cancerous lesion, originating in his genitals, slowly took over his body and wracked him with pain. To those who glimpsed his noisome, agonized condition, it seemed that the son was paying for the sins of his father.

After Timotheus's death the tyranny passed to his brother, Dionysius, named for his father's dictatorial model. This Dionysius, much like his namesake, enjoyed fine food and wine, so much so that he grew enormously fat. He took to concealing his body behind an armoire when speaking with Heracleans, allowing only his head to appear above the top. To ease the breathing troubles caused by his obesity, says one ancient source, his doctors ran long needles right through his folds of flesh, while he slept on, insensate. If the needles came too close to his organs, the pain woke him up and the procedure was stopped. Another source claims that the goal of the operation was to rouse Dionysius from sleep, for otherwise he could not be woken.

This sybaritic man reigned thirty-three years in peace and prosperity and came to be called Dionysius the Good. His dynasty somehow survived the upheavals of the age of the Sacred Band, including the one that brought that age to an end: the rise of a new, more expert warlord, Alexander the Great.

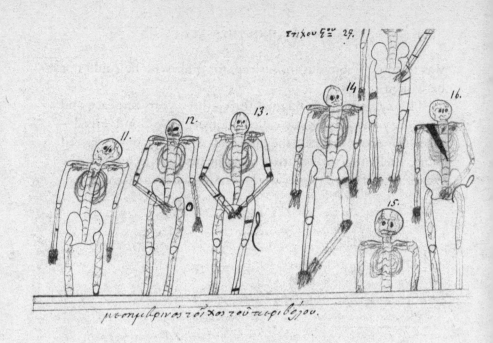

μεσημβρινὸς τοῖχος τοῦ περιβόλου.

CHAPTER 7

A Death in Arcadia

(364–359 BC)

In 1895, two years after the death from disease of John Addington Sy-
monds, Victorian England was rocked by the libel and indecency trials
of Oscar Wilde. These threw open to view, and to public disgrace, the
life of a gay Englishman. Among those deeply shaken by these trials,
and by Wilde's imprisonment, was another gay Englishman with phil-
hellenic tastes and literary ambitions, George Cecil Ives.

Ives had met Wilde a few years before and had tried to enlist him
in a league Ives was then forming, a secret society of gay men aimed
at millennial change. Ives sought to create a "new beautiful free earth,
freed from power, love-crowned . . . with the great salt sea not added
to by tears," as he wrote in his voluminous diary. He hoped that by
uniting "Hellenists," his term for those who found inspiration in Greek
male erôs, he could somehow bring this new world into being, though
just what actions were needed remained vague in his writings.

As Wilde was sent off to Reading Gaol to serve a sentence of hard
labor, Ives began to see his own struggle as a kind of combat, and this
led him to identify his league with the Sacred Band of Thebes. "I
have been reading the old Greek books, of the passionate comradeship,
world-old and eternal, which closed the ranks at Chaeronea and made
all flight and fear impossible," he wrote in July 1895, only weeks after
Wilde's incarceration. "And it must be so now . . . when I think of
the broken hearts and fallen victims strewn on this grim world's bat-
tlefields." In meditating on Chaeronea, Ives was pondering the Sacred
Band, whose mass grave there had been opened during his childhood.

Within a year or two of that diary entry, Ives began to date his journal's pages by years elapsed since 338 BC, the year of the Chaeronea battle. He labeled these new dates "Year of the Faith," "Year of the Greek Band," or "Year of the Band of Lovers." For him, the world's current epoch had begun not with the birth of Christ but with the death of the Sacred Band. He began to refer to his secret society as the Order of Chaeronea, and the name stuck. It is still used today, by an organization (not directly linked to that founded by Ives) calling itself "a fraternity of Lovers," claiming the Sacred Band as its point of origin, and showing the lion of Chaeronea on its emblem.

Though Ives's goals were opaque, his ardor was contagious. He recruited hundreds, mostly in England but internationally too, into his Order of Chaeronea, including leading intellectuals of his day. In 1899 he began using an elaborate rite of initiation, in which members vowed "that you will never vex or persecute lovers; that all real love shall be to you as sanctuary; that all heart-love, legal and illegal, wise and unwise, happy and disastrous, shall yet be consecrate." A heraldic emblem made prominent use of the calamus reed, presumably to evoke the Calamus poems of Walt Whitman. The Order was thus a kind of mystic religion, with the Sacred Band serving as its patron saints.

When Oscar Wilde returned from jail, broken in health, in 1897, Ives made a pilgrimage to see him, and the two men corresponded throughout the remaining three years of Wilde's life. A sentence from one of Wilde's letters to Ives is today widely quoted as prophetic: "I have no doubt we shall win, but the road is long, and red with monstrous martyrdoms." It was much what Ives himself had written seven years before, but with an emphasis more on hope than sacrifice. "The time is at hand—I know not who will live or who will die, but I believe that Liberty is coming," he confided to his diary in 1893. "I am more sanguine than I was once. . . . Now I sometimes think that some of us will live to see the victory."

He died in 1950, without having seen the "victory" he longed for.

• • •

Power, as the Greeks understood it, was not kept within limits, especially in interstate relations. Hegemony morphed easily into empire, empire into rule, rule into subjugation. "No one is free except Zeus," wrote an Athenian playwright, expressing the uniquely Hellenic idea that any secondary rank led, in the end, to enslavement.

Whether a democracy or an oligarchy wielded power, the grim outcome was the same. "Tyrant city" was the cry raised against Athens, liberal Athens, in its war against Sparta. And in truth, its naval empire had by then become a tyranny, a Pan-hellenic shakedown scheme maintained by force. Thucydides examined the dark side of that empire in his *History*, especially in the Melian Dialogue, a meditation on excesses of power. Melos, a small and unthreatening neutral state, dared to defy Athens and was annihilated—an atrocity approved by majority vote of a democratic city.

Did exercise of power *always* lead to abuse? Epaminondas, in the time he captained Thebes, sought a way out of that pattern. From the start of his career he eschewed extreme measures and argued for *philanthrôpia*, humaneness, in foreign affairs. When rebel cities were captured, he abated their punishments; when rightist regimes were defeated, he let their leaders remain in office. Perhaps he had learned this lesson from reading Thucydides, thereby fulfilling that author's goal of creating a "possession for all time," a study of universal principles of statecraft. Or perhaps it was Lysis, the last of the Pythagoreans, who taught him humanity and moderation, the qualities that moralists—Plutarch, Montaigne, Ralph Waldo Emerson—have long admired in him.

But moderation sometimes incurs the hatred of extremists, especially, in Greece, in the heated contest between *dêmos* and *beltistoi*. Thucydides had taught this lesson as well. "The citizens who were in the middle were destroyed by both sides, either because they didn't take part in the struggle or because their survival was resented," he wrote, in a nightmarish description of a fight to the death between haves and have-nots. Sixty years further on, those passions had not cooled. When Epaminondas had failed to walk a strict party line, his allies, the Arcadians, had grown angry and suspicious. Perhaps, they murmured, Thebes meant to control the entire Peloponnese—which meant, in Greek terms, to enslave it.

Had they been clever diplomats or eloquent speakers, the Thebans might have dispelled this anger and fear. Other superpowers organized councils at which smaller states could air grievances and hear official replies; the Thebans never took this step toward mutual trust. They were unused to the complex dance of interstate relations. In response to Arcadia's unease, they took the heavy-handed step of installing garrison posts in the Peloponnese—creating more unease and confirming suspicions. They fell back on their undisputed strength, their dominance in land warfare, exemplified by their remarkable Sacred Band.

Xenophon of Athens, at that time residing in Corinth, watched this evolution with a certain satisfaction. He'd scoffed at the Theban project from the start and hoped it would fail, and now he foresaw that his wish might come true. In his account of this period, in *Hellenica*, he uses *harmost* to refer to a Theban garrison captain—a word with ironic point, for men of that title had been hated across the Greek world when deployed by Sparta. It's as though Xenophon were mocking the pot for calling the kettle black. Epaminondas had taken the moral high ground when dealing with Sparta, but now his city was following Spartan patterns, and doing it poorly.

Xenophon was out of place in Corinth, a place famed for wealth, commerce, and elegant courtesans. He'd loved the rustic life of his Scillus estate: his hunting dogs, his horses, the festivals of the gods, the rhythms of planting and harvesting (or rather, watching his slaves do those things). An active life on open land—that was the Spartan way, the path of virtue he deeply admired. Walled cities, by contrast, were filled with idle crowds and the chatter of politicians. The invasions of Epaminondas had driven him out of the countryside and into a metropolis, much against his inclinations. It was yet one more reason for despising the Thebans.

Xenophon disdained Epaminondas for precisely the deed that other Greeks most admired: the building of a walled city, Messene. Xenophon does not speak of that feat in *Hellenica* and barely implies that Messene existed; he alludes to a second new construction, Megalopolis, only once, obliquely. To avoid such glaring historical facts—the creation of vast city-states—took real effort, but perhaps Xenophon hoped those places would soon be effaced from the earth. Agesilaus, his beloved former commander, was still at the helm of Spartan policy, even into his ninth decade, and had brought home much-needed funds after helping the Satraps' Revolt. His son, Archidamus, was proving an able field general. Messene might still be reclaimed and its walls pulled down, even if mercenaries had to be hired to do it. Megalopolis too might be crushed, and with it the Ten Thousand, the democratic body that led the Arcadian League.

Indeed Xenophon could see signs that the League, still less than a decade old, was losing cohesion. An oligarchic faction within Arcadian ranks was making its voice heard. Xenophon describes these dissenters as "those who were planning the best for the Peloponnese" or "those who cared about the Peloponnese," and the phrasing speaks volumes about his ideals. The Peloponnese, in his mind, was a bastion of agrarian virtue, a place run by landed nobility who followed the Spartan way. The Thebans, builders of walls, had overrun this precious enclosure and citified it. Clearheaded Arcadians, in Xenophon's view, regretted this crime and were reversing course.

The Arcadian League was indeed beginning to split, with

huge consequences for the Greek world. As the center of the Peloponnese, and the principal ally of Thebes, Arcadia was a bulwark of the new democratic order. Its breakup would endanger that order and release the Spartan lion from its cage. Xenophon watched from his perch in Corinth and left a breathless record of what he observed, in the last chapters of *Hellenica*—a whirlwind finish to that fifty-year tale of war, civil strife, and decay.

A remarkable strategist was heading the Arcadian League at this time or else had just recently stepped aside. Aeneas of Stymphalos is named by Xenophon as *stratêgos*, or "general," of the Arcadians—a unitary executive post filled by yearly election. Probably he is the same man as the "Aeneas" who wrote *How to Survive under Siege*, the sole surviving volume from what was once a series of tactical studies. This slim treatise, the earliest known Greek military handbook, gives startling insight into the instability of the 360s BC and the challenges facing a leader who tried to navigate through it.

How to Survive under Siege reveals the dark side of Greek warfare: the prevalence of trickery, treachery, plots, and subterfuge. Aeneas, its author, is master of a thousand ruses, many of them wondrously ingenious. He knows no fewer than twenty ways to sneak secret messages past a foe. Among these is the story of the tattooed man: around 500 BC, a Greek ruler had the head of his slave shaved and tattooed with a message, then allowed the hair to grow back; the message was read when the hair was shaved off again. That tale was well-known in the time of Herodotus, but nowhere else do we find the idea that an animal's bladder can be blown up like a balloon, then written on, then deflated, so the writing becomes too small to be read by the naked eye. For extra security, the bladder can be inserted inside a flask that is then filled with oil, so that no one inspecting it will even know the bladder is there.

Aeneas reveals that a *stratêgos* such as himself had to be always watchful, not just to defend against attack but to stave off internal revolt. He stresses again and again the problem of dissenters and fifth columns. At one point he seems to want a ban on all lanterns and night lamps in private homes because "those desiring a revolution"—members of the *dêmos* unhappy with oligarchic government, or *beltistoi* disliking democracy—can use these to set alight heaps of bedding and thus send fire signals to confederates outside the walls. He advocates rewards for informers, prizes for assassins, and—surprisingly—payment of private debts from public coffers, to reduce the disaffected bankrupt class. Unfortunately we do not know his tricks for obtaining the requisite funds, for he says he deals with this problem in his *Receipts*, a work subsequently lost.

Perhaps among those tricks was one that Arcadia was using, in the years just after Aeneas's generalship. When the League defeated Elis at the Battle of Olympia, a huge new revenue stream opened up. Olympia was rich beyond measure with dedications to Zeus: gold and silver goblets, vessels, and statues, accrued over centuries. These objects were sacred to Zeus, but also extremely tempting to a nation depleted by war. Arcadian magistrates—perhaps Aeneas among them—approved the tapping of these reserves to pay expenses. Someday, they no doubt argued, they'd pay it all back.

The policy was driven by politics. The inflow of wealth went largely to the poor, through salaries paid to the standing Arcadian army, the Eparitoi. Many who manned this force had moved to Megalopolis from nearby subsistence farms. The Eparitoi gave gainful employment, perhaps even upward mobility, to a newly urbanized *dêmos*. To fund it was to fund democracy.

But not all Arcadians favored their democratic regime, which had waged war on Elis and truckled to distant Thebes. At Mantinea, where Lycomedes had stirred up anti-Theban feeling, a cadre of *beltistoi* had gathered strength, wealthy land-owners resentful of Arcadian policy moves. An overstep by the democracy—embezzlement of the sacred wealth of Zeus—was just what these opponents needed to undermine it. They got the Mantinean assembly to vote against tapping Olympic funds and instead raise money from home to pay the Eparitoi. That set the city at odds with the rest of the League.

The Arcadian League made common decisions at assemblies of the Ten Thousand, at this moment meeting at Tegea, twelve miles from Mantinea. That federal body was outraged at the recalcitrance of a member state. It condemned the Mantineans for acting unilaterally and summoned their leaders to appear for questioning. When the Mantineans refused to hand over these men, the Ten Thousand sent soldiers to arrest them, but Mantinea barred its gates. With that move it virtually seceded from the League.

Xenophon's record of these events is spotty and rushed, a sign that as he neared the end of *Hellenica*, he was glad to be done. Our only other source, Diodorus, is so badly confused by events that he switches the roles of the two principal cities, Tegea and Mantinea. None of our sources makes clear how things went downhill so fast. It seems that the moves made by Mantinea provoked a general backlash, perhaps a crisis of conscience. The mood of the Ten Thousand shifted. That body reversed course and voted to end the Olympic subsidy. Those who had tapped the funds—a group of elected magistrates—now feared they would be punished when their terms of office expired.

"You must gather troops who are well-disposed and satisfied with the established constitution," wrote Aeneas of Stymphalos, in some of the opening words of *How to Survive under Siege*. "They will serve as a fortress"—literally, an acropolis—"in opposing the plots of others." He had seen many coups in his lifetime, especially when the rich came together and seized power from the *dêmos*. He recounts some of these in his treatise, revolutions successful and not, putsches and upheavals unknown to history except for his testimony. Now the lethal disease had set in on his home turf. The node from which it started was a clustering of *beltistoi*, in Mantinea; its spread was threatening the survival of the League.

With Olympic drawdowns at an end, pay for the Eparitoi, the elite federal troops of Arcadia, began to run dry. Poorer members were forced to leave the corps, while wealthier men took their place. The army tilted rightward, portending a possible coup. The democrats centered at Tegea became panicked. They sent to Thebes, their distant ally, and warned of a brewing crisis: without Theban help, they said, Arcadia might break apart, perhaps even revert to alliance with Sparta. The Boeotian army *must* come back, a fourth time, to the Peloponnese.

That was a message to furrow the brow of Epaminondas, especially when another one followed soon after. The rightists who now controlled the Ten Thousand sent their own envoy, close on the heels of the one sent by the magistrates. This second messenger told Thebes to ignore the first. The Ten Thousand wanted no more interventions; Thebes should keep its nose out of Arcadian affairs. Two messages tending opposite ways were an unmistakable sign of a schism. For the moment, though, the Thebans did not make a move.

Thebes already had a small presence in the region: a squad of three hundred hoplites—not the Sacred Band, but another troop of the same number—was stationed in Tegea, under a Theban officer. That man's name has gone unrecorded, remarkably, given the outsize role he was about to play. Fate had placed him smack in between two Arcadian factions that were spiraling toward civil war.

Tegea was hosting a feast of celebration at this time, to mark the signing of a peace treaty with Elis. At the behest of the *beltistoi*, the assembly of the Ten Thousand had forged this

peace and given back control of Olympia. Since Elis was oligarchic, and a Spartan ally, the treaty marked a further rightward
move, and also a thumb in the eye of Thebes—for, in defiance
of treaty terms, Thebes had not been asked for consent. The
revels at Tegea thus bore a strong anti-Theban, and antidemoc-
racy, stamp.

Mantinean rightists had turned out in numbers for this celebration, for Tegea was a day's walk from their home. The leaders of Tegea, their terms of office now ending, saw a chance to
strike a decisive blow and save their own skins. At a signal, they
ordered the gates of the city closed. They sent troops through
the streets—whatever Eparitoi were still on their side—to arrest the gloating Mantineans and throw them in makeshift
prisons. The three hundred Theban soldiers took part in this
sweep, under orders from their commander—orders he would
soon regret.

The Tegeans had not prepared for a citywide purge. So
many Mantineans were seized that no civic building could
hold them, and some simply walked away from the town,
helped over the walls by sympathizers. Others had already left
Tegea before the gates closed. When the dust settled, the Tegeans were startled to find they had captured so few. But they'd
certainly stirred up a hornet's nest of Laconist anger.

The Mantineans launched into action, sending troops to
close off the passes leading north from the region. This made
the Thebans in Tegea hostages to their wrath. With this new
leverage, they forced the Theban officer there to release his
prisoners. The hapless man explained that he'd only made the
arrests in fear of a Spartan takeover, but no one—according to
Xenophon—believed him.

The pressure on Thebes to act was becoming intense, especially when an envoy from Mantinea arrived there, demanding
that the offending officer be put to death. Half of Arcadia—the
Mantinean half—was clearly sliding toward Sparta, while the

Tegean half had stayed loyal to Thebes. The conflict that had riven much of Greece for two decades, since the time of the Spartan takeover of the Cadmea, was playing out among proxies within the Arcadian League. Suspicions rose on both sides that Thebes or Sparta or both were going to get involved. The Mantineans feared a new invasion by Thebes, and a faction of that city—the rightists who'd taken over the Eparitoi—signed a pact with the Spartans to enlist their help in defense. The stage was set for a new round of Sparto-Theban war.

Epaminondas had warned his countrymen that, so long as he stayed in office, they'd have to keep their hand on their *porpax*, the hand grip of their shields. The truth of that warning could now be clearly seen. In eight years he'd led them three times to the Peloponnese, as well as into Thessaly and the eastern Aegean. All that had not been enough. Epaminondas again prepared the Boeotian army, with its Sacred Band, to march.

Contingents of soldiers began streaming toward the central Peloponnese. Each of the two "Arcadias" had great powers pledged to defend it, and each of those powers had allies. On one side, the pro-Spartan states—Athens, Elis, Achaea, and Sparta itself—aligned with Mantinea, while on the other, with Tegea, stood Thebes, Argos, Messenia, Euboea, Thessaly, and Locris. Most of Hellas was in the field, over fifty thousand troops in all, including the two top commanders of the age, Epaminondas and Agesilaus, poised for a reprise of their decade-long duel.

For the first time in *Hellenica*, Xenophon takes a real interest in Epaminondas, but casts him in an unflattering light. He quotes a belligerent speech from the Theban—the only words he assigns him—that makes *him* the instigator of this war. But Xenophon also suggests the Thebans gave Epaminondas a strict time limit, a "clock" that enfeebled him and forced poor choices. Then in a personal comment, he praises Epaminondas for strategic acumen, but adds, "I would not say he was lucky [*eutuchês*]." The Greek word denotes a state of good fortune that comes from the gods, who, in Xenophon's eyes, had not favored Thebes.

Whether blind chance or the gods were against him, Epaminondas *was* exceptionally unlucky. Twice in the war's first phase, he nearly delivered a knockout blow, but both times missed his chance by an hour or less.

Epaminondas had marshaled his forces at Tegea, midway between two enemy strongholds, Sparta and Mantinea. A report came his way that the Spartans, under Agesilaus, were marching north toward Mantinea to join their allies. Epaminondas gave his troops dinner as though retiring for the night, then took his strongest units and struck off south, in the dark, at top speed. An all-night march could bring him to Sparta while it was undefended. The plan had every hope of success, but someone—a Thespian deserter, some said—found his way to Agesilaus and told him what was afoot.

Agesilaus turned and raced back to Sparta, first sending a messenger to Mantinea for reinforcements. Epaminondas arrived at Sparta to find he was expected. A pitched fight broke out on the outskirts of the city, closer than any invader had come before. The Thebans attacked but were charged by Archidamus, leading a corps of a hundred troops. Children and old men lent their hands to defense, hurling tiles from the roofs, filling sacks and baskets with rubble to block off the streets. The Thebans finally gave ground with heavy losses. Xenophon recounts with a sneer how "those breathers of fire, those who had beaten the Spartans, despite having numbers and high ground on their side, nonetheless did not withstand the charges of Archidamus's men, but retreated." He clearly relished this small payback for Leuctra.

Plutarch captures a memorable image from this battle. A Spartan teenager named Isidas, the son of Phoibidas (who had captured the Cadmea twenty years before), had been at home, in the midst of rubbing his body down with cleansing oil, when the Theban attack began. He rushed out to defend his city without pausing to put on armor or even clothes. Both Spartans and Thebans were astonished at seeing this tall, handsome youth dealing blows with sword and spear in the Spartan front lines, stark naked. He seemed to onlookers to be a god, or to have the protection of one. Despite his lack of gear he never received a wound.

Epaminondas withdrew from the fight, not beaten as Xenophon hoped, but preparing for another surprise attack. He knew that Mantinean troops were now on their way to Sparta, to aid its defense. Why not try the same trick a second time? He set a small crew to tend watch fires as though he had camped for the night, then set off again in the dark, making for Mantinea this time. He sent his cavalry ahead for the sake of speed, while he and the infantry took a few hours' rest at Tegea.

The horsemen arrived about noon at a shrine of Poseidon, a mile south of Mantinea. Their plans had not been betrayed; the farmers were still outside in the fields, unperturbed. Once these were rounded up and made prisoners, with the army still far away, the fall of the city would be all but guaranteed. But just as the populace glimpsed they were under attack, they also spotted *other* horsemen, their allies, coming over a hill to their north. The Athenians had arrived, after riding all night through the Isthmus. They had not known they'd be needed; their appearance at this moment was purely a matter of chance.

The Athenian horsemen were tired. They were planning to eat, make camp, and care for their horses as soon as they arrived at Mantinea. But before they had even dismounted, some Mantineans dashed up and pointed out, in the distance, the approaching Thebans. Ignoring the need for food and rest, the Athenians went into action. Xenophon celebrates their feat in anthemic tones. "Who would not be amazed at the virtue of these men?" he asks rhetorically. He gives no hint that his sons, Gryllus and Diodorus, were in that Athenian cohort; they'd been readmitted by Athens, despite their father's continuing banishment. "Those among them who died were brave men," intones Xenophon, never letting on that Gryllus was one of the slain.

The Thebans were outfought in this cavalry skirmish and, once again, had to withdraw. In three days' time Epaminondas had twice missed taking enemy strongholds, either of which might have instantly won him the war. As things were, he'd have to fight in the open field where dangers were greater. But Thebes, by any measure, still held the advantage. He collected his tired riders—they'd traveled hard through two consecutive nights and fought on two consecutive days—at Tegea. There, he made preparations to march into the plain, with all his men, and offer battle.

Uniquely, Xenophon pictures the eve of battle from behind Theban, not Spartan, lines. Hoplites there were making ready by sharpening spears and swords, cavalrymen by whitening their helmets. Arcadians were painting clubs on their shields, a Theban emblem, in solidarity with the power that had forged them into a league. These painted shields, and perhaps the whitened helmets as well, would help them distinguish friend from foe. A complex collision of fifty thousand men, the armies of a dozen states and regions, was hours away.

The Theban coalition marched out from Tegea and made their way toward their enemies, now in battle formation a few miles north. But then it veered off and went west, toward a ridge of low hills. There it grounded arms as though making camp for the night so as to commence battle the next day. Those on the Spartan side observed this and broke ranks, ambling about in relaxed mood and unbridling horses. Suddenly the Thebans armed up again and came straight at them, making them scramble back into phalanx positions.

Once again Epaminondas had put his strongest units, his Thebans, on the *left* wing and greatly increased their depth, while holding his right wing back. Xenophon's language here shows he had finally gotten the point: "like the prow of a trireme, ramming its foe amidships," he writes of the Theban left wing. Epaminondas planned to "ram" the enemy's right, where the Mantineans were stationed and, alongside them, the tiny contingent of Spartans. Almost certainly he stationed the Sacred Band at the point of the ram, though none of our sources, strangely, gives notice of this.

Both sides posted cavalry units flanking their wings, and these went into action first, engaging midfield. The Thebans, as before at Leuctra, had the best of these clashes. Meanwhile the massive phalanxes were drawing ever closer. The dust raised by the horses obscured their view of each other, as Epaminondas intended: he did not want his foe to glimpse his ram before feeling its impact.

As the strong Theban left made contact, the Mantineans and Spartans gave way. They turned to flee, and their line began to collapse, the prelude to full-scale rout. Epaminondas urged his troops to move forward in pursuit. But just then a spear, jabbed at him from the Spartan ranks, slammed into his chest. Its shaft snapped off on impact, leaving the lance head buried deep in the flesh. The general fell, and the Thebans halted. Their enemies escaped, unpursued, with only light losses instead of a crippling defeat.

No other wound dealt in any Greek battle was as consequential as this one. Epaminondas was carried off the field, alive and still conscious. The embedded blade as yet blocked his inevitable loss of blood; his doctors warned him that removing it would be fatal. He asked that his shield be brought to him, for to be without this—even at death's door—made an infantry soldier uneasy.

He inquired about the outcome of the battle. Those around

him gave news that the Thebans had won—not the full truth, but what he needed to hear. "Then I have lived long enough; for I die undefeated," he said, and yanked the blade from his chest. A gush of blood poured out, and with that, he was dead.

The Battle of Mantinea surprised all of Hellas, as Xenophon records in the last words of *Hellenica*. With so many troops in the field, with the great powers fully committed, it seemed a clear leader *must* emerge from the fray. Yet at day's end, both sides erected trophies, and both asked leave to collect the dead, simultaneously claiming victory and admitting defeat. Nothing had been resolved.

"There was even more tumult and *akrisia* in Greece after the battle than there had been before," laments Xenophon as he brings *Hellenica* to a close. *Akrisia* is a rare word, found only once before in all of surviving Greek, in a handbook on diseases. There, it denotes the state of suspense when a fever has not yet broken and its course remains unclear. Hellas, in Xenophon's eyes, was a fever-ridden patient, awaiting a turn for the better or else a decline toward death.

At Mantinea, the body of Epaminondas was interred in a grove called Pelagos, "sea," at the spot where the armies had clashed. The oracle of Delphi had told Epaminondas to beware of the sea, and he had long avoided travel by ship. It turned out that Pelagos was instead the site of his tomb. A column was erected on the mound and to it was affixed a shield with a dragon in high relief, evoking the Spartoi, the men sown from dragons' teeth, from whom he was descended. The burial was paid for by the Theban state, for Epaminondas had died in the poverty in which he'd lived; in his empty house was found a single iron coin of small value.

Next to the general was laid a youth who'd died fighting beside him, Caphisodorus, his *erômenos* at the time of the battle. This was the second of two *erômenoi* with whom Epaminondas was linked. The first, who had fought with him at Leuctra, was Asopichus, who afterward painted an image of the Leuctra battle trophy on his shield. That shield was later displayed by Asopichus in Delphi, as a memorial both to the Leuctra victory and to an undying love.

Sparta and Mantinea, whose troops had stood together to face the Thebans, vied for the glory of Epaminondas's death. Both said a certain Machaerion had wielded the lethal spear and both claimed him as *their* citizen. The Spartans awarded the man's descendants freedom from taxation in perpetuity, a reward for the service he'd done for the state. In Plutarch's time, five hundred years later, the privilege was still in force. In Athens meanwhile, a mural depicting the battle, commissioned for the famous Painted Stoa, showed Xenophon's son Gryllus killing Epaminondas in a cavalry duel, but this was a fiction, for Gryllus was dead by that time.

Epaminondas had never married and had no children, though legend has it he claimed a beautiful "daughter," whose name was Leuctra, or perhaps two "daughters," Leuctra and Mantinea. His loveliest "child," however, was Messene, the well-walled city that housed the former helots. As long as that fortress stood, the province around it, Messenia, stayed free. The Spartans might bend every sinew to retrieve it, as in fact they were doing, but would never succeed.

While the armies were still in the field, one side at Tegea and the other at Mantinea, their leaders came together and crafted an agreement, part armistice, part Common Peace. No record survives of their process except for the note that exhaustion helped move things along. The treaty required all troops to de-mobilize and return to their homes, and allowed signatories to "keep what they had" at that moment—a mutual stand-down based on the status quo. Under this clause, Messene became a fully legitimate state, since it already "had" its own land. Sparta could not abide that idea and excluded itself from the treaty.

Unlike previous pacts, the Peace of Mantinea was framed without the Great King, Artaxerxes, and did not assign him any enforcement role. The Greeks finally stood on their own two feet in policing themselves. When a Persian envoy arrived the following year, they sent back to the King a declaration of independence. "By sending embassies to one another, the Greeks have dissolved their disputes and made Common Peace," read the message, a copy of which was inscribed on a stone stele. Their goal, the message proclaimed, was "to be done with internal wars and to make their cities prosperous and as great as possible."

The armies made their way from Arcadia back to their homes both north and south of the Isthmus. The Sparto-Theban wars had not been resolved, but neither side was eager for them to resume. After two decades of conflict, and terrible losses, a détente was at hand. Perhaps the death of Epaminondas, in his prime and on the verge of victory, gave Agesilaus the revenge he'd sought for thirty-three years.

Among the troops making their way from Mantinea were mercenaries of Pherae, the men hired by Alexander to support his despotic rule. He'd stayed true to his treaty with Epaminondas and fought on the side of the Thebans, though that side included many who hated him with a passion. Now that Epaminondas was dead, the treaty could not be enforced, and Alexander of Pherae felt free to resume his marauding. Soon he was again leading his army of toughs deep into free Thessaly.

Maintaining six thousand mercenaries was expensive. Alexander minted beautiful coins to pay his hired troops, some stamped with his name—the first Western coinage to bear the full name of a living person. But his own currency was not meeting his needs; he had to have more. In the year after Mantinea, he staged an impudent raid that made him, in effect, the world's first recorded bank robber.

Like many warlords, Alexander of Pherae used elegant
coins in large denominations to dazzle hired soldiers.
On this coin Alexander imprinted his own name—a
way to lay claim to the loyalty of those whom he paid.

The Greeks had no banks in the modern sense. But they
did have "tables," *trapezai*, where coined money was kept, to be
lent at interest, taken on deposit, or exchanged for other kinds
of currency. Thus the word *trapeza* means both "table" and
"bank" in modern Greek. (*Bank* itself is derived from an Italian
word for "bench," recalling a stage of finance when coins were
similarly stored on broad wooden planks.)

The center for *trapezai* in Greece was Piraeus, the harbor
town of Athens. In this hub of commerce, lenders laid out
cash for shippers and traders, and travelers changed their coins
for those struck on the Attic standard, the most widely used
currency in Hellas. One could barely get off a ship there before encountering *trapezai*, just as one today meets exchange
bureaus in airport arrival halls. This proximity of "banks" to
docks caught the notice of Alexander.

By now the tyrant of Pherae had acquired a small navy,

which he used for plundering and slaving in coastal towns. Some of these raids had struck at Athenian interests, for Alexander and Athens were no longer friends, despite the bronze statue of the tyrant in the Athenian market square. Alexander had become a law unto himself, "a pirate by land and sea" as Xenophon termed him. Thebes, in the days of Pelopidas and Epaminondas, had tried to bring him to heel, but those men were dead and that time was over.

This pirate fleet lost a battle to ships of Athens in the seas off Thessaly. Alexander knew the victorious Athenians would take their time getting home. So he secretly sent his fastest ships, laden with troops, toward Piraeus. These rowed into the harbor unnoticed; trade ships came and went every day, and besides, what madman would try a marine attack on a leading naval power? Scythian archers, the police of their day, patrolled the streets of Piraeus but had no way to prevent what ensued: groups of armor-clad men got off Alexander's ships, raced to the *trapezai*, and scooped up sackfuls of cash, their swords drawn against interference.

Some Athenians went on the run to inform the Council of what was happening. But Piraeus was miles from the upper city. By the time a response could be mounted, the bandits were on the high seas, headed back to Pagasae, the harbor serving Pherae. Alexander had got clean away with his smash-and-grab theft.

Athens turned more resolutely against Alexander. An order was issued to break up the stone slab containing its treaty with him, and a new stele was set up in its place, an alliance with Alexander's foes, the Thessalian League. That League had been formed by Pelopidas, when Thebes had served as the shield of Thessalian freedom. But Thebes without its two visionary leaders was a shadow of its former self.

Alexander was not alone in his quest for money for troops. Other states, even established powers, were on the hunt for such funds, even Sparta, where coinage had long been disdained.

Regaining control of Messene, the Spartans' obsessional goal, required far more manpower than they could field, but mercenaries might make up the difference. So it was that Agesilaus, the lame king of Sparta, set sail for Egypt, at age eighty-three, on an unlikely mission: to help the ruling pharaoh, whom the Greeks called Tachos, make war on the Persian Great King.

Tachos had just ascended the Egyptian throne and was eager to go on the march, seeing that the Satraps' Revolt, recently suppressed, had set Persia back on its heels. He had a huge need for Greek soldiers, in particular skilled commanders with proven records. He offered handsome pay to Agesilaus, as well as to the Athenian Chabrias, the swashbuckling commander who'd once defeated the Spartans by resting his shield on his knee, to help him invade Phoenicia, in the Levant, a region subject to Persia. He also hired ten thousand Greek infantrymen, whom he paid in their native coin by importing metal dies from Athenian mints.

Four decades of leadership had made Agesilaus a legend, and the Egyptian royal court rushed to meet him after his ship had docked. No one expected to see a shrunken old man lying down on the ground on a simple straw mat, dressed in a threadbare cloak. "The mountains labor, and bring forth a *mouse!*" they jested, quoting a proverb that mocked too-high expectations. Their own monarchs were attended by pomp and riches, accoutered in purple and gold. They could not comprehend that this ragged, tired creature was, or had once been, the Greek world's most powerful man.

Agesilaus expected to hold supreme command in Egypt, but Tachos had reserved this post for himself. Agesilaus was assigned only the ten thousand hired Greek soldiers. Tensions over his brief increased when Tachos refused to take his advice: to stay in Egypt and guard the throne, rather than go to Phoenicia in person. Tachos came north to the front. Agesilaus found it irksome to serve under this upstart king, a man several decades his junior yet vain and self-important. Chabrias the Athenian bore his subservience better, for he was in charge of the fleet and could stay well offshore.

The Egyptians too disliked Tachos, and while he was away, they supported his nephew Nectanebo in a bid to usurp the throne. The two Greek captains now found themselves caught between rival pharaohs and differed as to whom they would serve. Chabrias wanted to stay with Tachos, but Agesilaus was tempted to sign on with Nectanebo. Tachos became panicked and begged Agesilaus not to desert him, but Nectanebo sent messengers from Egypt who promised huge rewards. The Spartan finally went over to the usurper, and Tachos fled for his life.

Both Xenophon and Plutarch pause to examine this change of allegiance, and the divide between their views is as wide as a chasm. Xenophon, in his *Agesilaus*—a hagiographic portrait—interprets the move as a patriotic act. The Spartan king, claims Xenophon, took the side of the ruler more likely to injure the Persians and therefore to help the Greeks. Plutarch's assessment, by contrast, is scathing. "Agesilaus used the interests of his country as a veil for this bizarre and unnatural episode," he writes, "but if we remove this pretense, the most fitting name for it is 'treachery.'" But so it always was with Spartans, he continues, who knew no other justice than what benefited their city.

Egypt's politics became still more complex. A new usurper, unnamed by our sources, arose in the city of Mendes and tried to woo Agesilaus away from Nectanebo. The king was ashamed (as Plutarch claims) to change sides again, but also wary of Nectanebo's passivity. Instead of giving battle to the Mendes forces, as Agesilaus advised, the new pharaoh fled to a fortified town and prepared for a siege. Agesilaus was forced to watch from inside the walls as Mendesians surrounded the place with a trench. He was trapped, and worse, Nectanebo, trapped with him, had not laid in proper provisions.

Agesilaus had not come so far and striven so hard only to

be starved into surrender in his eighties. He watched for an opening and seized it when it came, attacking at a point where the ditch was not yet complete. Just as it prevented those inside from escaping, so the ditch stopped the Mendesians from advancing. Agesilaus defeated one squad when the rest could not come to its aid. Then he lured the others into a trap, a confined space where their numbers were of no use. With two quick blows, the Mendes rebellion was crushed.

Nectanebo was grateful, and generous. He sent Agesilaus home with over two hundred talents of silver, enough to hire an army of three thousand for a year—resources for a new attempt on Messene. Agesilaus had taken one step, albeit a small one, on the long road back from Spartan irrelevance.

But that step had taken a toll on his aging frame. His ship had barely got underway, just reaching the so-called Harbor of Menelaus, on the North African coast, when Agesilaus fell ill and began to fail. The lion of Sparta, the spearhead of the wars against Thebes, was dying.

With his last words Agesilaus asked that no artist render his features—"no clay and no paint" was his brusque instruction—so that his deeds alone would be his memorial. Then, after forty-one years at Sparta's helm, having seen his city surpassed by Thebes and twice nearly extinguished, he breathed out his last.

Plutarch, aware that a great reign had ended, delivers a solemn eulogy at this point in his *Life* of Agesilaus. But the preamble to that *Life*, a comparison of Agesilaus and the Roman leader Plutarch chose as his parallel (Pompey), tells a different story. "In his desire to enslave Thebes, and to strip Messene of its inhabitants, he all but destroyed Sparta," Plutarch writes there. "And he *did* destroy its leadership position."

Custom demanded the body of a Spartan king be buried in native soil, but that was a long journey off. Since it was already winter, the ship's crew could find no honey in which to preserve the corpse, so they encased it instead in wax. In that beeswax shroud, Agesilaus returned home to Sparta. His son, Archidamus, took over his throne—the other was held by the son of Cleombrotus, not yet fully grown—and the task of resurrecting the ailing state.

In Thebes, the Boeotian League, still reeling from the deaths of Pelopidas and Epaminondas, groped for direction. The League clearly had to pull in its horns. It had already let Thessaly go, for Alexander of Pherae now terrorized that land without restraint. The navy Epaminondas had built to sail the Aegean was stored in its ship sheds. The Sacred Band continued to train, but its missions had grown scarce.

The last, most essential task left for Thebes was what it had been for a decade, suppression of Sparta. Thebes had hemmed Sparta in by transforming the Peloponnese, creating a cordon of three democratic cities, Mantinea, Megalopolis, and Messene. But Mantinea had defected, rejoining the Spartan side; Messene was still under threat. The third city, Megalopolis—the central square of the tic-tac-toe board—was crucial to Theban goals as never before.

Megalopolis had been built as the capital of the Arcadian League, and as its name, "great city," suggests, its scale was enormous. Its assembly hall, the Thersilion, could hold perhaps ten thousand people under its roof; its theater, the largest in Hellas, could seat twice that number under the open sky. Yet not all Megalopolitans were happy in this vast setting. Some missed the life of the farm and the pasture and cared little for the League that demanded their transplantation. By a tendentious reading of the new Peace, which called for all powers to demobilize and bring troops home, they began packing up their households and going "home," that is, to native towns and villages nearby.

A leading Theban, Pammenes, had helped build Megalopolis

eight years before. Now it fell to Pammenes to keep this construction intact. In 361, the year after Mantinea, he led the Theban army back to the Peloponnese, its fifth expedition there in less than a decade.

This fifth invasion was hardly a noble affair. Pammenes used armed force to repopulate Megalopolis, even destroying nearby towns so they could not be resettled. Absent Epaminondas, Thebes had little soft power—moral authority, or diplomatic skill—in its arsenal. It relied on its infantry strength, including its Sacred Band. With strength alone, as the historian Ephorus observed, it might bully barbarians but could not hope to lead Greeks.

Pammenes understood the Sacred Band, for it was he, according to one account, who first thought to station its lovers side by side. Plutarch explains the rationale, in words that perhaps came from Pammenes himself: "Men abandon their clansmen and kinsmen, even—by Zeus!—their parents and children; but no enemy ever came between an *erastês* and his *erômenos*." Significantly, Plutarch here calls Pammenes an *erôtikos anêr*, a term of high praise in this context: a man devoted to matters of *erôs*.

We know too little about Pammenes to understand this remark, but one fact about his erotic life *has* made it into our records. A Greek source reports that Pammenes became the *erastês* of Philip, prince of Macedon, when Philip lodged at his house as part of a treaty arrangement. Philip was then in his midteens and Pammenes at least a generation older. If the two were lovers, or close enough friends to seem so, then it's likely Pammenes helped instruct his ward in warfare and statecraft. Philip no doubt watched the Sacred Band train and drill; observed Epaminondas and Pelopidas in their heyday; witnessed the failure of the Peace of Thebes. An entire education in governance was set there before him.

Philip returned to Macedon as an eighteen-year-old, two

years before the Battle of Mantinea. He must have carried with him the lessons he'd learned at Thebes. When he became king a few years later, those lessons informed his reign. Philip embarked on a massive army buildup and overhaul of tactics and weapons. He professionalized his infantry, forged them into a phalanx, and drilled them in complex maneuvers. He created a new elite squad, the shield bearers, to serve in part as a fast-strike weapon in combat. With revenues from his mines, he paid for the upkeep and training of these new units, enabling them to stay in his service year-round.

Inevitably, the Sacred Band, and Pammenes, its designer, led Philip in the direction of these innovations. Later (as we shall see), when Philip was consolidating his rule, Pammenes visited him in Macedon and fought by his side as an ally. Whether or not the two men were lovers, it seems clear that the seeds of Macedon's new armed might were planted by Thebes. No one could yet foresee that, some two decades hence, that armed might would be turned against the city that spawned it and aimed straight at the heart of the Sacred Band.

Alexander of Pherae, his funds replenished by the *trapezai* of Piraeus, continued to vex the cities of Thessaly, and also to trouble his wife, long-suffering Thebe. This half-Theban woman, the daughter of Jason, had angered her husband by failure to bear him a child.

Already he had tormented her by seducing her brother, and by executing his own *erômenos*, a beautiful youth of whom she was fond, simply because she had sought his release from jail. Now Alexander added a new form of emotional abuse. He began sending envoys to Thebes to convince his own aunt— the widow of Jason—to become his new wife. Thebe contemplated the prospect of being replaced by her *mother*.

It had been six years since Thebe had visited Pelopidas in prison and the two had communed over hatred of Alexander.

The words of that great Theban had struck her to the core: "I'm amazed *you* can endure Alexander while not in chains," he had said. The hopes Pelopidas had fired still burned in Thebe's breast. Alexander began to fear her; when he went to her bed-chamber, he sent an armed guard—a tattooed Thracian—to walk before him, carrying a drawn sword.

Thebe had three brothers who also lived at Pherae, the sons of murdered Jason, and Alexander feared these men too. He conspired to have them done away with, but one night, while drunk, he breathed word of the plot, and this got back to Thebe. She decided the time had come at last to act. She armed her brothers and hid them in the palace. That night, she plied Alexander with wine and dismissed his guards on grounds she needed to bathe. Then she snuck her brothers upstairs, having covered the staircase in cloth to muffle their steps.

Though Alexander was dead drunk and sound asleep in his bed, the sight of the ruthless tyrant unnerved the three brothers. None felt he could lift his hand. Thebe begged, then pleaded, then threatened to wake her husband and expose them if they did not do the deed. Finally they found their courage or else were overcome by shame. As Thebe held aloft a lamp, one brother pinned Alexander's feet, another pulled back his head, and a third plunged in his sword. The tyrant was dead.

Alexander's corpse was cast out in the street, to be trampled by the Thessalians he'd terrorized for thirteen years. Then, somehow, it found its way into the sea and was tossed on the waves, until a fisherman hauled it in with his nets. Thus Alexander at last received burial, "the first and only tyrant," as Plutarch notes, "to be destroyed by his wife."

Thebe convinced the chief of the guards to support the four assassins as Pherae's new rulers. She seems to have held considerable power in the new regime. One would hope she'd renounce the ways of her father and husband, but a letter from Isocrates, addressed to her and her brothers, suggests that tyranny, backed by armed force, remained the family tradition of this violent clan.

Meanwhile in Susa, capital of the Persian Empire, another great ruler was passing from the scene. Artaxerxes Mnêmon was over ninety; he'd been on the throne nearly five decades, through many policy shifts. Early in his reign he'd fought Agesilaus, then allied with him in the King's Peace, then fought him in the Satraps' Revolt, then fought him again in Phoenicia. He'd outlived his great Greek counterpart, but his own end was drawing near. The turmoil in his family, which he himself had helped cause, would finally finish him off.

By taking away the lovely Aspasia from his son Darius, Artaxerxes had pushed the boy into revolt. Darius made common cause with another groom stripped of a bride, not once but twice: Teribazus, to whom Artaxerxes had promised two of his daughters in turn, then taken them away and wed them both himself. Together Teribazus and Darius plotted to stab the Great King in his sleep, but Artaxerxes got wind of the plot and built a secret escape door in his bedroom. The assassins were caught by guards after the King disappeared through the door. Darius was convicted at trial and beheaded, by an executioner who'd had to be forced into doing his job.

That episode left Artaxerxes short of an heir. He had two other legitimate sons, Ariaspes and Ochus; a third, Arsames, was Artaxerxes' favorite among the 115 he'd sired with harem girls. Of these three sons, Ariaspes was widely esteemed for clemency and kindness, while Arsames was wise and much loved by his father. Ochus, the youngest, inspired fear with his wild and cruel nature, and naturally it was he who most wanted the throne.

To eliminate his rivals, Ochus enlisted Atossa, his father's daughter and wife, thus his own sister and mother-in-law, by promising to make her *his* wife and future queen. The pair started in on their brother Ariaspes, preying on the man's fears of court intrigues. They sent messages to him that Artaxerxes had secretly spoken against him and meant to have him killed in some cruel way. The messages varied fiendishly in urgency; some spoke of an imminent threat to Ariaspes' life, others of a reprieve. Paranoia and confusion drove Ariaspes to despair. He finally drank poison and did away with himself.

Artaxerxes suspected that one of his royal sons had hounded the other to his death but felt too old to confront the impetuous Ochus. Instead he drew closer to Arsames, his child of the harem. Ochus and Atossa noted this tightening bond and acted more quickly this time. A simple stabbing, carried out by an aggrieved courtier, took care of Arsames.

That was as much as nonagenarian Artaxerxes could stand. Already weak and failing, he expired the instant he heard of Arsames' death (or so Plutarch says). He ended his reign of nearly half a century in heartbreak and despair. He was interred in a grand rock-cut tomb, one of two seen today at Persepolis in southern Iran.

Ochus took the throne and ramped up his purge of his rivals. He killed his sister/wife/mother-in-law, Atossa, perhaps to prevent her bearing more children, by having her buried alive. Then, according to one source, he slaughtered his half brothers, the harem-born brood, by locking them in a palace courtyard and summoning his archers. Some eighty were killed in a horrific orgy of blood. Ochus became the cruelest ruler the Persians had ever known, earning the nickname Machaera, "the Dagger." Officially, he changed his name to his father's and is known to us as Artaxerxes III.

By now Chabrias, the swashbuckling Athenian soldier, had become a wealthy man. He'd led troops in nearly every conflict of the past forty years, sometimes as a *stratêgos* elected by Athens, other times as a privateer hired by the highest bidders.

He'd fought for the Spartans and against them, for the Thebans and against them, twice against the Persians on behalf of the Egyptians, and many times against the foes of Athens. His most recent post, as admiral for the pharaoh Tachos, had made him especially rich, for he'd shaken down estates and temples on behalf of his employer. The money subsidized his famously lavish lifestyle and also supported his wastrel son Ctesippus.

Chabrias fought with equal skill on land or on sea, depending on where he was needed, but Athens increasingly needed him on the sea. Its naval league in the eastern Aegean had begun to deteriorate. Four states there had left the alliance by the early 350s BC—perhaps in response to the visits, some years earlier, by Epaminondas. Chabrias sailed against the island of Chios, one of the places seceding, along with a sizable force. He may once again have been an elected *stratêgos*, though one source reports he'd remained a condottiere, captaining his own vessel and employing his own crew.

Decades had passed since Athens had used its fleet against rebellious allies. Most of the captains held back their attack upon Chios, but Chabrias was not one for negotiation. He rowed into the island's harbor and made ready to force a landing, expecting his comrades to follow his lead, but they didn't. Alone in the midst of a hostile fleet, Chabrias could not avoid getting rammed. His hull was smashed in by a Chian prow and his ship began to sink.

Chabrias could have jumped off and swum to Athenian ships nearby. Most of his crew did exactly that, but Chabrias stayed on board. Perhaps he imagined his countrymen would advance into the harbor, unwilling to let such an iconic figure die unassisted. But the fleet stayed where it was, out of harm's way. The last our sources record of Chabrias is that he went down fighting, one against many, as Chians swarmed onto his decks.

Athens somehow recovered the body and erected a marble monument as Chabrias's tomb. Chabrias's estate passed to Ctesippus, his prodigal son, including his *ateleia*, a kind of honorary tax exemption, awarded by Athens to heroes and their descendants. When a reformer tried to revoke this boon by ending its heritability, those who'd admired Chabrias fought for his son's right to keep it. Demosthenes, just now beginning his great career as an orator and statesman, delivered his first public address in this cause, a speech that survives.

It's not known whether Ctesippus held on to his *ateleia*, but he soon used up his father's estate in banqueting and high living. When the money was gone, Ctesippus put an inglorious endpoint to the story of Chabrias. To pay his debts, Ctesippus sold the marble stones of his father's tomb.

Xenophon was back in Athens by this time, reinstated, for unknown reasons, by the city that had exiled him. He too was nearing the end of his life, a life as complex as any in this age. He'd studied with Socrates, then led a mercenary army to safety through half of Asia, then fought under Agesilaus, then published writings in half a dozen genres. He'd made history and recorded it, and he'd also tried to alter its tone with his emphases and omissions. The chronicle he created, *Hellenica*, had been put aside and never continued, though its story—*akrisia*, the fever of Greece that would never break—rolled on.

Xenophon had watched as first Sparta, then Thebes, failed to unite and lead the Greeks. In his final years he looked hopefully toward Athens. In his last known work, *Revenues*, he takes a hard-nosed look at Athenian finances, knowing that in income lay strength. Shortfalls had led to short pay for Athenian soldiers, and that had damaged military morale. Athens needed money. Its naval alliance had by this time nearly collapsed, so the hope of funds from tribute and trade were dimming. But Athens still had its mines, rich silver deposits at Laureion, south of the city.

These mines were worked by private contractors, using teams of the slaves they owned. The work was arduous and dangerous, and financial risks were high, for shafts that were sunk often did not produce. Many had abandoned the mining business to spare their own slaves, and the yield to the state had declined. Xenophon recommends that Athens adopt a system like that of Sparta: mass purchase by Athens of *public* slaves, as many as three for every male citizen (a total of perhaps seventy thousand). The income these slaves produced, he calculated, would more than make up for their cost, even if they died from the strain of extracting it.

With *Revenues*, Xenophon showed his Laconist orientation one last time. Though he'd seen Sparta's power decline and nearly fall, he tried to bring part of its legacy home to his native Athens. Where Sparta had once used helots to farm its fields, Athens could now have helots to toil in its mines. State slavery, which had fed the Spartan army, could also fill the Athenian treasury.

With those grimly pragmatic proposals—ignored by Athens—Xenophon's voice falls silent. It's assumed he died in the mid-350s, though the date, and circumstances, are not known.

So many demises in such a short span—kings, generals, tyrants, warlords, and unclassifiable Xenophon—seemed to empty the Greek firmament of its brightest stars. But along with these deaths came a birth that lit up that sky like a lightning bolt.

In 356 BC, as the Thessalians were burying one Alexander, another arrived on the scene, in neighboring Macedon. King Philip had wed five women in his first four years of rule, among them a princess of Epirus (roughly, modern Albania) named Olympias. She soon gave birth to a boy—the son of Philip, it seemed, though some later claimed that a god, in the form of a serpent, had been seen in the queen's bed on the night she conceived.

Strange portents accompanied that conception, and others, stranger still, came on the day of the birth. On that day, in July, an arsonist destroyed the vast temple of Artemis in Ephesus, one of the seven wonders of the world. He did it only to gain celebrity, and the Greeks were determined not to let him succeed; they decreed he should never be named. The name leaked out anyway and is known to this day—Herostratus.

At the time, all eyes were on the fire in Ephesus and not the birth in Macedon, but later, in retrospect, the two events seemed linked. Some thought the blaze betokened the bringing of light to the world; others thought it signified ruin and destruction. In either case, it was felt, a boy born at that moment was certain to change Greece forever. And that he would certainly do, as Alexander the Great.

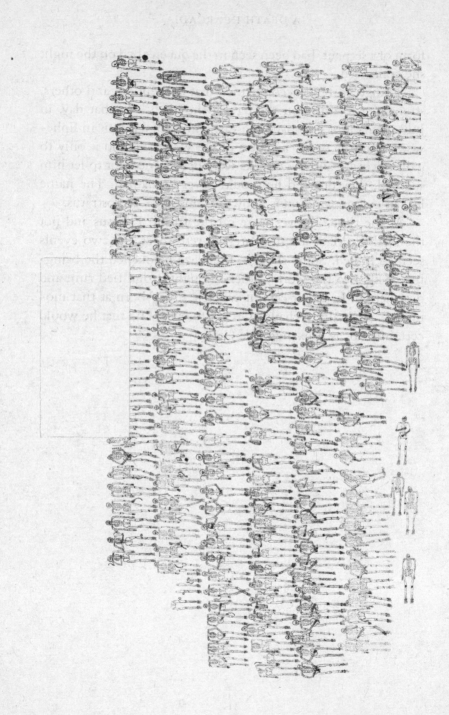

CHAPTER 8

The Sacred Wars

(358–335 BC)

On the Cadmea of Thebes, in the years after the Battle of Mantinea, the Thebans erected a statue of Epaminondas, right next to that of their legendary aulos master, Pronomus. Epaminondas too had played the aulos, the double-reeded pipe of the Greeks, and the lyre as well, we're told. Music was part of his philosophic training, for in music, Pythagoras believed, lay the deepest truths. The very cosmos, he taught, was filled with the music of the spheres; this harmony surrounds us constantly from birth to death, which is why we can no longer hear it.

The inscription at the base of the Cadmea statue was recorded centuries later by Pausanias. It captured only Epaminondas's military achievements, not his philosophic or musical training, his eloquence, or his high standards in matters of morality. In elegiac verses, the inscription read:

> By my counsels was Sparta shorn of its glory,
> Sacred Messene at last got her own children back;
> By Theban weapons was Megalopolis crowned with a city
>   wall,
> And all of Greece autonomous and in freedom.

The first three of these achievements were destined to endure, but the last and greatest, Greek freedom, was soon to come to an end.

Not long after his death, perhaps even in his life, Epaminondas was recognized as a singularity among the Boeotians, a uniquely gifted leader central to his nation's success. Ephorus, a contemporary historian, was the first to make this point. As soon as Epaminondas was gone, "the Thebans right away lost the hegemony—after they'd only just tasted it," he wrote. His praises of Epaminondas are partly preserved by Diodorus, a later chronicler who relied on Ephorus's work. In a ringing eulogy, Diodorus claims that in this one Theban, "all virtues were assembled: strength of body and sharpness of reason, brilliance of spirit, contempt for wealth, mildness, and what is greatest, courage and strategic insight. . . . When he was dead, his homeland was stripped of leadership, and thereafter every one of its changes was toward the worse."

Diogenes the Cynic, the sage said to have held a lantern aloft as he searched for an honest man, was also a witness to the rise of Thebes under Epaminondas and its decline without him. A moralist and social critic, Diogenes paid his own tribute to Epaminondas, when mocking superstitions about the Mysteries. Initiation into this secret religious rite was said to guarantee a happy afterlife. Diogenes, upon hearing a poem that expounded this doctrine, exclaimed with outrage, "What! You mean Pataecion, the infamous thief, will be better off after death than Epaminondas, merely because he got himself initiated?" In his search for a limiting case of moral virtue, Diogenes could find no better example.

Polybius, the Greek historian who charted the rise of Rome, continued the line of thought Ephorus had begun two centuries earlier. In refuting the idea that a nation's growth results from laws rather than leadership, Polybius cites Thebes (and Athens as well) as cases in point. It was "the virtue of one man, or even a second," by which Thebes had prospered, capitalizing on the policy errors of Sparta. "The achievements of Thebes grew, and flourished, and utterly collapsed along with the life spans of Epaminondas and Pelopidas," Polybius wrote. The speed of the descent had surprised the Thebans themselves: "While they still thought they were at the peak and likely to keep on prospering, their experience was instead of the opposite shift of fortune."

That shift of fortune forms the denouement of the story of Theban greatness. It played out over a quarter century and was marked by three great battles in three very different locales. The first was at holy Delphi, the seat of Apollo's oracle; the second was on the plains of Boeotia, "the dancing floor of Ares" as Epaminondas had termed it. The third was in the very streets and alleys of Thebes. The age of the Sacred Band had begun there, with the retaking of the city from Sparta in the solstice revolution. There too it was doomed to come to a crashing close.

357–356 BC

Though its power elsewhere was ebbing, Thebes as yet held pride of place with the oracle of Delphi. The priests there had granted the Thebans *promanteia*, a mark of high favor: the right to go first in consulting the oracle, even if others were waiting. Thebes had also gained control in the Amphictyonic Council, an interstate board that enforced the shrine's sacred laws. If an individual broke those laws, the Council could impose a grim death sentence: hurling from the Phaedriades, the "Shining" cliffs that loomed over the shrine and caught the dawn light on their faces. If a *state* was found guilty of wrong, the Council could levy a fine, then back that decision, if needed, by declaring a Sacred War.

In 357 the Council, guided by Thebes, decreed that Sparta had to pay reparations for the crime of Phoibidas, the seizure of the Cadmea, twenty-five years before. The amount was set at five hundred talents, but when a deadline passed and no payment was made, the fine was doubled. The people of Phocis, the region surrounding Delphi, were also fined at this Council meeting, for illegally farming the Cirrhaean fields, land set aside for Apollo. In case *this* fine was not paid, the Council warned, the Phocians' land would be consecrated such that it could never be farmed. Thebes, it seems, was using the Council as a lever of power, just as Sparta had long before done by exploiting the Common Peace.

A Phocian leader, Philomelus, a man of ambition and cunning, addressed the Phocian assembly on how to respond. The fine was too severe for the crime, he maintained, and in any case, the Phocians could not pay it. Phocis stood to lose its land if it did not act. The Delphic shrine had once been *theirs*, he told the Phocians, citing some verses from Homer in support. It could be theirs again, with its wealth of gold and silver—offerings sent to Apollo over centuries. The Phocians could borrow this wealth for their own use, as the Arcadians had already done at Olympia. Philomelus put himself forward as *stratêgos autokratôr*, general with full powers, and was elected on the spot to carry out the plan. Sparta, likewise defying a fine imposed by the Council, gave him money to hire troops.

Throngs of soldiers in Greece were looking for employment, hardened veterans made idle by the end of the major wars. Philomelus gathered an army of five thousand and captured the Delphic shrine without a fight. He executed some of the pro-Theban priests he found there, then began building walls and forts. As promised to Sparta, he smashed up the stele recording the Council's decrees.

Then Philomelus began to open the treasury houses and take inventory of what he found there. Through envoys, he promised the Greeks that Phocis would repay whatever wealth it borrowed and asked their support against the Council's decrees. Since Thebes had first moved those decrees, he was asking the Greeks, in essence, to spit in the face of the Thebans. Sparta and Athens hastened to join his cause.

The wealth of Apollo was untouchable due to religious laws, but also irresistible in its amplitude. Philomelus helped himself to a golden crown in the shape of a laurel wreath and gave it to Pharsalia, a dancing girl he fancied. Many years later, when Pharsalia had left central Greece for Metapontum in southern Italy, she wore the crown while walking in the market square. A voice suddenly issued forth from a bronze memorial there, alerting the town's soothsayers to the stolen object. They raised a cry, and the Metapontines fell upon Pharsalia and tore her to pieces. Such was the outrage aroused in the Greeks by thefts from Apollo. (Plutarch gives the story a different spin, claiming Pharsalia was killed by greedy youths fighting to claim the crown.)

The neighbors of Phocis to the east, the Locrians, were the first to come to the aid of Apollo's shrine. They crossed the border and attempted to liberate Delphi, but were soundly defeated by far more experienced troops. Philomelus took his Locrian prisoners and had them hurled from atop the Phaedriades, thus casting himself as Apollo's defender and his foes as transgressors. Clearly it was time for Thebes, and the Council it led, to enter the fight. Pammenes, the foremost Theban general at this time, began mustering an army of invasion. For only the third time in Greek history, the Council voted to launch a Sacred War.

Throughout this upheaval, the priestess who delivered Apollo's oracles, the Pythia, remained undisturbed at the shrine. She normally sat atop at a huge metal tripod, outside Apollo's temple, when she channeled the god. At some point Philomelus asked her to prophesy about his own prospects, but she refused to mount the tripod. Philomelus threatened her with force. "You can do as you please," said the priestess, still defiant. The words were not spoken in meter, as an oracle should be, but they suited Philomelus nicely, taken out of context. He proclaimed the utterance to all and had it inscribed on a stele. The god of Delphi, he boasted, had said he *could do as he pleased.*

The Theban army, led by Pammenes, approached Delphi and linked up with troops sent by the free Thessalians. On the slopes of Mt. Parnassus this combined force clashed with troops hired by the Phocians. No record of the battle survives beyond its being a decisive Theban win. The beaten mercenaries— by now ten thousand in number—were routed and driven up the wooded mountain. Philomelus, wounded and desperate, reached a cliff from which there was no escape and threw himself off to avoid capture. This was the top of the Phaedriades. Philomelus had carried out on himself the sentence for sins against Apollo.

It seemed Thebes had won the war with the very first battle. But here Pammenes made a mistake and forfeited all of his gains, as well as, almost certainly, his life.

Instead of following up his victory, Pammenes took five thousand Theban hoplites into Asia, hundreds of miles from home, to fight for a wealthy Persian satrap, Artabazus, in yet another revolt from the Great King. Pammenes assumed the Phocians were beaten and Delphi was safe. With the troops he had gathered, he planned to win money for Thebes by fighting in the East—the same move Agesilaus had made, a decade before, on behalf of Sparta. On his journey eastward, Pammenes stopped in Macedon to confer with Philip, now ruler of a growing empire. The two men campaigned together against a rival of Philip's, reaffirming their bond of friendship (or perhaps of love).

But in Delphi, the Phocians were proving they hadn't been beaten at all. Their second-in-command, Onomarchus, collected the remnants of Philomelus's army and got the Phocian assembly—now meeting at Delphi itself—to put him in charge, along with his brother, Phayllus. These two vowed to continue the war, silencing opponents with on-the-spot executions. They doubled the size of their army, to *twenty* thousand troops.

Pammenes meanwhile was winning battles in Asia, amply earning the wages that Artabazus had promised. But the Persian became suspicious of this Theban condottiere or else simply wanted to avoid making payment. He lured Pammenes to his camp on a pretext, then had him arrested and turned over to other satraps for safekeeping. No doubt Pammenes was then quietly done away with.

In this way the last of the men of '79 met his end: not charging his foes on a battlefield, like Pelopidas and Epaminondas, but slipping away into darkness, obscured from the eyes of the world. Somehow, one hopes, his five thousand hoplites made it back home to Thebes.

The Boeotians had lost their last great general. But at nearly the same moment, they gained an asset that was to become a wonder of their age, and many others. The city of Thespiae, a short distance from Thebes, revered the god Eros in his oldest known shrine. Now that shrine received a magnificent statue of Eros, a work inspired by a magnificent Thespian woman, the one they called Phrynê, "the toad."

Her real name was Mnêsaretê; Phrynê, a nickname inspired by her yellowish complexion, became an ironic joke, for there was nothing toad-like in her loveliness. She grew up poor—a gatherer of capers—but became wealthy indeed, through liaisons with A-list men. For Phrynê was a *hetaera*, literally a "companion," sometimes translated "courtesan," though the phrase "kept woman" comes closer. The typical *hetaera* was maintained by a male patron, to whom she provided sex, but also elegance, glamour, and wit. Her stature was so high that men vied for her favor and begged her to take their gifts. In an age that offered women no other careers, *hetaerae* were pioneers of female empowerment. Phrynê accrued the most power of them all.

Boeotia was too provincial a place for a woman of Phrynê's distinction. She relocated to Athens, the center of wealth and high culture, where beautiful, ambitious women such as her came to make their fortunes. There she met a sculptor, Praxiteles, the foremost artist of the day, and became his lover and muse. He carved his marble Eros to reflect his feelings for her, as he declared to the world in an inscription that adorned the statue's base. He thought it his most successful creation and gave it to Phrynê as a gift; she in turn donated it to her native Thespiae.

There, in the age-old shrine of Eros, the statue drew admirers and would continue to do so for centuries. Finally it attracted plunderers as well. In the first century AD the emperor Caligula had it hauled off to Rome, but his successor, Claudius, returned it. Then Nero pillaged it a second time. The violent deaths of both Caligula and Nero were seen by some as the vengeance of the god.

Phrynê was famed for her ability to inspire, especially when her beauty was seen au naturel. One day at the Eleusinia festival near Athens, an event that drew the elite from all Greece, Phrynê undressed, undid her hair, and walked into the sea for a swim. She was no exhibitionist—our sources make clear she dressed modestly and went light on makeup—but this skinny-dip, with its air of self-confidence and freedom, bowled over those who witnessed it. Praxiteles was among these. He later carved an image of the goddess Aphrodite emerging from a bath, taking Phrynê's naked body as his model. His *Aphrodite of Cnidus*, or the *Cnidia* as it came to be called, became a sensation in its day and long thereafter—the first large-scale female nude in European art.

Visitors flocked from all over Hellas to see the *Cnidia*, and legends and poems sprang up around it. One epigram, attributed (no doubt falsely) to Plato, imagines Aphrodite herself viewing the image and asking, "When did Praxiteles see me naked?" Admirers were said to have fallen in love, Pygmalion-like, with the statue or even to have attempted to make love to it. The *Cnidia* was apparently first displayed in a space that allowed only a frontal view, but a door could be opened by special permission to see the goddess's backside. The image became an early case of artistic mass production. Copies and imitations flooded the ancient world, several of which have survived (the original perished in a fire). The city of Cnidus, now greatly enriched by tourism, put an image of the statue on its coins.

Praxiteles was not the only artist inspired by Phrynê's ocean swim. The sight transported a leading painter, Apelles, who apparently was also attending that festival. He painted a scene depicting the moment that Aphrodite arose, newly created, out of the sea, using Phrynê as his model for the goddess. This painting, like the *Cnidia*, became famous throughout Greece. The Roman Caesars later stole it for display in one of their temples, and a Roman writer who saw it there described it for posterity. From that description, in a long but direct line of de-

This coin of Cnidus captures the sensuousness of Praxiteles' Aphrodite and also advertises the city's blockbuster tourist attraction.

scent from Phrynê's skinny-dip, came Botticelli's iconic *Birth of Venus* in the Florentine Renaissance.

In Athens, the price for Phrynê's favors rose in proportion to her fame. When a suitor complained of the cost, Phrynê replied that she'd gladly give discounts if *she* desired the encounter. She was a sharper businesswoman than Laïs, the only *hetaera* said to have rivaled her. Unusually, Laïs prorated her services for poorer customers and gave herself to Diogenes the Cynic, an ascetic sage who had nothing but an old cloak and a ragged pouch for his bread, for free.

Phrynê had several famous lovers besides Praxiteles. A leading orator, Hyperides, was among these, a wealthy swell who reportedly kept three *hetaerae* at a time in his three homes. When Phrynê was hauled into court on a charge of impiety, Hyperides acted as her defense attorney and, in a legendary legal stratagem, had her disrobe before the jurors (or, in another version, unclothed her himself). Dazzled by her naked breasts, the jury instantly voted to acquit.

One man alone was said to have resisted Phrynê's charms, even when he was freely offered a one-night stand. Xenocrates was a member of Plato's Academy, a sober philosopher known for abstemious ways. Phrynê evidently saw him as a challenge. She knocked on his door one evening, pretending she needed shelter from pursuers, then stayed until morning. Xenocrates had only one small bed to his name and graciously shared it, but during the long night he left his bedmate untouched. Phrynê later claimed it was not a man, but a statue, who had taken her in.

This remarkable woman brought her hometown, Thespiae, enduring fame as the home of Praxiteles' Eros. The Thespians responded in kind, commissioning a portrait statue of Phrynê herself.

Executed by Praxiteles, this extravagant work—plated in gold and placed atop a column of white marble—was placed where all

The so-called Venus of Arles is a Roman statue
representing the goddess Venus, but some art
historians believe it was copied from Praxiteles'
portrait of Phrynê.

of Greece would see it, the oracular shrine of Apollo at Delphi. It
stood between statues of two great kings of the age, Archidamus
of Sparta and Philip of Macedon. Its simple but proud inscription
read, "Phrynê of Thespiae, the daughter of Epicles."

355–346 BC

As the Sacred War dragged on, the Phocian warlords who occupied Delphi, Onomarchus and Phayllus, ramped up their drain
on the shrine's treasures to a level that shocked later Greeks.
Gold and silver vessels were smelted for coinage, bronze statues
for weapons. The money went to hire more troops, but also to

bribe other states to stay out of the war and to reward the support of Athens and Sparta. Some funds also went to research and development: Onomarchus devised a new class of artillery weapons, small catapults that could fire five-pound stones. These were designed for sieges but could also be used in open-field battles, as the Phocian-led army would soon demonstrate.

Ancient treasures came to light from the sacred buildings of Delphi. Philomelus had, before his defeat, already melted down a golden shield given by Croesus, ruler of Lydia (who's remembered in the phrase *rich as Croesus*). Now the two new Phocian *stratêgoi* extracted far older objects. One gold necklace they found was said to have been worn by Helen of Troy. Another had reportedly been made by the god Hephaestus—the necklace of Harmonia, Thebes's first queen, stashed there to nullify its curse. The wives of the two Phocian generals squabbled over who would get to wear which mythic chain. Friends and lovers received gifts as well: four golden combs went to the *erômenos* of Onomarchus, a beautiful boy from Sicyon, and a golden crown in the form of an ivy wreath went to a flute girl on whom Phayllus doted.

Amid his fevered search for precious metals, Onomarchus had a dream that seemed to promise great things. In the temple at the heart of the shrine stood a bronze statue of Apollo, paid for out of fines once levied on the Phocians. In his dream Onomarchus saw himself reshaping the statue with his hands, making it much bigger than before. He took this to mean that Phocis would become great under his leadership, never thinking it might be the *fines* that would increase. Phayllus, for his part, dreamed that while combing through the shrine's treasures, he found a statue of a rotting corpse, its flesh falling away in chunks from exposed bones. There was no mistaking *that* for a positive omen.

The pious among the Greeks believed that all who plundered the shrine, as the Phocians were doing, would suffer

Apollo's wrath in the fullness of time. Yet the god had thus far done little to punish the raiders. The Thebans were hard put to stop them and were even losing ground: Onomarchus and his brother were carving away at northern Boeotia, threatening to break up the League and even, perhaps, to march on Thebes itself. Not even the Sacred Band could stand up to twenty thousand skilled veterans, whose plunder of Delphi left them no exit from the Phocian cause. For no decent state would consent to take in *hierosuloi*, "temple robbers," in Greek eyes the worst class of transgressors.

Faced with this army of desperadoes, and lacking in leadership, Thebes looked certain to lose the Sacred War and lose its League. But just then, events took a new turn, in northern Greece.

The free Thessalians once again were battling the outlaw Pherae regime, now run by Alexander's assassins, Thebe and her brothers. The Thessalians had formerly looked to Pelopidas as their champion, and he'd given his life in their defense. No Theban stepped forward to help them now, so they turned instead to Philip of Macedon, the new strongman to their north. This brought a complex chain of alliances into play. The Pherae regime was backing the Phocians in the Sacred War, so Onomarchus felt obliged to aid that regime against Philip. He took his hired army northward, relieving pressure on Thebes.

In Thessaly, Onomarchus won an initial battle with Philip, thanks to his new catapults—the first battlefield artillery seen in that region. Philip retreated but returned the following year, "like a ram withdrawing to butt harder," as he declared. In this second clash, dubbed the Battle of Crocus Field, Onomarchus's troops were routed. Onomarchus himself lost his life— apparently killed by his own disillusioned troops—and Philip hung the body on a cross, then performed a mass execution by herding his Phocian prisoners into the sea to drown by the thousands. This form of death meant their bodies could not be recovered, a punishment meant to display Philip's hatred of temple robbers. Phayllus died soon after, of disease, as his dream had foretold.

The Phocians had now lost three *stratêgoi* in four years, and some began to suspect Apollo's wrath was at work. Yet even so, a fourth commander came forward to ransack Delphi and carry on the war. Phalaecus, son (or perhaps nephew) of Onomarchus, proved the most determined member yet of his warlord clan. He recruited new mercenaries and dug deeper into Delphi's riches. Phalaecus knew of a verse in Homer's *Iliad* that spoke of "things that the threshold of archer Apollo encloses, in rocky Delphi." The word used there for "archer," *aphêtôr*, was obscure and ambiguously placed; some on his staff thought it really meant "treasury," and the "things" were its riches. So Phalaecus and his troops tunneled under the temple, digging by night to avoid detection. Only when tremors were felt, the sign of the god's growing anger, did they give up the search.

For years, Phalaecus's army whittled away at Boeotia from the north and also bested the armies of Thebes whenever the two forces met. *His* troops were replaceable, given that more could be hired, while the fighting men of Thebes—citizen troops—were not. The grinding conflict was becoming, as one modern scholar has termed it, the suicide of Hellas. Finally the Thebans sent out a call for help. They dispatched envoys to Philip of Macedon, asking his aid in the war—as an ally of Thebes this time, not Thessaly. Philip agreed, and this changed the war's dynamic instantly. Athens, playing up to Philip for its own reasons, suddenly withdrew its support for the Phocians and accused them (ten years late) of temple robbing.

The Phocians sensed the endgame was drawing near. They feared the might of Philip, who'd so brutally punished their troops at Crocus Field. To appease him they stripped Phalaecus of his command and made a show of auditing Delphi's treasures; over ten thousand talents were found to be missing—enough to build twenty Parthenons. A few administrators were tried and executed, but the real predators, the warlords and their inner circle, were too clever to be caught in this trap. Phalaecus holed up in forts the Phocians had built near Thermopylae, together with eight thousand troops. They were now an army without a country, but they had one superb bargaining chip: control of Philip's only route south, the pass of Thermopylae, a passageway Philip had already sought for years.

While diplomats from all the Greek states arrived to curry favor with Philip—a new Common Peace was under consideration—Phalaecus proposed a separate deal for himself and his men. He'd swap control of the pass for safe conduct out of the region. Philip eagerly granted his terms. After years of waiting, the Macedonian king gained Thermopylae without striking a blow. He could march into central Greece whenever occasion arose—and it would arrive soon enough.

With the last of the Phocian warlords gone, the Sacred War came to an end. At Delphi, in a solemn ceremony, the weapons left by Phalaecus's men were hurled off the top of the Phaedriades. Some wanted all male Phocians thrown off those cliffs as well, but Philip, now sitting on the Amphictyonic Council, arranged better terms of surrender. The Phocians were left to live on and pay recompense to the shrine, at a pace that stretched out for more than a century. Their lands were barred to their use, their walls were pulled down, and their population was scattered into settlements of no more than fifty houses each. They were forbidden to own horses or weapons. Phocis became a ruin; in only a few years' time, a traveler saw "a land emptied of those in the prime of life; a few women and children only and pitiable old men."

Phalaecus and his desperadoes now lay under a curse, meaning no city in mainland Greece would hire them. They took ship for Italy, then detoured to Crete, where new wars offered new opportunities. In a siege of the city of Cydonia, their siege engines were kindled by a lightning strike and Phalaecus was burned to death.

It seemed everyone who had gained from the plunder of Delphi paid the price in the end, according to the pious reckoning compiled by Diodorus. Even the two women who received the mythic gold necklaces, the wives of Onomarchus and Phayllus, ended up wretched: one was burned alive in her home when her son went mad and set it on fire, while the other, widowed and impoverished, became a *hetaera* of low repute. Thus was the wrath of Apollo, the god of Delphi, appeased.

345–339 BC

Slowly, Delphi began to recover from the ravages of war, even as it continued to heal from the earthquake of thirty years earlier. Nothing better conveys the state of mid-fourth-century Greece, its confusion and nearness to collapse, than the damage done to this shrine and the Herculean efforts at reparation. A replacement for the ruined temple, funded by all the cities of Hellas, was almost complete after decades of construction. But meanwhile the treasuries had been emptied of precious objects dating back to mythic times. Hellenism's very core had been monetized and dispersed to warlords and thugs. The Phocian repayment plan restored less than 1 percent per annum, and even this amount was soon reduced.

Where once the priests of the shrine had favored Thebes, they now leaned toward their new protectors, Philip and his Macedonians. Though the Greekness of these northerners was in doubt—officials had once excluded them from the Olympic Games on grounds they were foreigners—the priests of Delphi awarded them *promanteia*, the right to "cut the line" when consulting the oracle. Even the answers delivered by the Pythia, Apollo's priestess, seemed to be tilting in Philip's favor. That,

at least, was the view of Demosthenes, by now the leading orator of Athens. When Athens sought to consult Delphi about
an ill-omened event—some men who'd been washing a sacri-
ficial pig in the sea had been bitten by a shark—Demosthenes
quashed the proposal, claiming the oracle was tainted by bias.
"The Pythia *philippizes*," he told the assembly, coining a potent
new word connoting betrayal of Greece.

The makeup of Greece's triangular power struggle had
changed. Now Athens, Thebes, and Macedon vied for control,
eyeing one another warily to see which two would ally against
the remaining one. Sparta was out of the game; it cared only
about the Peloponnese and the recovery of Messene, the fortress Epaminondas had built to protect its freed slaves. What
happened north of the Isthmus was of little concern to the
Spartans, still less what happened at Thermopylae, though its
famous "three hundred" had once died trying to hold that pass
against invaders. Now others would need to hold it against
Philip, if it could be held at all.

Whose side would the Thebans take, and what would they
fight for? That question became critical as Athens drifted
toward armed conflict with Philip. Theban loyalties were divided. In the recent Sacred War, Thebes had teamed up with
Philip, while Athens, until the last moment, had supported the
opposite side. For two decades before that, Thebes had fought
Athens whenever it fought Sparta, for the two cities had combined to counterweight Thebes.

Yet Athens had once been a friend in need, at the time of
the solstice revolution. Older Thebans still remembered those
days, when Athens had helped liberate their Cadmea, or when
Chabrias, at the head of Athenian troops, had led them in a
defiant gesture, resting their shields against one knee as the
Spartans advanced. Veterans who'd aged out of the Sacred
Band—replaced, no doubt, by younger couples to keep up unit
strength—had taken part in that display of fearlessness.

So Thebans could find reasons to side with Athens, not Philip, if they had to choose sides. They also did not trust the Macedonians, as seen in a move they made at this time to seal them off in the north. Philip, it seems, had secured Thermopylae, his route to the south, by garrisoning the fort of Nicaea at the southern end of the pass. At some point, probably in 339, Thebes ejected his garrison and occupied the fort with its own troops. Thebes could in this way lock Philip out of central Greece, and out of Boeotia—or such was the hope. In practice, though, things worked out differently.

339 BC

A *fourth* Sacred War was brewing that year, only seven years after the end of the third. The transgressor this time, in the eyes of the Council, was Amphissa, a small city just to the west of Delphi. Its people (like the Phocians before them) had trespassed on sacred lands and had then fought off Council troops who tried to evict them. The Council called a summit meeting, attended by neither Sparta nor Thebes, and war was declared. A summons went out to Philip, who now held a Council seat, asking *him* to lead a Greek army in defense of Apollo's shrine.

Philip marched south to transit the pass of Thermopylae, despite the Theban troops at its southern end. Those Thebans awaited a clash on which much would depend—the question of the autonomy of central Greece—but the clash never came. Using a little-known route through the mountains, Philip swerved to the west and forged his own path toward Amphissa, avoiding the Theban fortress entirely. Then he swerved again, to the southeast this time, and seized a city called Elatea, just north of the Boeotian border.

This move sent a wave of panic through mainland Greece,

for it could not be explained except as a threat. Elatea had little value in the fight against Amphissa, but it commanded the road leading south toward Thebes, forty miles distant, and toward Athens, forty miles farther on.

Philip had declared his intentions, and the time for Thebes to choose a side had come. Yet our evidence—some of it brought to light recently—suggests the Boeotian assembly was not at all sure which to choose.

Philip sent letters to be read to that assembly, laying out his terms. Thebes could join him in an attack on Athens and share in the plunder—or at least stay neutral and allow him to pass. If it chose to oppose his passage, however, Thebes too would come under attack. Then teams of diplomats arrived in Thebes to address the assembly. The Macedonians sent two of their own speakers and others from cities that had already been philippized. Athens, for its part, sent the two leading orators of the day, Demosthenes, head of the anti-Philip movement, and Hyperides, his ally. An all-star rhetorical contest was set to begin.

Philip's team spoke first, recalling to Thebes all the ways that Philip had helped it and all the harms done it by Athens. They spoke too of booty awaiting Thebes if Athens was sacked: herds of cattle and sheep, and slaves to be sold for hard cash. Thebes was asked only to open the path through Boeotia, and also to cease obstructing the pass of Thermopylae, by giving back to Philip's allies control of the fort at Nicaea.

The Athenian delegation had, for its part, brought a generous package of terms to offer the Thebans. In its own assembly meeting, a few days before, Athens had agreed to pay two-thirds of the cost of the war if Thebes fought on its side, and to cede to the Thebans command of the army. Most important, Athens would recognize, after decades of demurral, the legitimacy of the Boeotian League. Advised by Demosthenes, their leading politician, Athens had chosen to treat the Boeotians as equals, not as the rustics and boors the Athenians thought them to be. But no one knew how the Thebans would respond.

Demosthenes relayed these terms in his speech to the Theban assembly. Years later, when, in a legal defense of his record, Demosthenes recalled this speech and its results, he portrayed it as a diplomatic coup. He'd convinced the Thebans, he said, there and then, on the spot, to side with Athens. Ever afterward, this view of events, in which rhetorical genius had won the day, held sway among historians. But in the past two decades, an alternative voice has been heard. Hyperides, who was also part of the Athenian team, gave a different account in a later speech, "Against Diondas." That speech was recovered in 2002, when new imaging technology, X-ray fluorescence, was used to extract the half-erased text from beneath a medieval prayer book written over it.

We know now that the Thebans continued to waffle long after Demosthenes made his pitch. They were still negotiating with Philip months later, exploring just what he expected of them with regard to Nicaea, looking for a better deal. Late in the game—when the Athenian army was already on the march, preparing to take the field against Philip—Thebes finally joined with Athens. Demosthenes, for all his persuasive brilliance, had not fully turned them.

What tipped the scales for the Thebans, toward Athens and against Philip, in the most consequential policy choice they ever made? Historian John Buckler, who examined the era of the Sacred Band in minute detail, could not answer that question. "The Thebans could at one vote resolve their differences with Philip and enrich themselves at the expense of an old enemy," he wrote, referring to Athens. "Nothing in the historical record explains the Theban decision. They had much to gain by following Philip and everything to lose, if they did not." Something in Theban hearts and minds—a love of Greek freedom—set their feet upon the harder road.

The Thebans overturned and smashed the stele containing their treaty with Philip, who had up to that moment been, in name, at least, their ally. As the summer of 338 approached and Athenian troops arrived in numbers, the Thebans took over command of the coalition. The generalship went to a Theban named Theagenes—a man little known to our records, except that he had a brave and clever sister, Timoclea, whose tale is soon to be told.

338 BC

Over thirty-five thousand took the field against Philip, one of the largest coalitions the Greeks had ever mustered. The Sacred Band made up less than 1 percent of its numbers but far more than that of its strength. That storied regiment, nearly unbeaten in four decades, marched out of Thebes to the plain of Chaeronea.

In its two great battles under Epaminondas, Thebes had unsettled its foes by reversing right and left. Orthodox tactics, and long-standing codes of honor, called for an army's strongest unit to fight on the right wing, facing weaker contingents. Epaminondas had discarded that convention. He'd put the Sacred Band on his *left* and also fought there himself—matching strength against strength to "cut off the snake's head." That strategy had delivered a knockout blow at Leuctra and almost succeeded at Mantinea too, before a Spartan spear had found the great general's chest.

At Chaeronea, though, for reasons unknown, the Thebans abandoned that tactic, placing themselves and their Sacred Band on the *right* of the coalition. They chose not to face Philip themselves, but left that task to their Athenian comrades, a less experienced, less confident corps. No doubt they expected to lose that match but hoped to win on their own wing in time to "roll up the line" and come to the Athenians' aid. To do so they'd have to defeat Philip's son, Alexander, an eighteen-year-old apprentice fighting his first open-field battle.

As dawn rose on a day in early August, two armies lined up in formation, filling the plain of Chaeronea with nearly seventy thousand men. The battle commenced.

In past confrontations, the Sacred Band had charged on the run, smashing at speed into the enemy line. This time *Alexander's* troops hurtled forward, toward a gap that had opened between the Thebans and their allies. The Band found themselves cut off from their neighbors, unable to protect their left flank. Macedonian spears jabbed into their leftmost file, then, as those men fell, into the second from the left, then the third. With a skill and sangfroid out of step with his youth, Alexander carved away at the Band, stripping off layer after layer.

The skeletons in the mass grave at Chaeronea show what the Band went through on that morning. The Macedonians dug in with their *sarisas*, long pikes of cornel wood with fearsome flanged blades and heavy, spike-tipped butts. Spears penetrated so deep as to be hard to pull out; some victims were found with blades still lodged in pelvises and rib cages. If a *sarisa* could not be recovered, Alexander's men could draw a *machaira* or *kopis*, the swords they wore at their sides. The Sacred Band were assailed with these blades, which could cut right to the bone or, if swung down overhand, slice through helmets and split heads.

The multiple blunt-force traumas seen on recovered skulls tell the tale of that day's struggle. Some Band members clearly fought on with broken jaws or faces, or even with fractured crania, until a further blow finished them off. One man's facial fractures indicate he'd been hit by a heavy object swung up from below, presumably the rim of his opponent's shield. That must have killed him, but only after his skull had been bashed in from above and partly sliced off by a blade at the back of his head. This man, though battered from all sides, had been unwilling to die.

Another grim sign of the Band's travails is a skull with a quarter-inch hole, evidently made by the butt spike of a *sarisa*. The victim must have been kneeling or prone when the fearsome metal prong was thrust into his brain. The blow was so sharp that experts can detect a circular depression around the hole's rim, where the round flange at the base of the spike compressed the bone. This coup de grâce (as one expert, John Ma, has termed it) attests to Alexander's zeal to annihilate the Band. To him, *they* were the head of the snake, the emblem of Greek defiance. Lopping off this head might paralyze the rest of free Greece.

As the Band were assailed by pike blades and swords, half a mile away, on the other end of the line, the Athenians were under assault from troops led by Philip. Perhaps, if we believe Polyaenus, collector of stratagems, Philip lured them out of position by feigning retreat, then suddenly reversed direction and came straight at them. However that chanced, Athenian corpses began to pile up. A thousand were slain by the end of that morning's fighting, and twice that number were captured and taken prisoner—huge totals by the standards of the time. Demosthenes, fighting that day in his first-ever battle, turned and ran ignobly for safety (or so his political enemies claimed). In his terror he imagined, when his garment caught on a bush, that one of Philip's men was running him down; he begged his "captor" for quarter.

Victorious over Athens, Philip made his way to his son's position to see the results of the fight. There he found the Sacred Band's bodies heaped in a pile. All three hundred had been slain where they stood. If they'd asked to surrender on terms, no terms had been given; their utter destruction was Alexander's main task. Plutarch reports that Philip saw them "mingled together"—the word Plutarch selects has erotic overtones—and was moved to tears at the sight. "Perish all those who suggest that these men did or endured anything shameful," Plutarch quotes Philip as saying, as though moved by the thought of *erastai* and *erómenoi* embracing in death. Philip himself, in Plutarch's view, had once been the *erómenos* of Pammenes, the Theban general who'd arranged the Band so that lovers stood side by side.

The clash that decided the freedom of Greece was over by midday. Then began the sad task of interring the slain. Philip's losses had been light; he was able to cremate his dead, then entomb the remains within a vast burial mound, over two hundred feet in diameter. That hill stands today in the plain of Chaeronea, covered by cypress trees. Bones recovered from inside the mound, reduced to rubble by fire, can be seen in the museum of Thiva (modern Thebes).

By contrast the Thebans did not cremate the Sacred Band, but dug a mass grave at a site they had carefully chosen: near a temple of Heracles, where several roads came together, including the main road to Thebes. The spot was a distance away from the Macedonian mound; in death, the Band would remain disengaged from their foes. The bodies were carted across the Chaeronea plain, then laid together in the earth. They were assembled in at least seven tight rows, perhaps eight, as though in phalanx formation. That way they could "stand" together through time, as they had stood together in battle, right up to the end.

Amid the corpse-strewn field at Chaeronea, some bodies could not be found immediately, or perhaps some Band members died only later of wounds they'd incurred. At least, that's what we'd surmise from the strangely cramped and irregular layout of the last (bottom) row in the grave. As seen in the image that opens this chapter, five skeletons in this row lie perpendicular to the rest, while others have been jammed in between or partly on top of the legs of their neighbors. It seems likely the tomb's designers ran out of room as new bodies kept on arriving. At

The plain of Chaeronea, where the Sacred Band took the field for the last time.

first they squeezed in the surplus by laying corpses lengthwise, but finally could not avoid unseemly overlaps.

A few Band members had to be carted over in pieces. The Band's remains include pairs of feet that seem to have been deliberately hacked off, presumably by the Macedonian victors, and buried separately. Even complete skeletons show signs of hacking on the shins, done, in the opinion of osteologist Maria Liston, while the victim was prone, most likely already dead. No one knows why the Band's corpses would have been mutilated in this way.

Most men were interred with their strigils, the sickle-shaped tools they had used to scrape sweat from the skin—recalling the drill sessions they'd shared, or perhaps the gymnasia, sites of male *erôs*, where they'd exercised. A few drinking cups were buried with them as well. In several cases, pairs of corpses were laid out with arms linked at the elbow—a restoration in death of the bonds that had linked them in life. An individual soldier, or perhaps two or three—the officers leading the Band?—were cremated atop the bodies of the others. Then the enclosure was covered with earth.

The Sacred Band was no more. In its place, a different three hundred (that mystical number again!) came to power in Thebes: a cadre of exiled oligarchs brought back to the city by Philip. These men were installed as the new government; prior leaders, the pro-democracy Thebans who'd refused to "philippize," were thrown out or sentenced to death in a series of show trials. The Cadmea was garrisoned by Philip's troops to enforce the new decrees. As before, in the days of the Spartan occupation, the Thebans lived under rightist oppressors backed by an outside army. As before, their leading dissidents fled across Cithaeron and found refuge in Athens, a place as yet free of Macedonian troops.

337–336 BC

In Athens, the essayist Isocrates, now two years short of one hundred, published his last known work, an open letter to Philip. "I'm grateful to my old age for this one reason, that it has brought my life to this moment," he wrote, referring to Philip's victory at Chaeronea. For fifty years Isocrates had sought a leader to unify the Greeks. He'd reached out, in other open letters, to all the likely candidates of the age: to Dionysius of Syracuse, to Agesilaus of Sparta, to the children of Jason of Pherae (Thebe and her brothers). Now, on the point of death, it seemed Isocrates had at last found the strongman he'd sought.

In the letter he urged Philip to bind the Greeks together in a Common Peace, and Philip set out to do this. Representatives from all the cities except Sparta—still nursing its wounds and holding aloof—were summoned to Corinth, where they forged a Panhellenic league and made Philip its head and enforcer. Oaths were taken and stones were inscribed, as in the old days of Spartan synods (with Philip now playing the role of Agesilaus). The principle of autonomy, so often avowed and so little observed, was once again made the basis of relations. The League of Corinth, as it's now termed, was born.

Isocrates felt sure that, having mastered the Greeks, Philip would lead them in a campaign against the Great King of Persia—a campaign Isocrates had called for, in letters and speeches, for decades. Only with such a crusade, he thought, could the Greeks abide by the Peace and stay unified. He urged Philip to bend the Great King to his will and to "helotize" the peoples of Asia—a curious turn of phrase, implying that Macedon would become what Sparta had been. If Philip accomplished these things, Isocrates said, "there will be nothing left for you except to become a god."

Whether he heeded those words or not, Philip was indeed planning an Asian campaign, and also schooling himself in superhuman power, studying prior examples. The case of Dionysius especially interested him. While in Corinth, where he'd gone to head the Greek League, Philip met with that potentate's son, who was living in exile after an overthrow. Philip was eager to know just how the dynasty of Dionysius, fortified by wealth and huge caches of arms, could have fallen. It seems that, like Jason of Pherae and Clearchus of Heraclea before him, Philip regarded the Syracusan regime—with its cult of a godlike warrior-chief—as a template for autocracy.

Philip had at his court a talented but deranged doctor, a Syracusan, who'd likewise learned from the model of Dionysius. This man was named Menecrates but called himself Zeus, claiming that his power to heal the sick—that is, to give

life—made him equal to the greatest of the gods. Like Dionysius, under whom he'd once lived, he strolled about wearing
purple robes and a crown, but went his model one better: he
trailed behind him an entourage of men who'd agreed to serve
his will if he cured them. He dressed these acolytes as lesser
gods—Heracles, Hermes, Apollo—so he could have an Olympian retinue.

Philip was skeptical of this mad physician and once gave the
lie to his pretensions. He seated Menecrates and his "gods" at a
laden banquet table, but only burned incense before them instead of serving them food. Their obvious discomfort, as other
guests drank and ate, drew scornful laughter, until finally they
ran from the room in shame. Philip had unmasked these sham
deities, but all the same he was intrigued by the question they
raised: What sort of power could make a man a god?

As Philip continued preparing his march on the Great
King's empire, he undertook a carefully measured program
of self-deification. He erected a building in the sacred precinct of Zeus at Olympia, the Philippeion as it became known,
which featured statues of himself and his family, decked in gold
and ivory—cladding, before this, reserved for statues of gods.
Then, in a festal procession for the wedding of his daughter,
before spectators from all over Greece, he had images of the
twelve Olympians carried through the arena, followed by his
own image, a thirteenth.

"No one is free except Zeus"—the truth of that line, written
by an Athenian playwright, must have struck the Greek spectators at that procession. Now that a Zeus-like figure controlled
their destiny, their freedom was fast disappearing. Some cities
had been coerced by bribes, others pressured by threats, still
others controlled by troops and puppet regimes. Thebes had
been locked down hardest of all—garrisoned, purged of dissidents, entrusted to a cadre of philippizers. Its Boeotian League
was dissolved. With a wave of his hand, Philip had restored

the old Spartan ring of containment in Boeotia, rebuilding the walls the Thebans had once pulled down. A third Plataea had risen there and a second Orchomenus.

As Philip strode in person into the arena behind his thirteen gods, an aggrieved cadet rushed out from the crowd and stabbed him to death. At first glance it seemed that the fate of Greece had once again shifted, but the new Macedonian order was not so easily quashed. Philip's headship of the League, and his plan for the Asian campaign, passed to his twenty-year-old son, Alexander, who immediately reaffirmed them.

Over the next ten years this astonishing youth would defeat the Great King, don purple robes and a crown, and demand to be regarded as something more than human. He would set the template for centuries to come, as warrior-kings controlled the cities of Greece, in part by projecting an image of godlike power.

Before all that could occur, however, one city tried to stop the slide toward absolutism and hero worship—the city of Thebes.

335 BC

It was the first year of Alexander's reign. Forty-four years had passed since Pelopidas, returning from exile in Athens, liberated Thebes on a cold solstice night. The luster of '79 still burned bright in Theban minds.

A new generation of Theban exiles, thrust out by Philip of Macedon and residing in Athens, took inspiration from that glorious moment. They too, as they thought, could sneak into Thebes, carry out targeted killings, and force a foreign garrison to surrender. They too would have backing from Athens, as Pelopidas and his comrades did in that solstice revolution. Demosthenes, a leading Athenian statesman, had guaranteed his city's support, spurring the exiles on with promises of troops. History could repeat itself at a distance of two generations. Thebes could again throw off a foreign yoke.

Then reports arrived in Greece that Alexander was dead, killed in a battle near the river Danube. A plot took shape among the Thebans in Athens, very much like the one their grandfathers had laid. A group of exiles made their way across Cithaeron and entered Thebes under cover of darkness. The next day they struck. Two Macedonian officers were stabbed to death as they walked in the lower city, anticipating no danger. The *dêmos* of Thebes rose up; the puppet regime was deposed and democracy reinstated. A second Theban revolution, it seemed, was at hand.

A double palisade was set around the Cadmea, trapping the Macedonian garrison troops on that fortified hill. Soon, the Thebans expected, these would have to surrender and leave, much as the Spartans had done forty-four years before. But then Alexander appeared with his army, and everything changed.

Though eyewitnesses claimed to have seen him fall in battle, Alexander was very much alive, and he'd led a lightning march back from the Danube. He too had learned the lessons of history: Sparta had lost control of Thebes, forty-four years before, by responding to the solstice plot too slowly. Alexander traveled so fast that no one, at first, believed it could be him; they thought an army from Macedon had come, led by a different man named Alexander. The awful truth emerged soon enough.

A divided Theban assembly debated its next steps. Some thought surrender was prudent; others said the revolt had gone too far to turn back. The plotters, after all, had killed two Macedonians, a blood guilt that stained the whole city. Then too, this faction argued, Thebes could expect that Athens would join its revolt and send reinforcements. An assembly vote in Athens, steered by Demosthenes, had indeed approved the dispatch of Athenian troops; but that army, for reasons unclear, never entered Boeotia. Unbeknownst to the Thebans, Athens had pulled back from its vague commitment of aid.

Dire portents were seen and heard in the region surrounding Thebes. A nearby marsh produced strange noises at night, sounds like a bull's roar; a spring ran red with blood; a statue of Athena burst spontaneously into flame. In a temple of Demeter, a spider that spun in a certain doorway suddenly produced a web of rainbow colors. Some interpreters saw this as the sign of a kaleidoscopic "storm" of troubles. Yet Thebans who were inclined to fight thought the omens presaged Alexander's doom, not theirs. These men talked boldly of Leuctra and other Theban victories, the age in which their Sacred Band had astounded the world.

Alexander's army was over thirty thousand strong, Macedonian at core but augmented by Greek allies. Officially, these forces represented the League of Corinth, conducting an enforcement of that League's will. Among those assisting Alexander were Boeotians with cause to hate Thebes: Plataeans, driven out when their city was leveled in the 370s; Thespians, whose walls had been pulled down; Orchomenians, who as children had fled their city's *katalusis*. Phocians were there as well, men who perhaps blamed Thebes for starting the third Sacred War by levying heavy fines, and who certainly despised the way this war had ended. It seemed that all Thebes's enemies were now outside its gates—except Sparta, still holding aloof from events outside its region, still scheming to somehow get back its Messenian slaves.

For days Alexander camped in the plain before Thebes but held back his forces, hoping to find a bloodless resolution. Some reports say he promised amnesty to the Thebans if they surrendered just two of the revolt's leaders. The Thebans either didn't trust him or took his inactivity for weakness. They mounted the walls and shouted taunts, demanding, with sarcastic point, that Alexander give up two of *his* officers. They summoned the rest of the Greeks to join them in a battle for freedom. They called Alexander "the tyrant of Hellas," an epithet that, according to one source, drove the young king into a rage.

Finally the standoff gave way to open combat. Our sources give different accounts of how the battle started but agree that it was pitched and determined. The Thebans sallied out of their walls and fought with every sinew. They shouted to one another of Leuctra and Mantinea, of the need to protect their wives and families. The clash went on for a long time before the walls of Thebes. Alexander called in reserve troops, and the Thebans cried out he had shown he was beaten. But while they held off this fresh wave of attackers, a Macedonian squad found one of their gates undefended. This squad forced its way inside the city and made its way toward the Cadmea. Macedon's garrison troops had been watching from that hilltop, eager to help their beleaguered countrymen.

The Thebans outside the walls, learning of this penetration, rushed back to defend the city. They dashed through the gates, but these could not be closed before some of Alexander's troops also slipped past. The invaders got control of the walls, allowing their comrades to set scaling ladders and start climbing over. The fight for Thebes had now become a desperate struggle in streets, squares, and alleys. Alexander led the attack himself, mounting forays and charges wherever he met with resistance. The Macedonians on the Cadmea broke out of their palisade and made their way into the fight, their anger whetted by weeks of imprisonment. The slaughter of Thebes became total.

"The length of the day did not suffice for the savagery of their vengeance," says Diodorus of Alexander's army. By nightfall some six thousand Thebans lay dead, and an untold number had been wounded, robbed, or beaten. The ravaged city surrendered.

One episode, preserved by Plutarch, conveys the suffering of Thebes, and also the city's proud spirit. A woman named Timoclea, sister of Theagenes—the former commander at Chaeronea, presumably killed in that battle—lived in a wealthy home in the conquered town. A Thracian captain, one of many non-Greeks who fought under Alexander, broke into her house, got drunk on her wine, and raped her. Then he demanded the family's gold and silver. Timoclea had hidden her valuables in a nearby well (or claimed that she had), and she offered to show him the cache. The soldier climbed down the shaft to recover the goods. When he reached the bottom, Timoclea and her housemaids began hurling stones down the well, until he was battered to death.

A victorious Alexander considered the fate of the blood-soaked city and his thirty thousand captives. Officially, the League of Corinth had jurisdiction over this matter, but Corinth was over fifty miles away; to convene the League would take time. Alexander instead conferred with Greek troops fighting in his army, especially those who most hated Thebes. A list was compiled of Theban transgressions going back seven generations, to the time of the city's primal sin, its support of the Persians 150 years before. A weighty decision was taken—probably guided, and certainly not overturned, by Alexander. The verdict was *katalusis*, annihilation.

The army pulled down Thebes's walls and leveled its buildings, sparing only the house of Pindar, the famous Theban poet, and the Cadmea, a future fortress. The now-empty land was parceled out among Alexander's Boeotian allies. Thebans who'd survived the onslaught were sold into slavery, so many that the price of slaves plunged to bargain levels. Any Thebans who had escaped were condemned as criminals, and the rest of the Greeks were forbidden to give them refuge. A single exception was made for Timoclea, the woman who'd murdered her rapist. Bound as a prisoner and taken to Alexander for justice, she refused to bow her head or plead for mercy. Alexander, impressed by her courage, let her go free.

The Theban cataclysm was the single greatest catastrophe the Greeks ever saw, according to Arrian, a later historian. Other disasters, he wrote, had struck armies but not their cities, or had been foreseen in advance, or had *damaged* a city but not threatened its survival. Only the fate of Thebes fulfilled all three of Arrian's grim criteria. It struck without warning, and right in the heart of the nation; its scope, by definition, was existential. The city of Heracles and Dionysus, of Oedipus and Antigone, of Epaminondas and Pelopidas, became a stretch of farmland and pasturage for cows.

The destruction of Thebes drew a famous remark from Phrynê, the Boeotian beauty who'd become the most desired woman of her day. With the riches accrued in her glamorous career, Phrynê offered to pay to rebuild the walls of Thebes, but she imposed one condition. The new wall, she said, should bear an inscribed message: "Alexander knocked it down, but Phrynê the *hetaera* put it back up." That imagined epigraph put her on an equal footing with the most powerful man in the world.

No one took Phrynê up on her offer, but new walls *did* rise at Thebes, two decades after Alexander pulled them down. A civil war among the Macedonians, after Alexander's death, brought a new monarch, Cassander, to power in central Greece. To distance himself from the former regime, he refounded Thebes in 316, drawing in scattered survivors. The cities of Greece pitched in to restore walls and buildings (Athens, we're told, gave the greatest share of reconstruction funds).

But this second Thebes remained a paltry place, depopulated and demoralized. After losing a battle some decades later, with heavy casualties, the Thebans, according to Polybius, lost all motivation and took to feasting and drinking instead of nation building—"Boeotian swine" once again.

The low wall around the Lion of Chaeronea encloses the mass grave of the Sacred Band.

Though otherwise shorn of honor, Boeotia retained two landmarks that recalled the days of its triumphs. One was the Eros of Praxiteles, in the shrine at Thespiae—the testament of the artist's love for Phrynê. The other was the Lion of Chaeronea, erected at some point after Cassander's refounding of Thebes.

That magnificent figure was also a tribute to Eros, for it stood atop the grave of the Sacred Band, the warriors of love who had briefly made Thebes great. It stands there today, a silent, mournful witness to the deaths of the Sacred Band and the last, desperate fight for Greek freedom.

Acknowledgments

This book would not have been possible without a Public Scholars Fellowship from the National Endowment of the Humanities, and I want to thank the NEH for that crucial support. This relatively new grant program seeks to narrow the gap between academic researchers and the reading public, and I hope this book helps achieve that. My work was further supported by the American Philosophical Society, Bard College, and the Center for Hellenic Studies in Washington, DC, which generously opened its doors to me on three research forays.

I have many people to thank at Scribner, but first and foremost my editor, Sally Howe, who steered this book away from Sicilian shoals on which it might well have foundered. Her sound judgment and fine ear have improved every page, along with the sharp eye of Steve Boldt, the design sense of Erich Hobbing, and the production skills of Katie Rizzo. My agents, David Kuhn and Nate Muscato, of Aevitas Creative Management, strengthened me with their enthusiasm for this project and helped at many turns to bring it to completion.

Friends and colleagues in many corners of Classics have contributed expertise and encouragement, including Daniel Mendelsohn, who first gave me the confidence to undertake this story; Pam Mensch, Jim Ottaway, and Eve Romm, whose comments on a first draft have greatly improved later ones; and Paul Cartledge, Josh Ober, and Adrienne Mayor, who were never too busy to answer importunate questions. Other scholars and writers have generously sped me on my way, including:

John Bintliff, Shane Butler, Rob Cioffi, Kevin Daly, Michael Flower, Sam Gartland, Tom Hubbard, Stephanie Larson, John Ma, Mary Norris, A. E. Stallings, and Sarantis Symeonoglou.

A special vote of thanks goes to researcher Brady Kiesling and digital illustrator Markley Boyer, who together made possible the image that opens my eighth chapter: a visualization of the remains of the Sacred Band, as seen (but never photographed) when the Band's mass grave was opened in 1880. This astonishing "group portrait" was made by carefully fitting together some eighty of the excavator's sketches to reflect the position in which each skeleton had been found. As a result we can now behold what historian John Ma has termed "a phalanx of the dead," just as it was interred in 338 BC. Seldom has a single image brought the Greek past back to such vivid life. The generous assistance of Athina Chatzidimitriou and other staff at the Historical Archive of Antiquities and Restorations, a branch of the Hellenic Ministry of Culture and Sports, helped make this image possible.

My loving family has helped in ways small and large to improve this book (and its author), most of all my wife, Tanya Marcuse, who has captured, in photographs seen here, the drama and beauty of Messene and Chaeronea. To view the Greek world by her side—or our own world, for that matter—is to see afresh what is meaningful and true.

Guide to Further Reading and Notes

The works listed below are foundational studies in English of various topics covered in *The Sacred Band*. A few other sources are cited in the endnotes that follow, especially where they help resolve a point of dispute. A supplementary bibliography, listing specialized materials and those in foreign languages, is available on my website, jamesromm.com.

On Thebes and Boeotia

Berman, Daniel W. *Myth, Literature and the Creation of the Topography of Thebes.* Cambridge, 2015.

Buck, R. J. *Boeotia and the Boeotian League, 423–371 BC.* Edmonton, 1994.

———. *A History of Boeotia.* Edmonton, 1979.

Buckler, John. *The Theban Hegemony, 371–362 BC.* Cambridge, MA, 1980.

Cartledge, Paul. "Boiotian Swine F(or)ever? The Boiotian Superstate 395 BC." In *Polis and Politics: Studies in Ancient Greek History*, edited by Pernile Flensted-Jensen, Thomas Heine Nielsen, and Lene Rubinstein, 397–418. Copenhagen, 2000.

———. *Thebes: The Forgotten City of Ancient Greece.* London, 2020.

Demand, Nancy. *Thebes in the Fifth Century: Heracles Resurgent.* London, 1982.

Gartland, Samuel D., ed., *Boiotia in the Fourth Century BC.* Philadelphia, 2016.

Hack, Harold. "The Rise of Thebes: A Study of Theban Politics and Diplomacy, 386–371 BC." PhD diss., Yale University, 1975.

Harding, Philip. *From the End of the Peloponnesian War to the Battle of Ipsus.* Cambridge, 1985.

Lewis, John David. *Nothing Less than Victory.* Princeton, 2010, chap. 2.

Munn, Mark. "Thebes and Central Greece." In *The Greek World in the Fourth Century BC*, edited by Laurence Tritle, chap. 4. London and New York, 1997.

Rockwell, N. *Thebes: A History.* London and New York, 2017.

Roy, J. "Thebes in the 360's." In *The Cambridge Ancient History*, vol. 6, edited by D. M. Lewis et al., chap. 7. Cambridge, 1993.

Schachter, Albert. *Boiotia in Antiquity: Selected Papers*. Cambridge, 2016.

Symeonoglou, Sarantis. *The Topography of Thebes from the Bronze Age to Modern Times*. Princeton, NJ, 1985.

On the Fourth Century BC in Greece

Anderson, J. K. *Military Theory and Practice in the Age of Xenophon*. Berkeley and Los Angeles, 1970.

Buckler, John. *Aegean Greece in the Fourth Century B.C.* Leiden and Boston, 2003.

Buckler, John, and Hans Beck. *Central Greece and the Politics of Power in the Fourth Century BC*. Cambridge and New York, 2008.

Dillery, John. *Xenophon and the History of His Times*. London, 1995.

Hamilton, Charles D. *Agesilaus and the Failure of Spartan Hegemony*. Ithaca, NY, 1991.

———. *Sparta's Bitter Victories*. Ithaca, NY, 1979.

Heskel, Julia. *The North Aegean Wars, 371–60 B.C.* Stuttgart, 1997.

Nails, Debra. *The People of Plato*. Indianapolis and Cambridge, 2002.

Rice, David. "Why Sparta Failed." PhD diss., Yale University, 1971.

Ryder, T. T. B. *Koinê Eirênê*. London, New York, and Toronto, 1965.

Scott, Michael. *From Democrats to Kings*. New York, 2010.

Steinbock, Bernd. *Social Memory in Athenian Public Discourse*. Ann Arbor, 2012.

Strassler, Robert, ed. *The Landmark Xenophon's Hellenika*. New York, 2009.

Strauss, Barry. *Athens After the Peloponnesian War*. Ithaca, NY, 1986.

Stylianou, P. J. *A Historical Commentary on Diodorus Siculus Book 15*. Oxford, 1998.

Tuplin, C. J. *The Failings of Empire*. Stuttgart, 1993.

Westlake, H. D. *Thessaly in the Fourth Century BC*. London, 1935.

On the Leading Historical Figures

Badian, Ernst. "Xenophon the Athenian." In *Xenophon and His World*, edited by C. J. Tuplin, 33–54. Stuttgart, 2004.

Cartledge, Paul. *Agesilaos and the Crisis of Sparta*. Baltimore, 1987.

Cawkwell, G. L. "Epaminondas and Thebes." *Classical Quarterly* 22 (1972): 154–78.

De Voto, J. G. "Agesilaus II and the Politics of Sparta, 404–377 BC." PhD diss., University of Chicago, 1982.

Georgiadou, Aristoula. *Plutarch's Pelopidas*. Stuttgart and Leipzig, 1997.

Hanson, Victor. *The Soul of Battle*. New York, 1999, pt. 1 (on Epaminondas).

Higgins, W. E. *Xenophon the Athenian.* Albany, NY, 1977.
Roisman, Joseph. *The Classical Art of Command.* New York, 2017, chap. 7 (on Epaminondas).
Sanders, L. J. *Dionysius and Greek Tyranny.* London, New York, and Sydney, 1987.
Shipley, D. R. *A Commentary on Plutarch's Life of Agesilaos.* Oxford, 1997.
Shrimpton, G. "The Epaminondas Tradition." PhD diss., Stanford, 1970.
Sprawski, S. "Alexander of Pherae: *Infelix* Tyrant." In *Ancient Tyranny*, edited by S. Lewis, 135–48. Edinburgh, 2006.
———. *Jason of Pherae.* Cracow, 1999.

On the Sacred Band of Thebes and Greek Sexuality

Cantarella, Eva. *Bisexuality in the Ancient World.* New Haven, CT, 1992.
Compton, Louis. "An Army of Lovers." *History Today* 44 (1994).
Davidson, James. *The Greeks and Greek Love.* New York, 2009.
De Voto, J. G. "The Theban Sacred Band." *Warfare in Antiquity* 23 (1992): 3–19.
Dover, K. J. *Greek Homosexuality.* New York, 1980.
Garrison, Daniel. *Sexual Culture in Ancient Greece.* Norman, OK, 2000.
Halperin, David. *One Hundred Years of Homosexuality.* London and New York, 1990.
Hubbard, Thomas, ed. *Greek Love Reconsidered.* New York, 2000.
Leitao, David. "The Legend of the Sacred Band." In *The Sleep of Reason*, edited by Martha Nussbaum and Juha Sihvola, chap. 5. Chicago, 2002.
Ma, John. "Chaironeia 338: Topographies of Commemoration." *Journal of Hellenic Studies* 128 (2008): 72–91.
Masterson, Mark, Nancy Sorkin Rabinowitz, and James Robson, eds. *Sex in Antiquity.* London and New York, 2018.
Ogden, Daniel. "Homosexuality and Warfare in Ancient Greece." In *Battle in Antiquity*, edited by Alan B. Lloyd, chap. 3. London, 1996.

Chapter 1. Love's Warriors

1 *George Ledwell Taylor carried with him a copy of Pausanias:* Taylor published an account of the episode in his autobiography; summarized by Frank Sanborn in *The New England Journal* 22 (March 1897): 97–103, the source for the details that follow.

4 *largely accepted today, though occasionally doubted:* The vast consensus of scholarly comment on the Band affirms Plutarch's account; however, a recent article by a careful scholar (Leitao 2002) has claimed that the erotic makeup of the Band is a fiction, developed out of Greek philosophic

ideas. This article has not yet received the reply it deserves, but flaws have been pointed out in incidental comments by Ma (2008, 83n79) and Andrew Lear (in Masterson, Rabinowitz, and Robson 2018, 133n54). My objections to Leitao's thesis are many but the main ones are these: (1) Arguments from silence carry little weight in discussions of Xenophon; (2) Xenophon clearly indicates in *Symposium* that Thebans and Eleans stationed lovers side by side in battle and also mentions in *Hellenica* an elite corps of Eleans called the Three Hundred; (3) the Theban polyandrion at Chaeronea is almost certainly that of the Sacred Band; (4) Plutarch's use of "they say," "some say," and "it is said" in his discussion of the Band (*Pelopidas* 18–19) need not indicate skepticism or lack of evidence. (On this last point see Brad L. Cook, "Plutarch's Use of *legetai*," *Greek, Roman and Byzantine Studies* 42 [2001]: 329–60).

5 *had forbidden its citizens to serve:* Xenophon, *Hellenica* 5.2.27.

5 *had been since well before Ismenias:* The anonymous, fragmentary history known as the *Hellenica Oxyrhynchia* makes clear that Leontiades had preceded Ismenias in power (17.2). Commentary by I. A. F. Bruce, *An Historical Commentary on the* Hellenica Oxyrhynchia (Cambridge, 1967). For discussion see Steinbock 2012, chap. 4.

6 *By a prearranged plan:* Historians are in agreement on this point, even though Xenophon (clearly wishing to exonerate Sparta) depicts Leontiades proposing the move on the spur of the moment. Phoibidas had no reason to march so close to Thebes unless Thebes was his real objective.

6 *a* balanagra *or "bolt puller":* The workings of this obscure device have been ingeniously reconstructed by S. A. Handford in *Journal of Hellenic Studies* 46 (1926): 181–84.

6 *"Do not despair":* Leontiades' words are reported by Xenophon, *Hellenica* 5.2.30, where it is also stated that confederates had been stationed there in advance.

7 *the fate that awaited hundreds:* Xenophon reports that, more than three years after this time, 150 were prisoners in the Theban jail, mostly for political reasons; and since imprisonment was often a prelude to execution, we can guess that many times that number had been arrested over the years.

7 *It welcomed the Thebans by official decree:* A piece of the decree has been recovered (see Steinbock 2012, 255–56).

8 *at a spot later shown to tourists:* Pausanias (*Description of Greece* 9.12.3) was shown the spot in the second century AD.

11 *According to Plutarch, who cites Aristotle:* The Aristotelian text has not survived. Plutarch reports the rite at *Pelopidas* 18 and *Amatorius* 761d.

12 *"a man and a youth live together":* Quoted from Xenophon, *Spartan Constitution* 2.12.

13 *"One might tell many stories":* Xenophon, *Hellenica* 5.4.1.

14 *Today's scholars largely concur:* See for example George Cawkwell, "Ages-

ilaus and Sparta," *Classical Quarterly* 26 (1976): 77–78; Cartledge (1987, 156); and Stylianou (1998, 222).

15 *a lack of contrition that shocked later ages:* See, for example, Polybius 4.27.4.

18 *What follows is based largely on Plutarch's texts:* The occupation and subsequent liberation of Thebes were huge events for both Xenophon and Plutarch, though they wrote from different perspectives. Xenophon (*Hellenica* 5.2.25–36, 5.4.1–13) saw the occupation as an act of tragic hubris on Sparta's part, for which it incurred divine retribution. Plutarch by contrast (*Pelopidas* 5–13 and *De genio Socratis*) celebrates the courage of the Theban liberators. The second of these Plutarchan works is a philosophic dialogue about the "sign" that supposedly guided Socrates, set among the conspirators seeking to liberate Thebes, at the moment the plot goes into motion; the work is a mixture of fact and fiction, but contains important details not recorded elsewhere. Plutarch's two accounts (not always in agreement) are privileged over Xenophon's, in my retelling, because Xenophon's patent suppression of the role of Pelopidas reveals his disdain for the Thebans. See H. D. Westlake, "The Sources of Plutarch's *Pelopidas*," *Classical Quarterly* 33 (1939): 21–22; J .G. De Voto, "The Liberation of Thebes in 379/8 BC," in *Daidalikon*, ed. R. Sutton (Wauconda, IL, 1989); and Dillery 1995, 216–31.

22 *beauties and women of standing:* Xenophon is clear on this point (*Hellenica* 5.4.4) though its significance is unclear. Normally the women attending such drunken parties would be demimondaines.

23 *The phrase became a popular tagline:* See Plutarch, *Quaestiones Conviviales* 619d–e (where Archias stuffs the note not under a pillow but a ceramic jar).

24 *This gold vessel . . . may well depict Pelopidas's attack:* The link between the vase and the assault on Leontiades was made by E. Borthwick, "The Scene on the Panagjurischte Amphora: A New Solution," *Journal of Hellenic Studies* 96 (1976): 148–51.

24 *Leontiades was already arming himself:* Xenophon paints a very different picture in the *Hellenica*, perhaps to minimize Theban bravery: Leontiades, he says, was sitting quietly at home with his wife, suspecting nothing.

25 *Some sort of smoke screen was used:* Attested by a single word in the last chapter of Plutarch's essay *De genio Socratis*; but the text may be damaged, and some editors prefer to change this word. However, both Epaminondas and Pelopidas are reported (by the military writer Polyaenus) to have used smoke screens in other cases (my thanks to Adrienne Mayor for this observation).

26 *Athenians had been of two minds:* The role of Athens in the liberation—unclear from our sources—is examined by R. J. Buck in "The Athenians at Thebes in 379/8 BC," *Ancient History Bulletin* 6 (1992): 103–9.

26 *the "sister" of this one:* Reported by Plutarch as the general view of the Greeks (*Pelopidas* 13.2). See Steinbock 2012, chap. 4.

26 *It's not clear whether they authorized these troops:* Evidence discussed by Stein-
    bock (2012, 260–67).

27 *the Spartans took further revenge by killing the man's mother:* Executions of
    female family members are not otherwise known at Sparta. This one was
    reported by the historian Theopompus in a now-lost work (Athenaeus
    609b). Theopompus claimed that Chrysê, Lysanoridas's aunt (or perhaps
    sister), was also put to death.

28 *one of his loftiest sentences:* Quoted from *Pelopidas* 13.4.

28 *One leading member, Gorgidas, stepped forward:* Plutarch attributes the for-
    mation of the Band to Gorgidas (*Pelopidas* 18); Athenaeus, less reliably,
    names Epaminondas as its organizer (*Deipnosophistae* 602a).

28 *he refused to take the Spartans:* Unique information supplied by Plutarch in
    De genio Socratis 5.

29 *"A squad held together by* erôs*":* Quoted from Plutarch, *Amatorius* 17.

29 *run faster than single horses:* It's not at all clear this is true, though I note
    that a recent, well-researched video game, *Assassin's Creed: Origins*, gives
    chariot teams a 5 percent edge in speed over horses. The Plutarch passage
    is found at *Pelopidas* 19.4.

Chapter 2. Boeotia Rising

31 *this was thought to affect the brains of Boeotians:* The Roman poet Horace
    (*Epistles* 2.1.244) speaks of a literary dullard (Alexander the Great) as re-
    sembling "one born in Boeotia's thick air."

31 *and called them* kroupezophoroi, *"clog wearers":* The term comes from a now-
    lost play by Cratinus (frag. 310). Athenaeus (417b–418b) collects eleven
    insults on Boeotian manners, mostly concerning their interest in food.

32 *"Thick and strong," said a Roman, Cicero:* Quoted from *De Fato* 7. The
    Nepos quote that follows is from *Alcibiades* 11.3.

32 *In his eyes the Boeotians lacked* paideia: Ephorus's comments are preserved
    by the geographer Strabo (9.2).

34 *thanks to a lucky papyrus find:* The *Hellenica Oxyrhynchia*, so named for the
    site in Egypt at which it was found, contains portions of a fourth-century
    historical treatise by an unknown author. The surviving portions record
    much detailed information about the Boeotian League. See the discussion
    in Cartledge 2000.

36 *"Knowing that he was captive to matters of* erôs*":* Quoted from Plutarch,
    Agesilaus 20.6.

36 *the march proved a difficult:* Episode related by Xenophon, *Hellenica* 5.4.17–18.

38 *a typically Spartan male bond, part love affair, part political alliance:* See Paul
    Cartledge's discussion in "The Politics of Spartan Pederasty," *Proceedings
    of the Cambridge Philological Society* 30 (1981): 17–36.

38 *some pointed to an oracle:* Plutarch, *Agesilaus* 3, and Pausanias, *Description of Greece* 3.8.9.

39 *who seems to have put her up to competing in the race:* Plutarch (*Agesilaus* 20) claims that Agesilaus's goal was to show, by a kind of lampoon, that mere money could achieve anything, even a female chariot victory. We may guess he had other, more self-serving motives.

40 *perhaps in an effort to show the Thebans he could:* I concur with the view of Stylianou (1988, 125): "He was perhaps making a gesture of Spartan annoyance and strength in view of the Thebans' rejection of his call for contingents from other cities."

40 *They spoke of it thirty years later:* Xenophon, *Hellenica* 7.1.34.

43 *The obvious move for Sparta was to part ranks:* Xenophon, an eyewitness, praises Agesilaus for not doing this (*Hellenica* 4.3.19), but Xenophon's tone suggests he is defending the king against criticisms of his strategy; in *Agesilaus* (2.12) Xenophon states that criticism himself.

43 *"One could see the ground stained red":* Quoted from *Agesilaus* 2.14.

44 *Agesilaus withdrew and took ship for home:* None of our sources discusses the route homeward of Agesilaus after Coronea, but Xenophon places him in Delphi a short while later. Presumably he and his forces were shipped home from there across the Gulf of Corinth.

47 *Epaminondas and Pelopidas, set off for the Peloponnese:* Evidence for Theban participation in a battle at Mantinea is thin (only Plutarch, *Pelopidas* 4, and Pausanias 9.3.1, with no confirmation from Diodorus), and some historians have questioned it. I concur with Cawkwell (1972, 257) that such questions are needlessly skeptical. For the contrary view, see J. Buckler, "The Alleged Theban-Spartan Alliance of 386 B.C.," *Eranos* 78 (1980): 179–85. The Loeb edition of Plutarch's *Pelopidas* improbably assumes that the two men fought at Mantinea in 418 BC, a time when they were children or not even born, rather than in 385.

47 *Agesilaus was forced to travel at night:* Xenophon, *Hellenica* 4.5.18.

47 *the Spartans went into action:* The account that follows is based on Plutarch, *Pelopidas* 4.

49 *"Sparta's rule was well and securely established":* Quoted from *Hellenica* 5.3.27.

50 *Xenophon, thought the Thebans had urged Sphodrias on:* Xenophon, *Hellenica* 5.4.20. Plutarch and Diodorus by contrast thought that Cleombrotus initiated the plot, a theory first advanced by Ephorus (and Xenophon confirms that Cleombrotus had put Sphodrias in place in Thespiae). An interesting article by R. M. Kallett-Marx suggests that Sphodrias had never expected to reach Piraeus, but only to fire a shot across the Athenians' bow ("Athens, Thebes, and the Foundation of the Second Athenian League," *Classical Antiquity* 4 [1985]: 127ff). Helpful also is David Rice, "Xenophon, Diodorus and the Year 379/378 BC: Reconstruction and Reappraisal," *Yale Classical Studies* 24 (1975): 95–130.

52 *Chabrias was seen leaving the court:* Anecdote from Plutarch, *Regum et imperatorum apophthegmata* 47.

52 *They'd built an enormous stockade of brushwood and pointed sticks:* On this unusual strategy see J. G. De Voto, "Agesilaos in Boiotia in 378 and 377 BC," *Ancient History Bulletin* 1 (1987): 75–82; and Mark Munn, "Agesilaos' Boiotian Campaign and the Theban Stockade of 378–377 BC," *Classical Antiquity* 6 (1987): 106–38.

54 *"A solid mass of scarlet and bronze":* Quoted from *Agesilaus* 2.7.

54 *Chabrias chose to be portrayed in this moment of insouciance:* The leadership of Chabrias in the crucial engagement, and the resulting statue at Athens, are analyzed by John Buckler in "A Second Look at the Monument of Chabrias," *Hesperia* 41 (1972): 466–74.

54 *They muttered about leaving farms and homes:* As seen in an anecdote related by Plutarch (*Agesilaus* 26), probably to be dated to this second Boeotian invasion. The quip that follows, from Antalcidas, is found in the same chapter and in three other Plutarchan texts.

56 *the "dancing floor of Ares," the open Boeotian plains:* The phrase is attributed to Epaminondas by Plutarch (*Marcellus* 21). Greek dances were performed on flat, broad, circular surfaces, often surrounded by the steep banks of an amphitheater in the same way that Boeotian plains are surrounded by hills.

57 *Pelopidas himself was filled with* erôs, *as Plutarch meaningfully says:* Statement found at *Pelopidas* 4.3 (where it also applies to Epaminondas). The anecdotes that follow come from the preceding chapter and from 20. On Plutarch's view of *erôs* generally, see Philip Stadter, "'Subject to the Erotic': Male Sexual Behavior in Plutarch," in *Ethics and Rhetoric*, ed. Doreen Innes, Harry Hine, and Christopher Pelling (Oxford and New York, 1995), 221–36.

60 *Plutarch—himself a Boeotian—marks the moment's significance:* The following quote (and the preceding battle account) come from *Pelopidas* 17.

60 *The chronicler Diodorus reaches a similar conclusion:* Quote taken from Diodorus's *Library* 15.37.

Chapter 3. Philosophers in Arms

64 *Müller's Dorian study was published in England:* The influence of Müller in England is detailed by Robert Ackerman, "K. O. Müller in Britain," in *Zwischen Rationalismus und Romantik*, ed. William M. Calder III and Renate Schlesier (Hildesheim, Germany, 1998), 1–18; and by Linda Dowling, "Ruskin's Pied Beauty and the Constitution of a 'Homosexual' Code," *Victorian Newsletter* 75 (1989): 1–8.

64 *Jowett, himself asexual and homophobic:* Attested by Geoffrey Faber, *Jowett: A Portrait with Background* (Cambridge, MA, 1958), chap. 5, with quote

from an 1896 letter by a friend of Jowett's: "He had a 'horror naturalis' of sentimental feelings between men" (90).

64 *texts he helped introduce into the Oxford curriculum:* See Linda Dowling, *Hellenism and Homosexuality in Victorian Oxford* (Ithaca, NY, and London, 1994), 67–80.

65 *Whitman was also a reader of Plutarch's Lives:* Documented by Whitman's close friend William Sloane Kennedy, who specifically connected "I dream'd in a dream" with the Sacred Band account in Plutarch's *Pelopidas* (noted by Juan Herrero Brasas, *Walt Whitman's Mystical Ethics of Comradeship* [Albany, 2010], 113).

65 *The poem has been compared to Martin Luther King's "I Have a Dream" speech:* See Gary Schmidgall, *Walt Whitman: A Gay Life* (New York, 1997), 146.

66 *an episode that intrigued Xenophon:* Found in *Hellenica* 5.4.56–57.

67 *his larger concern with male erôs generally:* For Xenophon's complex view of *erôs*, see two important articles by Clifford Hindley: "*Sophron Erôs:* Xenophon's Ethical Erotics," in *Xenophon and His World*, ed. C. J. Tuplin, (Stuttgart, 2004), chap. 3.3, and "Xenophon on Male Love," *Classical Quarterly* 49 (1999): 74–99.

68 *He first met Socrates as the two were passing in an alley:* Diogenes Laertius, *Lives of the Eminent Philosophers* 2.48.

69 *Xenophon quotes Socrates praising* enkrateia *as "the foundation stone of virtue":* Xenophon, *Recollections* 1.5.4–5. The Choice of Heracles parable is found at 2.1.21 and following.

72 *Agesilaus provided him with a model of this restraint:* The incident is discussed by Xenophon at *Agesilaus* 5.4–6.

74 *a late essay, the* Spartan Constitution: Thought by some to be by a different author than Xenophon, but accepted by most scholars as genuine.

76 *according to one rumor, he built an underground chamber:* Diogenes Laertius 8.41.

77 *may even have become his legal adoptees:* Unique information supplied by Diodorus, *Library* 10.11.

78 *Once when a friend invited him to a festive meal:* Anecdote found in Plutarch, *Regum et imperatorum apophthegmata* 71.4.

79 *He preferred to wait for the chance to free his city "with justice":* Plutarch, *De genio Socratis* 25.

80 *the* dêmos, *to humble his pride, appointed him* telmarch: Plutarch, *Praecepta gerenda reipublicae* 15.

85 *Isocrates, an Athenian essayist, berated his countrymen:* The speech, known as the *Plataicus* or *Plataean Oration*, is officially listed as speech number 14.

85 *Thebes pulled down the walls of Thespiae, a less aggressive measure:* Theban moves against Thespiae have been portrayed as more severe than this, based on a too-literal reading of tendentious Athenian texts (see Buck 1994, 104, 157–58nn12–13).

86 *Xenophon records three speeches they delivered:* See *Hellenica* 6.3.1–13, a

uniquely detailed presentation of diplomatic maneuvering (analyzed by Ryder 1965).

87 *He'd watched in disgust:* The account of Plutarch, *Agesilaus* 27.4–28. It's noteworthy that Plutarch explores Epaminondas's state of mind even in a biography devoted to Agesilaus.

88 *Xenophon says the Thebans went home "entirely despondent":* Hellenica 6.3.20. The editor's note to this passage in the Landmark edition (Strassler 2009) puts this statement in its proper context: "Some, perhaps most, of the Theban delegation may have been despondent, but its leader Epaminondas must have realized beforehand that his provocative stand would lead to war."

89 *"It seems that* to daimonion *was leading them on":* Quoted from *Hellenica* 6.4.3.

Chapter 4. *Otototoi!*

92 *The story of the Leuctridae is found in several ancient versions:* Plutarch recounts the story twice, in slightly different forms (*Pelopidas* 20, the basis of my retelling, and *Amatoriae narrationes* 773b–774d); other versions are in Xenophon (*Hellenica* 6.4.7) and Diodorus (*Library* 15.54).

93 *Epaminondas . . . did not put much credence in portents:* Diodorus 15.52.

93 *(Other sources accuse the Theban himself of contriving the "omens"):* Diodorus (15.53), Xenophon (*Hellenica* 6.4.7), and Polyaenus (2.3.8 and 12) concur in making Epaminondas responsible for the reports.

95 *he collected them into an anthology:* The work known as *Apophthegmata Laconica.* The quip reported here is found in chapter 44.

96 *their strongman was out of action, still nursing a phlebitic leg:* In *Hellenica* 6.4.18, Xenophon speaks of Agesilaus's "weakness" (*astheneia*), presumably that of the leg. Interestingly, John Buckler suspects he may have suffered from combat trauma.

96 *he may have fortified himself by getting drunk:* Xenophon reports this as a rumor, perhaps in an effort to scapegoat Cleombrotus (*Hellenica* 6.4.8).

96 *As his soldiers watched, he crushed the creature's head:* Polyaenus 2.3.15. Victor Hanson has raised questions regarding the innovativeness of Epaminondas's tactics; see "Epameinondas, the Battle of Leuktra (371 B.C.) and the 'Revolution' in Greek Battle Tactics," *Classical Antiquity* 7 (1988): 190–207, but his argument is handily refuted by Buckler (2003, 293n56).

97 *the causes of which are debated to this day:* Aristotle (*Politics* 2.9) began the discussion by attributing the decline to laws regarding land ownership. A recent study by Timothy Doran (*Spartan Oliganthropia* [Leiden, 2018]) summarizes the state of research.

98 *helots continued to join Spartan ranks:* Paul Cartledge presents an interesting view of this phenomenon in "Rebels and Sambos in Classical Greece: A

Comparative View," *Spartan Reflections* (London, 1985), 127–52. See also Peter Hunt, "Arming Slaves and Helots in Classical Greece," in *Arming Slaves*, ed. C. Morgan and P. Brown (London and New Haven, CT, 2006), 14–39.

99 *The sun had already passed noon:* Reconstructions of the Battle of Leuctra vary widely, in particular with regard to the arrangement of the Theban left wing. Three accounts survive (from Plutarch, Xenophon, and Diodorus) but differ widely, and none are clear. We know too little about where the Sacred Band was stationed in relation to the rest of the Theban army, or how exactly it made its decisive move. I have relied primarily here on the views in J. F. Lazenby, *The Spartan Army* (Warminster, England, 1985), chap. 9; C. J. Tuplin, "The Leuctra Campaign: Some Outstanding Problems," *Klio* 69 (1987): 72–107; and John Buckler, "Plutarch on Leuctra," *Symbolae Osloenses* 55 (1980): 75–93.

100 *They simply assigned horses, on the day of battle:* As described by Xenophon, *Hellenica* 6.4.11.

102 *The next day, however, he regretted his indulgence:* Anecdote found in Plutarch, *Regum et imperatorum apophthegmata* 71.11.

104 *That word . . . went on to serve, in other tragic plays:* Later playwrights added a fifth and sixth *ot* to the word's length. The five-syllable version was used in print as recently as October 17, 2016, by Elizabeth Kolbert in the *New Yorker*.

104 *Word of Leuctra arrived at Sparta:* Plutarch, *Agesilaus* 2; and Xenophon, *Hellenica* 6.4.16.

107 *Jason had been born into a wealthy Thessalian family:* On Jason of Pherae, see Westlake (1935), Sprawski (1999), and Sian Lewis, *Greek Tyranny* (Bristol Phoenix Press: Exeter, UK, 2009), chap. 3. The fundraising stories reported here are found in Polyaenus, *Stratagems* 6.1.

107 *Xenophon has preserved a portrait of Jason's character and methods:* *Hellenica* 6.1.4–16, a remarkably long and detailed speech (quite likely invented or embellished but based on Xenophon's own observations).

108 *The story was told long afterward:* E.g., by Cicero (*De natura deorum* 3.70) and Plutarch (*De capienda* 6).

109 *The "gigantic bluff" by which Sparta intimidated all of Hellas:* The phrase is from Lazenby, *Spartan Army*, 188.

110 *K. J. Dover, dated* Symposium *to just before the creation of the Band:* In both his article in *Phronesis* 10 (1965): 1–20, and in the introduction to his edition of Plato's *Symposium* (Cambridge, 1980), sec. 5.

111 *The Dion ode, however, seems genuine:* See the discussion by C. M. Bowra, "Plato's Epigram on Dion's Death," *American Journal of Philology* 59 (1938): 394–404.

112 *Pausanias and Agathon . . . stayed together, in an exclusive bond:* The two men are known to have emigrated together from Athens around 407 BC, after

they'd been together for two decades. Our sources lose sight of them at that point.

118 *in the judgment of its sole chronicler, Diodorus:* See *Library* 57; the same term is employed by Plutarch, *Praecepta gerendae reipublicae* 814b.

119 *no fewer than twelve hundred* beltistoi*:* Plutarch (in the passage cited) says fifteen hundred.

119 *"a prize of virtue, for those willing to compete for it":* Diodorus 15.60.

Chapter 5. The Three Free Cities

123 *Symonds, at age seventeen, discovered "the revelation I had long been waiting for":* Quote from *The Memoirs of John Addington Symonds*, ed. Phyllis Grosskurth (New York, 1984), 99. Grosskurth's biography of Symonds, *The Woeful Victorian* (New York, 1965), has also been drawn on in this segment.

124 *Symonds wrote an impassioned letter to Jowett:* Symonds, *Memoirs*, 100–102.

124 *Whitman humored him for a while but finally slammed the door:* Episode discussed in Grosskurth, *Woeful Victorian*, 272–75, with quote on 273–74.

125 *another city was being laid out, Arcadia's new capital:* The date of the founding of Megalopolis is given differently by different sources, leading to uncertainties today; I have left the matter vague. See Simon Hornblower, "When Was Megalopolis Founded?," *Annual of the British School at Athens* 85 (1990): 71–77.

126 *the Eparitoi . . . is said to have numbered five thousand:* The number, given by Diodorus (15.62, for a corps he calls by the related term *epilektoi*), has been called into question but is defended by Buckler (1980, 292n3).

126 *almost certainly built by Thebes in the years after Leuctra:* Identification is contested, but see Frederick A. Cooper, "The Fortifications of Epaminondas," in *City Walls*, ed. James Tracy (Cambridge, 2000).

127 *"Yes, for women, not men, to live in":* Remark reported by Plutarch, *Apophthegmata Laconica* 2.

129 *what Plutarch called a* kludôn, *a billowing wave:* Plutarch, *Apophthegmata Laconica* 2.

129 *King Agesilaus was ruing a boast he had often made:* Details in the account that follows are taken from Plutarch's *Agesilaus* (31–32) and Xenophon's *Hellenica* (6.5.25–32).

131 *Epaminondas crossed the Eurotas, unopposed:* Thus says Xenophon, but Diodorus (15.65) reports a contested crossing in which many Thebans were killed.

132 *(as Xenophon snidely reports):* Hellenica 6.5.50, clearly meant to imply that the Theban-led invasion was little more than a plundering raid, and those who had gotten their share of booty had no further interest in it.

135 *thus earning the contempt of Xenophon: Hellenica* 6.5.51–52, an unusually personal comment.

136 *"an unjust pirate on both land and sea": Hellenica* 6.4.35. Xenophon calls Alexander "an enemy to the Thebans and the Athenians," presumably meaning "in turn" since both cities fought him at different times.

136 *perhaps an adaptation by Shakespeare of this story:* The connection of the anecdote (found in Plutarch's *Pelopidas*) to Hamlet's speech was noted as early as 1746 by John Upton, according to Arthur Johnston, "The Player's Speech in *Hamlet*," *Shakespeare Quarterly* 13 (1962): 27–28.

141 *(Plato's own description, if the* Seventh Letter *is his work):* The quote is from *Epistle* 7 326b. Controversy has raged for centuries over the authenticity of this, and other, Platonic letters, and no firm conclusion is possible. It is often supposed that Plato's visit to the court of Dionysius formed the basis of his portrait of tyrannical government in Books 9 and 10 of the *Republic*.

141 *"Take me back to the quarries":* Anecdote reported by Diodorus (15.6), who adds a follow-up: Philoxenus later gave a crafty double-edged answer to Dionysius when asked the same question, calling the tyrant's verses *oiktra*—both "inspiring pity" and "pitiful."

142 *The story, later recounted by Cicero:* In *Tusculan Disputations* 5.61. The Dionysius in question is sometimes supposed to be Dionysius II but was more likely his father.

142 *within thirty years they had spread throughout Greece:* As shown by Josh Ober, "Toward a Typology of Greek Artillery Towers," in *Fortificationes Antiquae*, ed. Symphorien Van de Maele and John M. Fossey (Amsterdam, 1992), 147–69. Ober shows that the defensive towers of Messene, built in 370, had openings wide enough to permit *gastraphetae* to swivel back and forth on stands.

142 *Dionysius devised ingenious schemes to raise cash:* Described by Aristotle in *Economics* 1349a ff.

142 *an Athenian orator denounced "the tyrant of Syracuse":* The speech was by Lysias, partly preserved as the Olympic oration (33) and also mentioned by Diodorus (14.109).

143 *Two inscribed stones record Athenian decrees:* Tod 133 and 136*, translated and discussed in *Greek Historical Inscriptions*, ed. P. J. Rhodes and Robin Osborne (Oxford and New York, 2003), 160–68.

144 *the Sacred Band—whom he calls "the picked men of the Thebans":* There is little doubt that Xenophon refers to the Sacred Band in this passage (*Hellenica* 7.1.19), as shown by the footnotes to that effect in the two most recent editions of the work (by George Cawkwell in the 1979 Penguin Classics edition and by John Marincola in the Landmark edition).

146 *the Boeotian army mobilized and prepared for a rescue mission:* The expedition is related by Diodorus (15.71), Nepos (*Epaminondas* 7), and Pausanias (9.15.2).

146 *he reportedly promised to sell to Athens:* As related by Plutarch, *Regum et imperatorum apophthegmata* 71.

148 *"Man's virtue is done for":* Anecdote found in Plutarch, *Apophthegmata Laconica* 20.

149 *"If you follow the Thebans blindly":* Quoted from Xenophon, *Hellenica* 7.1.24.

150 *Agesilaus . . . began to weep tears of relief:* Account of Xenophon (*Hellenica* 7.1.32), nearly seconded by Plutarch (*Agesilaus* 33.5).

150 *the grimmest, ugliest fundraising effort the Greeks had ever seen:* Recorded by Diodorus (15.75). Plutarch reports that Alexander conducted a similar massacre at Meliboea (*Pelopidas* 29.4).

151 *a messenger arrived from Athens:* Diodorus 15.74.

Chapter 6. A Death in Thessaly

154 *his domineering mother, Parysatis, killed his wife Stateira:* Plutarch, *Artaxerxes* 19. The torture of the troughs, in the next paragraph, is described in chapter 16 of the same work.

155 *Mithridates had in fact dealt Cyrus a serious, but not fatal, wound:* As attested by Ctesias, who was at the battle (Plutarch, *Artaxerxes* 11). Xenophon records the eye wound but does not know who dealt it (*Anabasis* 1.8.27).

156 *a way to demonstrate her son's absolute power:* Plutarch, *Artaxerxes* 23. The information tallies with a story in Herodotus (3.31) in which an earlier Persian king had married his sister as a way to place himself above human law.

156 *Ctesias told of a team of counting cows:* Information from the work *Persica* (frag. 34), also mentioned by Plutarch, *De sollertia animalium* 974d. The story of the marvelous spring in the next section comes from *Persica* also (frag. 45).

157 *perhaps Artaxerxes, though more likely one of two previous monarchs named Xerxes:* The dispute over which Persian king should be identified with Ahasuerus goes back to antiquity. The Septuagint Bible and Josephus, a Jewish historian who wrote in Greek, settled on Artaxerxes I (*Jewish Antiquities* 11.6). The case for Artaxerxes II, dating back at least to the sixth century AD, has been advanced in modern times by biblical scholar Jacob Hochsander (*The Book of Esther in the Light of History* [Oxford, 1923]). Most modern scholars prefer an identification with Xerxes I or II.

158 *Ismenias stealthily dropped a ring:* Anecdote from Plutarch, *Artaxerxes* 22.8. This chapter, as well as *Pelopidas* 30 and Xenophon, *Hellenica* 7.1.33–37, are the sources for this treaty conference.

160 *Disgraced and disillusioned, he starved himself to death:* Plutarch reports this suicide as though it followed the peace conference of 366, and I have fol-

lowed his chronology. Some scholars have argued Antalcidas died some years later.

160 *Xenophon recounts the episode in* Hellenica: 7.1.38–40.

163 *in words Xenophon gives them in* Hellenica: 7.4.9.

163 *A remarkable speech survives from the time of this Sparta-Corinth parley:* The *Archidamus* of Isocrates survives intact (Speech 6). The quote that follows is from sections 73–76.

164 *what was recorded by Plutarch and another Greek writer, Aelian:* See Aelian, *Varia Historia* 12.1 and chapters 26–28 of Plutarch's *Artaxerxes*. I am grateful to Monique Cardell for the paper "Aspasia of Phocaea" published on Academia.edu.

166 *"the Phocaean woman, said to be wise and beautiful":* Xenophon, *Anabasis* 1.10.2–3 (also the source for the second Greek woman, a Milesian, in Cyrus's train).

167 *the Persians were fiercely possessive of women:* As attested by Plutarch, *Artaxerxes* 27.

168 *"if I'm your general, you'll have to go on the march":* This quote and the next are both from Plutarch, *Regum et imperatorum apophthegmata* 71.18.

170 *Diodorus even says Thebes made these places "its own":* Library 79.1

170 *an Athenian orator would claim Epaminondas had aimed at a takedown of Athens:* Aeschines, Speech 2 (105).

170 *Heraclea on the Black Sea, called on Epaminondas:* Attested by Justin, 16.4.3.

171 *Sostratus of Sicyon, dubbed Akrochersitês, or "the Fingertipper":* Pausanias 6.4.1.

172 *Eubotas of Cyrene:* Pausanias 6.8.3. Details of the battle of Olympia are taken from Xenophon, *Hellenica* 7.4.28–32, and Diodorus 15.78.

174 *Xenophon mentions a squad called the Three Hundred:* At *Hellenica* 7.4.31 (also mentioned at 7.4.13).

175 *"Epaminondas and Pelopidas never killed anyone after a victory":* Quoted from the *Comparison of Pelopidas and Marcellus,* chap. 1.

178 *Amazingly, the final line begins "Lysippus . . .":* As noted by J. Bousquet, "Une Statue de Pélopidas à Delphes Signée de Lysippe," *Revue Archéologique* 14 (1939): 125–32. The first line of the inscription seems to have identified Pelopidas as the destroyer of Sparta.

179 *Warlordism was contagious in the age of the Sacred Band:* I'm grateful to the recent discussion by José Pascal González, "Commanders and Warlords in Fourth Century B.C. Central Greece," in *War, Warlords and Interstate Relations in the Ancient Mediterranean,* ed. Toni Ñaco del Hoyo and Fernando López Sánchez (Leiden and Boston, 2018), 89–112. The importance of Dionysius as model is stressed by Lionel Sanders, "Dionysius I of Syracuse and the Origins of the Ruler Cult in the Greek World," *Historia* 40 (1991): 275–87.

179 *Soon a third Greek tyrant arose, the most cunning and ruthless yet:* My portrait

of Clearchus of Heraclea comes from Justin 16.4.5, Polyaenus 2.30.1–3, and Memnon. Discussion by Stanley Burstein, *Outpost of Hellenism: Heraclea on the Black Sea* (Berkeley, 1976), 47ff.

181 *"When Clearchus was at my school"*: Quoted from Isocrates, *Letter to Timotheus* 12.

182 *He took to concealing his body behind an armoire*: This and the following anecdote come from Aelian, *Varia Historia* 9.13. The variant version of the latter story comes from Memnon.

Chapter 7. A Death in Arcadia

185 *a "new beautiful free earth, freed from power, love-crowned"*: Quoted from Ives's diary, entry of October 8, 1893 ("Thoughts on Hellenism," 17:110).

185 *"I have been reading the old Greek books"*: Diary entry of July 7, 1895 (24:93).

186 *A sentence from one of Wilde's letters to Ives*: The letter is dated March 1898 in Karl Beckson, *London in the 1890's: A Cultural History* (London and New York, 1992), 229.

186 *"I am more sanguine than I was once"*: Diary entry of July 2, 1893 (5:127).

187 *"No one is free except Zeus," wrote an Athenian playwright*: Line 50 of *Prometheus Bound* (attributed to Aeschylus but probably not by him).

187 *"The citizens who were in the middle were destroyed by both sides"*: Thucydides 3.82.8.

188 *he uses* harmost *to refer to a Theban garrison captain*: At *Hellenica* 7.3.4, the only place where the word is applied to a non-Spartan. Hatred of harmosts by other Greeks is revealed at 3.5.13. The harmost differed from other sorts of administrative envoys in his use of force to control the city in which he was stationed.

189 *"those who were planning the best for the Peloponnese"*: *Hellenica* 7.4.35 and 7.5.1. George Cawkwell calls attention to the significance of the phrase and of Xenophon's contempt for walls in general (*Xenophon: A History of My Times* [New York, 1979], 39).

190 *Probably he is the same man as the "Aeneas" who wrote* How to Survive under Siege: The identification is not certain but most scholars have deemed it likely, including, most recently, David Whitehead in the introduction to his translation of the work (*Aineias the Tactician: How to Survive under Siege* [Bristol, 2002], 11–13).

191 *When the League defeated Elis at the Battle of Olympia*: The narrative that follows is based principally on Xenophon, *Hellenica* 7.4.33ff, with discussion by W. Thompson, "Arcadian Factionalism in the 360's," *Historia* 32 (1983): 149–60.

195 *He quotes a belligerent speech from the Theban*: *Hellenica* 7.4.40. In the section that follows (7.5.2), Xenophon makes clear that anti-Theban rumors were

rife in the Peloponnese, and these may well have been the source of the quote.

196 *a Thespian deserter, some said:* Plutarch, *Agesilaus* 34.4. Xenophon (*Hellenica* 7.5.10) says the informer was a Cretan, and Diodorus (15.82.6) says that a mysterious "King Agis" (otherwise unknown) somehow guessed Epaminondas's intentions.

196 *filling sacks and baskets with rubble:* Detail from Aeneas's *How to Survive under Siege.*

196 *"those breathers of fire":* A rare case of Xenophontean sarcasm, quoted from *Hellenica* 7.5.12.

196 *Plutarch captures a memorable image from this battle: Agesilaus* 34.4.

200 *"Then I have lived long enough; for I die undefeated," he said:* The last words of Epaminondas are variously recorded, as are the details of his death. The version given here is that of Nepos (*Epaminondas* 9). Pausanias reports that Epaminondas watched the end of the battle before dying and that therefore the place his wounded body had lain was afterward called *Skopê* or "lookout point."

200 *a single iron coin of small value:* Plutarch, *Fabius Maximus* 27. Plutarch calls the iron piece a "spit" (*obeliskos*) but this seems to be used metaphorically of a small coin.

201 *Both said a certain Machaerion had wielded the lethal spear:* Thus Pausanias (8.11.5–6); Plutarch (*Agesilaus* 35) gives the man's name as Anticrates, but also notes his descendants were called Machaeriones, "swordsmen." Perhaps Machaerion, the name found elsewhere, was a kind of nickname or title.

201 *Epaminondas had never married:* Only one anecdote, from an unreliable source, associates Epaminondas with any woman or wife (Polyaenus, *Stratagems* 3.1). Plutarch by contrast makes clear Epaminondas's refusal to marry (*Pelopidas* 3.3).

201 *he claimed a beautiful "daughter," whose name was Leuctra:* Anecdote from Nepos, *Epaminondas* 10.

202 *"By sending embassies to one another, the Greeks have dissolved their disputes":* Text of inscription Tod 145, lines 4–5 (Ryder 1965, 143).

202 *he staged an impudent raid:* Story told by Polyaenus, *Stratagems* 6.2.

205 *Agesilaus, the lame king of Sparta, set sail for Egypt:* The details that follow come from the final chapters of Plutarch's *Agesilaus* and Xenophon's work of the same name.

207 *"he all but destroyed Sparta":* Plutarch, *Comparison of Agesilaus and Pompey* 3.2.

208 *the son of Cleombrotus, not yet fully grown:* The birth date of Cleomenes II is not known, but given that he reigned sixty years, he is likely to have been fairly young when he came to the throne.

209 *as the historian Ephorus observed:* Comments preserved by Strabo (9.2).

209 *Pammenes understood the Sacred Band:* See Plutarch, *Amatorius* 17 (the source of the quote that follows).

210 *He must have carried with him the lessons he'd learned at Thebes:* Also the opinion of André Aymard. "Philippe de Macedoine Otage à Thèbes," *Revue des Études Anciennes* 56 (1954): 15–36.

210 *and also to trouble his wife, long-suffering Thebe:* Details that follow taken from Plutarch, *Pelopidas* 25 and *Amatorius* 768f; Cicero, *De Officiis* 2.25; and Valerius Maximus, 9.13 ext. 3.

213 *according to one source, he slaughtered his half brothers:* Quintus Curtius 10.5.23; see also Justin 10.3.1.

215 *a speech that survives:* Speech 20, *Against Leptines*, was probably given in 355 BC when Demosthenes was approaching thirty. From its very first sentence the speech is cast as an effort to aid Ctesippus.

215 *Ctesippus sold the marble stones of his father's tomb:* Athenaeus, *Deipnosophistae* 4.60.

217 *they decreed he should never be named:* As attested by Valerius Maximus (8.14 ext. 5).

Chapter 8. The Sacred Wars

219 *The inscription at the base of the Cadmea statue:* Quoted by Pausanias 9.15.6.

220 *"the Thebans right away lost the hegemony":* Strabo 9.2.2, quoting a lost work of Ephorus's.

220 *Diogenes paid his own tribute to Epaminondas:* Anecdote from Plutarch, *Quomodo adulescens* 4.

220 *Polybius cites Thebes (and Athens as well) as cases in point:* Polybius 6.43.

223 *Plutarch gives the story a different spin:* De Pythiae oraculis 8, a variant version of Athenaeus, *Deipnosophistae* 13.83.

225 *Her real name was Mnêsaretê:* Athenaeus, *Deipnosophistae* 13.59–60, the source for much of my account of Phrynê. The reason for the nickname is given by Plutarch, *De defectu oraculorum* 14. A brief biography of Phrynê is given by Christine Mitchell Havelock, *The Aphrodite of Knidos and Her Successors* (Ann Arbor, 1995), 42–47. On the Phrynê legend, see Patricia Rosenmeyer, "(In-)Versions of Pygmalion: The Statue Talks Back," in *Making Silence Speak*, ed. A. Lardinois and L. McClure (Princeton and London, 2001), 240–60.

226 *as he declared to the world in an inscription:* Quoted by Athenaeus, *Deipnosophistae* 13.59.

226 *He thought it his most successful creation:* Pausanias 1.20–21.

227 *even to have attempted to make love to it:* Pliny the Elder (*Natural History* 36.21) reports that this attempt left a visible stain on the statue.

228 *One man alone was said to have resisted Phrynê's charms:* Anecdote from Diogenes Laertius, *Lives of the Eminent Philosophers* 4.2.

230 *Ancient treasures came to light from the sacred buildings of Delphi:* Details from Athenaeus, *Deipnosophistae* 6.22, and Diodorus, *Library* 16.60–61.

231 *apparently killed by his own disillusioned troops:* So says Pausanias (10.2.5), though Diodorus (16.35.5) seems to imply that he drowned while trying to swim to safety.

232 *Phalaecus knew of a verse in Homer's Iliad:* Diodorus 16.56. Strabo (*Geography* 9.3) connects the story to Onomarchus rather than Phalaecus.

233 *at a pace that stretched out for more than a century:* The yearly compensation that Phocis was assessed, sixty talents, would have paid back the missing wealth in 166 years. The amount was reduced by half soon after it was levied.

233 *They took ship for Italy:* Diodorus 16.62–63.

235 *"The Pythia philippizes," he told the assembly:* As attested by Aeschines, *Against Ctesiphon* 130. Demosthenes uses *philippize* again in his reply to Aeschines, *De Corona* 176; these are the only two instances of the word in extant Greek.

238 *Demosthenes recalled this speech and its results:* In *On the Crown* 213–15.

238 *in a later speech, "Against Diondas":* For the account of the debate given by Hyperides, see the articles by Judson Herrman and S. C. Todd in the *Bulletin of the Institute for Classical Studies* 52 (2009): 161–74, 175–85.

238 *"The Thebans could at one vote":* Buckler 2003, 499. See also D. Mosley, "Athens' Alliance with Thebes 339 B.C.," *Historia* 20 (1971): 508–10.

240 *Alexander's troops hurtled forward:* It's unclear from surviving accounts whether Alexander fought on horseback or on foot, and I have chosen to leave this question unresolved. Scholars who have recently written about the remains of the Sacred Band have argued for a Macedonian cavalry charge: see Maria Liston, "Skeletal Evidence for the Impact of Battle on Soldiers and Non-combatants," in *New Approaches to Ancient Warfare,* ed. Lee Brice (Hoboken, NJ, 2020), chap. 7; and Matthew Sears and Carolyn Willekes, "Alexander's Cavalry Charge at Chaeronea," *Journal of Military History* 80 (2016): 1017–35.

240 *recovered skulls tell the tale:* As described by Maria Liston (see above note) and John Ma (2008), 75–76.

242 *at least seven tight rows, perhaps eight:* John Ma (2008, 84) speculates there may be an eighth row, not unearthed by excavators, which would bring the grid into line with typical phalanx depth.

244 *"I'm grateful to my old age for this one reason":* Quoted from Isocrates' second letter to Philip (*Letters* 3.6).

245 *Philip had at his court a talented but deranged doctor:* Athenaeus, *Deipnosophistae* 7.33–35.

248 *History could repeat itself at a distance of two generations:* "It almost seems as though the Theban exiles in 335 used the account of the Theban counter-coup (of 379) as a script," writes Steinbock (2012, 273). The account that follows, of the siege and capture of Thebes, is taken from the (conflicting) accounts of Diodorus and Arrian.

251 *One episode, preserved by Plutarch:* The story is told in *Mulierum virtutes* 24.

252 *the single greatest catastrophe the Greeks ever saw, according to Arrian: Anabasis* 1.9.

252 *the Thebans . . . lost all motivation and took to feasting and drinking:* Polybius 20.4.6–7. The battle in question took place in the mid-third century BC.

Image Credits

P. 1: Courtesy of the Royal Pavilion Museums, Brighton and Hove

P. 12: © Jonah Romm

P. 24: Photograph by Nicholay Genov

P. 46: Courtesy of the American School of Classical Studies at Athens

Pp. 55, 103: Digital illustration by Markley Boyer

Pp. 69, 82, 140, 155, 229: Wikimedia Commons

P. 88: Photograph by Jeff Vanderpool, courtesy of the Epigraphical Museum, Athens

P. 94: Courtesy of CNG Coins

P. 127: Alamy Limited

Pp. 134, 243, 253: Photograph by Tanya Marcuse

P. 178: Courtesy of the École Française d'Athènes

P. 203: Courtesy of the Trustees of the British Museum

P. 227: Courtesy of the American Numismatic Society

Index

Page numbers in *italics* refer to maps and illustrations.

Achaea, in Mantinean alliance, 195
Achilles, 112, 113
Aelian, 164, 166, 167
Aeneas of Stymphalos, 190–93
Aeschylus, 10, 104
"Against Diondas" (Hyperides), 238
Agamemnon, King of Mycenae, 40
Agathon, as Pausanias's *erômeos*, 111–12, 114
Agave, 9, 11
Agesilaus, King of Sparta, 35–36, 85, 105, 127
  and acquittal of Sphodrias, 50–51
  Artaxerxes' support for, 148
  in attempts to stop anti-Spartan movement, 117, 119
  and Boeotian invasions of Peloponnese, 129
  Cleombrotus overshadowed by, 95–96
  at Coronea battle, 43
  coup attempts foiled by, 130–31
  death of, 207
  in Egyptian invasion of Phoenicia, 205–6
  Epaminondas respected by, 130
  and exoneration of Phoibidas, 15
  in Great Satraps' Revolt, 169, 189
  as likely architect of Spartan capture of Thebes, 14
  as Lysander's *erômenos*, 38
  Lysander's rivalry with, 41–42
  in Mantinean alliance, 196
  Mendesians defeated by, 206–7
  as model of *enkrateia*, 72
  personal vendetta toward Thebes of, 36, 40–41, 43, 44, 52, 61, 85, 202
  phlebitic leg of, 56, 65, 89, 96
  as proponent of machtpolitik, 14
  as proponent of Spartan expansionism, 38, 39
  recalled from Persian campaign, 42
  in response to Leuctra battle, 105–6
  Spartan invasion of Boeotia led by, 52–56
  Spartan throne claimed by, 39
  Sparta's Asian campaign led by, 39–40, 72
  Thebes excluded from 371 peace treaty by, 87
  371 peace conference hosted by, 86
  Xenophon as adjutant of, 73
  Xenophon's lionizing of, 72, 115
Agesilaus (Xenophon), 206
Agis, King of Sparta, 37, 38
agôgê (Spartan military training), 28, 32, 74
akrasia (lack of self-control), 114, 115
Alcetas, 66–67, 75
Alcmene, 19
Alexander II, King of Macedon, 138
Alexander of Pherae, 159, 180
  assassination of, 211
  Athenian alliance of, 146–47
  coinage of, 202, *203*
  in failed peace talks with Pelopidas, 137–38
  mercenary troops of, 202, *203*

Alexander of Pherae (*cont.*)
  money needs of, 150, 202
  navy of, 203–4
  Pelopidas imprisoned by, 138–39,
    145–46, 179
  Pelopidas's 364 campaign against,
    175–79
  in raid on Piraeus *trapezai*, 202,
    203–4
  Scotussa citizens massacred by,
    150–51
  as *tagus* of Thessaly, 136
  Thessaly subjugated by, 208, 210
  in treaty with Epaminondas and
    Boeotians, 179, 202
Alexander the Great, xvii, 183
  accession of, 247
  birth of, 216–17
  Chaeronea victory of, 2, 240–41
  false report of death of, 248
  as League of Corinth head, 247
  in lightning march to Thebes, 248
  Philip's planned Persia invasion
    taken up by, 247
  in Thebes battle, 249, 250
Amatorius (Plutarch), 78
Amestris, 166
Amphictyonic Council:
  Philip as member of, 233, 236
  Phocis fined by, 222–23
  punishment of Phocians by, 233
  Sacred War against Amphissa
    declared by, 236–37
  Sacred War against Phocis launched
    by, 223
  Spartan reparations ordered by,
    221–22
  Theban control of, 221–23
Amphissa, Sacred War against, 236–37
Amphitheus, 19, 25
Anabasis (Xenophon), 67
Androclidas, 7, 16
Antalcidas, 45, 55, 130, 154, 160
Antigone, 10–11
Antigone (Sophocles), 10

Antigone's Drag Track, 10–11, *12*
Apelles, portrait of Phrynê by,
  227–28
Aphrodisia (Theban festival), 16–17, 22
Aphrodite, 8, 22, 165, 166, 167
Apollo:
  Delphic oracle of, 7, 200, 221, 223,
    234–35
  wrath of, 230–31, 232, 234
Apology (Xenophon), 68
Arcadia, *xi*, 116–17
Arcadian army, 126
  Spartan slaughter of, 149–50
Arcadian League, 117
  Argos's alliance with, 119, 139
  breakup of, 189–200
  as democracy, 126, 191–92
  Megalopolis as capital of, 125–26,
    128, 208
  in Olympia battle, 172, 191
  Olympia's sacred objects used to pay
    Eparitoi by, 191–92, 222
  in peace treaty with Elis, 193–94
  pro-Spartan vs. pro-Theban factions
    in, 194–95
  Theban aid sought by, 128
  Thebes's fraying alliance with,
    148–49, 160, 161–62
Arcesus, 25, 26–27
Archias, 15, 19, 20, 22
  assassination of, 23
Archidamus, 148, 163, 189, 196
  as king of Sparta, 208
  Spartan army commanded by, 149
  Spartan reinforcements commanded
    by, 106, 109
Argos, *xi*, 118
  Arcadian League's alliance with,
    119, 139
  in Tegean alliance, 195
Ariaspes, 212–13
Ariobarzanes, 169
Aristotle, 13
Arrian, on destruction of Thebes, 252
Arsames, 212, 213

Artabazus, 224, 225
Artaxerxes II (Mnêmon), Great King
    of Persia, xvi–xvii, 37, 41, *155*,
    202
  Common Peace blueprint of, 45
  concubines of, 156
  Cyrus's attempted overthrow of, 70,
    154, 166
  death of, 213
  and death of Tiridates, 166–67
  Delphi conference convened by, 148
  Egyptian revolt against, 51, 52, 81,
    153–54
  and Great Satraps' Revolt, 169, 189
  Greek envoys to, 151, 154, 157–60
  Greek mercenaries needed by, 45,
    153
  Greeks paid to fight one another by,
    41, 44–45
  and Peace of 375, 81
  and sedition among western satraps,
    159
  as Spartan ally, 153–54
  Theban alliance of, 159–60
  Theban navy funded by, 159, 169, 170
Asopichus, 78, 201
Aspasia of Phocaea, 212
  beauty and intelligence of, 165
  in choice of Darius over Artaxerxes,
    167
  Cyrus's love affair with, 165–66
  fame of, 164
  as priestess of Anahita, 167–68
  Tiridates' place in Artaxerxes' bed
    assumed by, 167
Athena, 11
Athenian naval alliance, 49, 56, 81–82
  rebellions against, 214
  as tyranny, 187
Athenian navy, 57, 146, 159, 169
Athens, Athenians, *x, xi*, 40
  in alliance with Alexander of
    Pherae, 146–47
  anti-Macedonian plotters abandoned
    by, 249

as beacon of democracy, xviii, 5,
    16, 39
  Boeotian League as threat to,
    34–35
  celebrated history of, xv
  at Chaeronea battle, 241
  Dionysius as ally of, 143
  Laconists in, 85, 128
  Macedonian garrison at, 244
  in Mantinean alliance, 195,
    197–98
  mineral wealth of, 215–16
  Phocians supported by, 232
  Plataea's alliance with, 83
  regime of the Thirty in, 15–16
  solstice plotters reinforced by, 26,
    235
  Spartan alliances of, 131–32, 143
  Theban alliances with, 5, *46*, 51, 52,
    235, 237–39
  Theban exiles in, 7, 15–16, 247–48
  Theban intervention repudiated by,
    27
  Theban request for aid after Leuctra
    rebuffed by, 106
  as threat to Persia's Aegean holdings,
    159
  and 371 peace conference, 86
  Xenophon banished by, 72
  Xenophon's return to, 215
Atossa, 156, 166, 212, 213
Attica, *x, xi*
Atticists, 7, 17, 19, 38, 46
Aulis, 85, 109
  Agesilaus's thwarted sacrifice at,
    40–41, 43
authority, Xenophon on need for, 68
Autocles, 86–87

Bacchae, The (Euripides), 9
Bacchylidas, 94, 96
beltistoi (best men), 37, 161–62, 191–94
  in conflict with *dêmos*, 117–19, 162,
    170–71, 180, 187–88, 192–93
Birth of Venus (Botticelli), 227–28

boeotarchs, 34, 49, 79, 128, 145, 168, 175
 and Leuctra battle, 93–94, 96
Boeotia, Boeotians, *x*, 8
 Athenians' mockery of, 31–32
 Cicero on, 32
 coinage of, *94*
 Philip's control of, 247
 Spartan bases in, 15
 Spartan campaigns in, 52–61, 105–6
 Spartan relief force in, 35–36
Boeotian League, 38, 208, 237
 administrative structure of, 34
 Alexander of Pherae's treaty with, 179, 202
 common currency of, 34
 in Common Peace conclaves, 35
 in Coronea battle, 42–44
 dissolution of, 246
 in failed attack on Corinth, 144–45, 168
 fifth Peloponnese invasion of, 208–9
 as first European federal state, 33–34
 first Peloponnese invasion of, 128–35
 fourth Peloponnese invasion of, 195–202
 King's Peace as attempted breakup of, 45–46, 49
 large army of, 34
 Orchomenus's joining of, 116
 Phocians as threat to, 231
 post-Leuctra strength of, 115–16
 rebuilding of, 83, 85
 restoration of, 49
 second Peloponnese invasion of, 139–40, 143–45
 seen as threat by both Athens and Sparta, 34–35
 Thebes as founder of, 33
 Thessalians' request for aid from, 137
 third Peloponnese invasion of, 161
 see also Thebes, Thebans

Boeotian (Corinthian) War (305–387 BC), 42, 44–45, 60, 97
Botticelli, Sandro, 227–28
Boyer, Markley, xiii
Buckler, John, 238
Bura, 91
Byzantium, 170

Cabirichus, 23
Cadmea (Theban acropolis), xv, 4–5, 8, *12*, 235, 251
 Macedonian garrison in, 244, 248, 250
 solstice plotters' recapture of, 26, 49
 Spartan garrison at, 6–7, 13, 25, 48
 Spartan seizure of, 6, 221
 statue of Epaminondas at, 219
Cadmus, 7–10
 dragon's teeth planted by, 8
 palace of, 8, *12*, 13
Calamus poems (Whitman), 64–65, 124, 186
Caligula, Emperor of Rome, 226
Caphisias, 77, 79
 in solstice plot, 20
Caphisodorus, 78, 200–201
Caravaggio, 140
Carthage, Sacred Band of, 174*n*
Caryae, Caryans, 129, 149
Cassander, King of Macedonia, Thebes rebuilt by, 252, 253
Cebes, 110
Celts:
 in Spartan army, 147, 149–50
 in Syracusan army, 142, 143, 145
Cephisodorus, 24
Cephisodotus, Eirênê statue of, 81–82, *82*
Chabrias:
 Athenian attack on Chios commanded by, 214
 in Athenian-Spartan alliance, 132
 as Athenian *stratêgos*, 51, 52
 as commander of Egyptian navy, 205–6, 214

death of, 214–15
in defense of Boeotia, 52–54, 235
Isthmus barricade constructed by, 143
memorial statue of, 54, *55*
mercenary army in Egypt led by, 51–52
military career of, 213–14
in Spartan-Athenian alliance, 143
Chaeronea, Battle of (338 BC), *x, xi,* 2, 186
Alexander's victory at, 240–41
Athenians in, 241
Philip in, 241–42
Sacred Band in, 239–41
Theban employment of orthodox tactics in, 239–40
Chaeronea, Sacred Band burial ground at, xiii–xiv, 123, 185, *243,* 253
linked arms at, 244
lion's head at, *1,* 2–4, 63, 186, 253, *253*
location and layout of, 242–43
Macedonia burial mound at, 242
Stamatakis's excavation of, xiii–xiv, 3, 185
strigils burial alongside bodies at, 243–44
Taylor's discovery of, 1–2, *1,* 63
trauma to skeletons at, 240–41, 243
Charon:
as boeotarch of liberated Thebes, 79
in meeting with Archias, 22
in solstice plot, 17–19, 21–22
Chion, 182
Chios, 170, 214
Chlidon, in failed attempt to call off solstice plot, 18, 21
Choice of Heracles, the, 69–70, *69*
Cicero, 142
on Boeotian character, 32
Cinadon, in failed revolt against Sparta, 98–99

Cithaeron, Mt., *x,* 9, 11, 21, 26, 56, 57, 94–96, 106, 109, 126, 244
class strife (*stasis*), 117–18, 120
Claudius, Emperor of Rome, 226
Clearchus, 245
assassination of, 182
tyrannical regime of, 180–82
Cleombrotus, King of Sparta, 85
in belated attempt to break Cadmea siege, 26–27, 35–36
failed invasion of Boeotia led by, 56
indecisiveness of, 94–95, 96
in Leuctra battle, *see* Leuctra, Battle of
in march to Leuctra, 89
as overshadowed by Agesilaus, 95–96
Spartan army in Phocis commanded by, 86, 88, 89
Clepsydra (Ithomê spring), 132, 134
Cnidia (*Aphrodite of Cnidus;* Praxiteles), 226
Cnidus, Aphrodite coin of, 227, *227*
Colchis, 8
Common Peace, Greek search for, xvi–xvii, 85, 201–2, 233
Artaxerxes' blueprint for, 45
Boeotian League in, 35
Philip and, 245
371 conference on, 86–88, 115
see also King's Peace; Mantinea, Peace of; Peace of 375; Thebes, Peace of
Comon, 133
Copais, Lake, 31, 42, 59
Corcyra, 118
Corinth, Corinthians, *x, xi,* 13, 33, 143
in conference with Spartans over Messene, 163–64
failed Boeotian attack on, 144–45, 149, 168
Peace of Thebes rejected then signed by, 161, 162, 164
in Spartan army, 130
Theban alliance with, 42

Corinthian War (395–387 BC), 42, 44–45, 60, 97

Coronea, Battle of (394 BC), *x*, 42–44, 60, 97

Creon, 10

Crocus Field, Battle of (392 BC), 231, 232

Croesus, King of Lydia, 230

Croton, 75
massacre of Pythagoreans at, 77

Ctesias, 156–57

Ctesippus, 51, 214, 215

Cunaxa, Battle of (401 BC), 166

Cydonia, 233–34

Cynisca, 39

Cynoscephalae, Battle of (364 BC), 176–77

Cyrus, 70, 154
Aspasia's love affair with, 165–66
in attempted overthrow of Artaxerxes, 166
death of, 166

Damocles, Dionysius and, 141–42

Darius (son of Artaxerxes II), 167, 168
execution of, 212

Datames, 159, 169

Delphi, *x*, *xi*
Amphictyonic Council of, *see* Amphictyonic Council
Athena's shrine at, 10
destruction of Apollo's temple at, 91, 126
Locrians' failed attempt to liberate, 223
Macedonian control of, 234
oracle at, 7, 91, 120, 200, 221, 223, 234–35
Pammenes' defeat of Phocians at, 223–24
Pelopidas's commemorative statue at, 178, *178*
Philomelus's capture of, 222–23
Phocians' plunder of, 229–35

Praxiteles' statue of Phrynê at, 228–29, *229*

Pythian Games at, 120

Theban-Spartan peace conference at, 148

Theban treasure house at, 126

371 BC earthquake at, 91

treasures at, 222–23

Demeter, 4

democracy:
Arcadian League as, 126, 191–92
Athens as beacon of, xviii, 5, 16, 39
fourth-century flourishing of, xvii
Mantinea as, 125, 135
Megalopolis as, 125–26, 135
Messene as, 135
Thebes as, 108, 174

dêmos (masses), 33, 37, 68, 168, 191
in conflict with *beltistoi*, 117–19, 162, 170–71, 180, 187–88, 192–93

Demosthenes, 31, 215, 234–35
anti-Macedonian plotters supported by, 247–49
on Delphic oracle's bias, 235
Theban-Athenian alliance proposed by, 237–38

Diocles, 13

Diodorus, 88, 118, 170, 192, 198, 234, 250
on building of Messene, 135
on Epaminondas's singular gifts, 220
on Tegyra battle, 60–61

Diogenes the Cynic, 220, 228

Dion:
assassination of, 111
bond between Plato and, 111, 113

Dionysius of Heraclea, 182–83

Dionysius of Syracuse, 146, 179
as Athenian ally, 143
Damocles and, 141–42
death of, 151
dictatorship of, 139–40
Isocrates' praise of, 142–43
lavish building program of, 141

literary ambitions of, 140–41, 143, 151
money-raising schemes of, 142
as role model for Clearchus, 180
as role model for Philip, 245
as Spartan ally, 143
weaponry innovations under, 142, 148
Dionysus, 9, 11
Dirce, tomb of, 28
Dover, K. J., 110

Egypt:
  in Great Satraps' Revolt, 169
  Greek mercenaries in, 51–52, 205–7, 214
  Phoenicia invaded by, 205–6
  in revolt against Persia, 51, 52, 81, 153–54
Eirênê ("peace") statue, 81–82, 82
Ekêcheiria, 171, 172
Elatea, Philip's seizure of, 236–37
Eleusinia festival, 226
Eleusis, 17
Eleutherae, Theban fort at, 126, 127
Elis, xi, 12, 13
  in anti-Spartan coalition, 119
  in Mantinean alliance, 195
  in Olympia battle, 172–74, 191
  in peace treaty with Arcadian League, 193–94
enkrateia (self-mastery), 68, 69, 77–78, 102–3, 104, 114
  Agesilaus as model of, 72
  Socrates as exemplar of, 68
  as Spartan principle, 68
Epaminondas, 35, 39, 47, 58, 96, 164, 197
  in abstention from solstice violence, 20–21, 79
  Agesilaus's respect for, 130
  Alexander of Pherae's treaty with, 179, 202
  aloofness and solitary lifestyle of, 78, 80

appointed telmarch (supervisor of garbage collection), 80
  athleticism of, 78–79
  bad luck of, 196
  as boeotarch, 79, 93–94, 96, 128, 147, 168
  in building of Messene, 133–34, 189, 201
  Cadmea statue of, 219
  "cutting off the snake's head" as strategy of, 96–97, 239
  death of, 199–200, 202
  and death of Pelopidas, 179
  in decision to abandon assault on Sparta, 132
  enkrateia of, 78, 102–3
  erôs of, 78
  exonerated for exceeding term of office, 135
  in failed attack on Corinth, 144–45
  as favoring Leuctra battle, 94
  in first attempt to capture Sparta, 129–32
  first invasion of Peloponnese led by, 128–35
  fourth invasion of Peloponnese led by, 195–200
  generosity toward defeated enemies urged by, 116
  growing reputation of, 89
  as horrified by mass murder of Orchomenians, 175
  as indifferent to wealth, 79
  Isthmus barricade breached by, 143–44
  in Isthmus truce with Spartans, 44
  justice as core principle of, 79, 80, 87, 89
  in Leuctra battle, see Leuctra, Battle of
  Lysis's influence on, 77–78, 79
  in Mantinea battle, 47–48, 239
  in march to Ithomê, 132
  music as passion of, 80, 219
  omens as viewed by, 93

Epaminondas (*cont.*)
  Pelopidas's friendship with, 80
  philanthrôpia (humaneness) as
    principle of, 116, 161, 175, 187
  Plutarch's lost biography of, xvi
  in rescue of Pelopidas, 147, 179
  in second attempt to capture Sparta,
    196
  second invasion of Peloponnese led
    by, 139–40, 143–45
  as singularly gifted leader, 220–21
  in solstice plot, 17–18
  term of office exceeded by, 129, 132
  Theban alliances strengthened by,
    127
  Theban navy created and
    commanded by, 168–71
  third invasion of Peloponnese led
    by, 161
  at 371 peace conference, 86–89
  as warrior-philosopher, 75, 219
  Xenophon's scorn for, 189
Eparitoi (Arcadian army), 126, 195
  antidemocratic tilt of, 193
  payment of, 191, 192, 193
Ephesus, destruction of temple of
    Artemis in, 217
ephors (Spartan council), 104, 105,
    149
  as outraged by Spartan capture of
    Thebes, 14
Ephorus, 32, 220
Epidauros, *xi*
Epiteles, 133
erastês, erastai (older male lover), 38, 61,
    63, 66, 111–12, 113, 115
erômenos, erômenoi (adolescent male
    lover), 11, 13, 61, 63, 66, 111–12,
    113, 115, 209, 242
Eros (god), 225, 253
  Praxiteles' statue of, 226, 228, 253
Eros (Praxiteles), 253
erôs (passionate love), 57, 61
  between men, *see* male *erôs*
Esther, Book of, 157

Eteocles, 10
Euboea, *x, xi*, 116
  in Tegean alliance, 195
Eubotas of Cyrene, 172
Euripides, 9, 136
Europa, 7
Eurotas River, 129, 130
Euthycles, 154

gastraphetae (crossbows), 142, 148
Gauls, in Syracusan army, 142
Gigis, 154
Gorgidas:
  as boeotarch of liberated Thebes,
    79
  as Sacred Band commander, 53–54,
    61
  Sacred Band created by, 28–29
  in solstice plot, 17
Gorgoleon, 59
Great Satraps' Revolt, 169, 189
Greece (Hellas):
  Alexander's conquest of, 2
  fourth-century turbulence of,
    xvi–xvii
  search for Common Peace in, *see*
    Common Peace, Greek search for
Greek Archaeological Service, xiii
Greek War of Independence, 2–3
Gryllus, 198, 201

Haliartus, *x*, 57
  opening of Alcmene's tomb at, 19,
    25
Haliartus, Battle of, Theban victory
    over Spartans at, 41–42
Harmonia, cursed necklace of, 8–9,
    230
Helen of Troy, necklace of, 230
Helicê, 91
Hellas, *see* Greece
Hellenica (Xenophon), xv–xvi, xvii,
    14, 18, 48, 49, 61, 66, 67, 74, 99,
    158, 160, 161, 163, 188, 192, 195,
    200, 215

helots, 28, 98
as deserters from Sparta, 130, 132
loyalty to Sparta of, 131
Messene as refuge for, 134, 147, 148
Hephaestus, 8, 230
Heraclea:
civil strife in, 170–71, 180
Clearchus's tyranny in, 180–82
Timotheus as enlightened leader of, 182
Heracleia, Jason's destruction of, 120
Heracles, 11, 31, 58
Herippidas (Sparta commander), 25, 26–27
execution of, 27
Herodotus, 190
hetaera (kept woman), Phrynê as, 225–26, 228
hierosuloi (temple robbers), 231
History (Thucydides), 187
History and Antiquities of the Doric Race, The (Müller), 63–64
Homer, 61, 93, 222, 232
homosexuality:
in Victorian era, 123–25, 185–86
see also male erôs
hoplites (infantrymen), 28, 37, 45, 56
How to Survive under Siege (Aeneas), 190–91, 192–93
hubris (arrogant pride), 13, 78
Hydra, 11
Hyperides, 228, 237, 238
hypomeiones (former Spartiates), 98
Hypsistos, 12

Iberians, in Syracusan army, 143
"I Have a Dream" (King), 65
Iliad (Homer), 61, 232
Iolaus, 11
tomb of, 11, 12, 28
Iphicrates, 135
Isidas, 196–97

Ismenias (Theban envoy to Thessaly):
imprisonment of, 138–39, 145
in mission to Artaxerxes, 154, 157–60
Ismenias (Theban polemarch), 5, 16, 38, 41, 46, 48
arrest of, 6
trial and execution of, 15, 48
Isocrates, 85, 180, 211–12
"Archidamus" speech of, 163–64
in call for new war with Persia, 245
on Clearchus, 181
Dionysius praised by, 142–43
open letter to Philip from, 244–45
as suspected of supporting authoritarian rulers, 181–82
Ithomê, Mt.:
Epaminondas in march to, 132
as refuge from Spartan oppression, 132–33
Ives, George Cecil:
diaries of, 185–86
Order of Chaeronea founded by, 186
Sacred Band as inspiration for, 185
Wilde's letters to, 186

Jason of Pherae, 66, 79, 245
in alliance with Thebes, 108
assassination of, 120, 135
character and methods of, 107–8
chosen as tagus of Thessaly, 119
imperial dreams of, 108, 119–20
Leuctra truce arranged by, 108–9
private army of, 107, 119
Thessalians' fear of, 108
Thessalian tagus as goal of, 106, 108
Jocasta, Queen of Thebes, 9–10
Jowett, Benjamin, 123
on male erôs, 64, 123–24
Symonds and, 123–24, 125

katalusis (annihilation), 175, 251
katapaltai (crossbows), 148
Kiesling, Brady, xiii
King, Martin Luther, Jr., 65

King's Peace, 44–48, 49, 51, 52, 84, 130, 153, 160
  Athenian adherence to, 49
  Peace of 375 as successor to, 81–83
  Sphodrias's breach of, 50–51

Lacedaemonians, 98
Laconia, *xi*, 5*n*, 87
  Boeotia invasion of, 129–35
  see also Peloponnese; Sparta
Laconists, 5, 6, 15, 19, 46–47, 53, 78, 85
Laïs, 228
Laius, King of Thebes, 9–10
Larissa, 138
League of Corinth, 249, 251
  Alexander as head of, 247
  Philip as head of, 245
Leaves of Grass (Whitman), 64–65, 124–25
Lebadea, 1
Leonidas, 174
Leonides, 182
Leontiades, 15, *24*
  assassination of Theban exiles ordered by, 16
  as leader of Theban junta, 16, 19
  Pelopidas's assassination of, 23–24, *24*, 179
  Spartan capture of Thebes aided by, 5–6
  Theban rulership assumed by, 6
Leuctra, Battle of (371 BC), *xi*, 126, 159, 179, 196, 201
  cavalry action in, 100–101
  charge of Sacred Band in, 101
  Cleombrotus's bizarre use of cavalry in, 99
  collapse of Spartan army in, 101–2
  "cutting off the snake's head" strategy in, 96–97, 239
  Sacred Band at, 115
  Spartan cavalry driven from field in, 101
  Spartan right opposed by Sacred Band in, 97, 100

  Spartiate death toll in, 102, 105
  Theban trophy erected at, 102, *103*
  Thespians allowed to withdraw by Epaminondas, 99
  wounding and death of Cleombrotus in, 101–2
Leuctra, Battle of (371 BC), aftermath of, 103–4
  Athenian rebuff of Theban request for aid, 106
  growing strength of Boeotian League in, 115–16
  Jason's role in truce of, 108–9
  Spartan reinforcements ordered to Boeotia in, 105–6, 109
  Spartans' reaction to, 104–5
  Spartans return to Peloponnese in, 109
Leuctra, Battle of (371 BC), run-up to:
  boeotarchs' concerns about fighting on open ground and, 93–94
  Cleombrotus's indecisiveness and, 94–95
  Epaminondas's arguments in favor of field fight in, 94
  omens in, 91–92
  Theban decision to fight in, 96
Leuctridae, rape of, 92–93
Libya, 133
Liston, Maria, 243
Locris, Locrians, *x*
  in failed attempt to liberate Delphi, 223
  in Tegean alliance, 195
logos, logoi (reason), 32, 58, 177
Lycomedes of Mantinea, 117, 149, 191
  anti-Theban rhetoric of, 149, 153, 160, 162
  Athenian alliance promoted by, 162
  murder of, 162
Lysander:
  as Agesilaus's *erastês*, 38
  Agesilaus's rivalry with, 41–42
  as architect of Spartan Aegean empire, 38
  death of, 42

Lysanoridas (Spartan garrison chief):
  as absent from Thebes during
    Aphrodisia festival, 19, 25, 27
  exile of, 27
Lysippus, 178
Lysis, 187
  death of, 77
  enkrateia (self-mastery) of, 77–78
  influence on Epaminondas of,
    77–78, 79
  as Pythagorean, 75, 77
  tomb of, 19–20

Macedon, Macedonians, 224
  Athenian garrison of, 244
  Cadmea garrison of, 244, 248, 250
  Theban alliance of, 138
  Theban mistrust of, 236
  see also Alexander the Great; Philip
    II, King of Macedon
Macedonian army:
  Chaeronea burial mound of, 242
  Philip's professionalization of, 210
  shield bearers of, 210
  see also Chaeronea, Battle of
machtpolitik, of Sparta, 14, 29, 47
male *erôs*, 4, 63, 253
  chaste, 74, 112, 113–15
  lifelong (Uranian), 111–12, 113, 114
  Plato on, 11–12, 63, 110–13
  Theban view of, 4, 11–13, 28–29
  Victorian era views of, 63–64
  Xenophon on, 12, 66–67, 72–73,
    74–75, 113–15
Mantinea, Battle of (362 BC),
    198–200, 210, 239
  death of Epaminondas in, 199–200
  Epaminondas's tactics in, 199
  as stalemate, 200
  Theban-Athenian cavalry skirmish
    in, 197–98
Mantinea, Battle of (385 BC), 47–48
Mantinea, Mantineans, *xi*, 128, 208
  as anti-Spartan democracy, 117, 125,
    135

anti-Theban sentiment in, 191–92
beltistoi in, 191–94
burial of Epaminondas in, 200
in creation of Arcadian League, 117
in defense pact with Sparta, 195
in Leuctra battle, 99
new walls of, 125
pro-Spartan states aligned with, 195,
    196, 197
in refusal to submit to Arcadian
    League demands, 192
tapping of Olympic wealth opposed
    by, 192
Tegea revolt aided by, 118
Mantinea, Peace of, 201–2, 208
Marathon, Battle of (490 BC), *xi*, 83
Mausolus, 169–70
medism, 33
Megabates, 73
Megalopolis (Arcadian capital), 128,
    148, 189, 191, 298
  as anti-Sparta democracy, 125–26,
    135
Megara, *xi*, 26
Melian Dialogue (Thucydides), 187
Melôn:
  as boeotarch of liberated Thebes,
    79
  in solstice plot, 16, 23, 24–25
Melos, Athenian annihilation of, 175,
    187
Mendes, Mendesians, Agesilaus's defeat
    of, 206–7
Menecleidas, 145
Menecrates, 245–46
Messene, *xi*, 148, 179, 208
  as anti-Sparta democracy, 135
  independence of, 159, 160, 201
  as refuge for escaped helots, xvi,
    134, 147, 148
  Spartan obsession with capture of,
    163, 205, 207, 235
  Thebes in founding of, xvi, 133–34,
    189, 201
  walls of, 133–34, *134*

Messenia:
refugees from, 132–33
in Tegean alliance, 195
Mithridates, 155–56
mothakes (illegitimate sons of
Spartiates), 98
Müller, K. O., on male *erôs*, 63–64, 65

Nectanebo, Egyptian pharaoh, 169
Agesilaus's support for, 206–7
Mendesian revolt against, 206–7
neodamôdeis (freed helots), 98
Nepos, Cornelius, 32
Epaminondas praised by, 80
Nero, Emperor of Rome, 226
New York Times, Chaeronea excavation
reported by, 3–4
Nicaea, 237, 238
Theban garrison at, 236

Ochus (Artaxerxes III), King of Persia,
212–13
Oeconomicus (Xenophon), 68
Oedipus, King of Thebes, 9–10
Oedipus Rex (Sophocles), 10
Olympia, *xi*
Philippeion at, 246
sacred objects at, 191–92, 222
Temple of Zeus at, 171, 173
Olympia, Battle of (364 BC), 172–74,
191
Xenophon on, 174
Olympias (mother of Alexander the
Great), 216–17
Olympic Games (Olympiad):
Macedonians excluded from, 234
of 364 BC, 171–73
of 396 BC, 39
Olynthus, 5, 6
Onomarchus, 224, 231
in aid to Pherae against Philip, 231
in battles with Philip, 231
death of, 231
Delphic treasures plundered by,
229–31

dream of, 230
new catapult designed by, 230,
231
Orchomenus, Orchomenians, *x*, 15, 57,
85, 174, 247, 249
Boeotian League joined by, 116
Spartan garrison at, 58–59
Theban murder of all male citizens
and annihilation (*katalusis*) of,
175
Theban rivalry with, 58
Order of Chaeronea, 186
Orecchio di Dionisio, l', 140
Oreus, Spartan garrison in, 66–67
Orontes, 169

Pagasae, grain shipments to Thebes
from, 66–67
paideia (learning), 32
paiderasteia (bond between *erômenos* and
erastês), 66n
Pammenes, xii, 29, 61, 127, 210
arrest and presumed death of, 225
Asian campaign of, 224, 225
in campaign with Philip, 224
in defeat of Phocian army at Delphi,
223–24
fifth Boeotia invasion of
Peloponnese commanded by,
208–9
as Philip's possible *erastês*, 209, 224,
242
paradeisos (walled game park at Susa),
156
Parallel Lives (Plutarch), xvi, 65, 207
Parnassus, Mt., *x*, 224
Parysatis, 154, 156, 166
Patroclus, 112, 113
Pausanias, 1, 4, 219
as Agathon's *erastês*, 111–12, 114
on Chaeronea burial ground, 2
Peace of 375, 81–83
King's Peace replaced by, 81
withdrawal of garrison troops in,
81, 84

Pelopidas, *24*, 29, 35, 39, 47, 179
    Alexander of Pherae's imprisonment
        of, 138–39, 145–46, 179
    in assassination of Leontiades,
        23–24, *24*, 179
    as boeotarch of liberated Thebes, 79
    at Cynoscephalae, 176–77
    death of, 177–78
    in drafting of Peace of Thebes, 159,
        161, 179
    Epaminondas's friendship with, 80
    erôs of, 57, 61
    in escape from Thebes, 7
    in failed peace talks with Alexander
        of Pherae, 137–38
    in Leuctra battle, 101, 179
    Leuctridae dream of, 92–93
    Macedonian alliance signed by,
        138
    in Mantinea battle, 47–48
    in mission to Artaxerxes, 151, 154,
        157–60
    Plutarch's biography of, xvi
    rescue of, 146, 149
    as Sacred Band commander, 29,
        57–61, 97, 179
    as solstice plot leader, 16, 21–22,
        23–24, 25–26, 28, 57, 58, 79, 179,
        247
    in Tegyra victory over Spartans,
        59–61, 179
    Thebe's meetings with, 146
    in 364 BC campaign against
        Alexander of Pherae, 175–76
    thumos of, 7, 16, 21, 57–58, 61, 137,
        176, 177
Peloponnese, *x*, *xi*, 26, 235
    anti-Spartan strongholds in, 125–26,
        135, 147
    fifth Boeotian invasion of, 208–9
    first Boeotian invasion of, 128–35
    fourth Boeotian invasion of,
        195–202
    second Boeotian invasion of, 139–40
    Spartan dominance of, 128

Theban garrisons in, 188
    third Boeotian invasion of, 161
    uprisings in, 117–19, 120
Peloponnesian War, xv, 15, 83, 131
    expansion of Spartan hegemony
        after, 37–38
    Theban alliance with Sparta in, 38
Pentheus, 9
Pericles, 168
perioikoi (Spartan soldiers from
    surrounding towns), 98, 129
Persian Empire:
    Athenian threat to Aegean holdings
        of, 159
    Athens and Sparta as allies against,
        131
    Egyptian revolt against, 51, 52, 81,
        153–54
    in 480 BC invasion of Greece,
        32–33
    Great Satraps' Revolt in, 169, 189
    sedition in western satrapies of,
        159
    Sparta's 395 BC campaign against,
        39–42
Persians (Aeschylus), 104
Phaedo (Plato), 31
Phaedriades, 221, 223, 224, 233
Phaedrus, 110, 111, 112, 114
Phaedrus (Plato), 64–65, 123
    on male *erôs*, 63
Phalaecus:
    in attacks on Boeotia, 232
    death of, 233–34
    Delphi plundered by, 232
    in surrender of Thermopylae to
        Philip, 233
    Theban forces defeated by, 232
Pharsalia, 223
Pharsalus, 108
Phayllus, 224, 231
    death of, 232
    Delphic treasures plundered by,
        229–31
    dream of, 230

Pherae, 108
regime of Thebe and brothers in, 211, 231
see also Alexander of Pherae; Jason of Pherae
philanthrôpia (humaneness), 116, 161, 175, 187
Philesia, 74
Philip II, King of Macedon, xvii, 209, 216, 231
assassination of, 247
at Chaeronea battle, 241–42
Dionysius of Syracuse as role model for, 245
Isocrates' open letter to, 244–45
League of Corinth created by, 245
Macedonian army professionalized by, 210
mass drowning of Phocian soldiers ordered by, 231–32
as member of Amphictyonic Council, 233, 236
Pammenes in campaign with, 224
as Pammenes' possible *erômenos*, 209, 224, 242
Persia invasion planned by, 246
Sacred Band training witnessed by, 209
self-deification program of, 246
Theban alliance against Athens proposed by, 237–38
Theban mistrust of, 236
Theban plea for aid from, 232
Thermopylae controlled by, 233
as treaty hostage in Thebes, 138, 209
Philippeion, 246
Philiscus, 148
Philolaus, 13
Philomelus:
Delphic treasures plundered by, 222–23, 230
suicide of, 224
Philoxenus, 141
Phocaea, 165

Phocis, *x*, 222, 249
Athenian support of, 232
destruction of, 233
Sacred War against, 223–25, 229–33
Spartan army in, 86, 88, 89
Phocis, mercenary army of, 222–23
Pammenes' defeat of, 224
Philip's mass drowning of, 231–32
as temple robbers, 231–32
Phoibidas (Spartan commander), 48, 50, 57, 196–97
in capture of Thebes, 5–6, 221
exoneration of, 14–15
Xenophon's condemnation of, 14
Phrynê:
beauty of, 225–29
and destruction of Thebes, 252
as *hetaera*, 225–26, 228
Hyperides's defense of, 228
as Praxiteles' lover and muse, 226, 253
Praxiteles' portrait statue of, 228–29, *229*
Phyllidas, in solstice plot, 17, 20, 22, 25
Picture of Dorian Gray, The (Wilde), 64
Pindar, 251
Piraeus, *xi*
Alexander of Pherae's raid on *trapezai* of, 203–4
Sphodrias's failed march on, 49–50
Plataea, Battle of (479 BC), Thebans as allies of Persians in, 33
Plataea, Plataeans, *x*, 15, 26, 57, 247, 249
Athenian alliance with, 83
Boeotian League rejected by, 83
failed Thebes attack on, 83
Spartan destruction and rebuilding of, 83–84
Spartan garrison at, 49
Theban razing of, 84–85
withdrawal of Spartan garrison from, 84

INDEX

Plato, 31, 64–65, 68, 75, 180
  bond between Dion and, 111, 113
  Dion ode of, 111
  on male *erôs*, 11–12, 63, 110–13
  Pythagorean teachings adapted by,
    76
  as suspected of supporting
    authoritarian rulers, 181–82
  in visit to Syracuse, 141
Plutarch, xii, xvi, 11, 36, 65, 78, 95,
    104, 164, 170, 175, 178, 206, 207,
    211, 251
  on Agesilaus's respect for
    Epaminondas, 130
  on Epaminondas, 78, 79, 80
  on Leuctra battle, 92–93
  on Pelopidas's character, 177
  on Philip's reaction to Sacred Band
    deaths, 241–42
  Sacred Band celebrated by, xvi, 29
  on solstice plot, 18, 28
  on Spartans' reaction to Leuctra
    defeat, 105
  on Tegyra battle, 59–60
  on Thebans' second failure to
    capture Sparta, 196
  on Theban view of male *erôs*, 12–13
  on 371 peace conference, 87
  on *thumos*, 57–58
polemarcheion (Theban council
    chamber), 20, 21
  Aphrodisia massacre at, 22–23
polemarchs:
  Spartan, 59, 61, 97, 101, 102, 109
  Theban, 5, 6, 17–18, 19, 22–23
Polyaenus, 95
Polybius:
  on achievements of Epaminondas
    and Pelopidas, 220–21
  on imprisonment of Pelopidas, 139
Polydorus, 135–36
Polynices, 10–11
Polyphron, 135–36
Poseidon, 91
power, Greek view of, 187

Praxiteles:
  Eros statue of, 226, 228, 253
  Phyrnê as lover and muse of, 226,
    253
"Problem in Greek Ethics, A"
    (Symonds), 123
Procles of Phlius, 132
Prothoös, 89
Proxenus, 70
Pythagoras, 219
  teachings of, 75–76
Pythagoreans, 75–76, 77
  massacre of, 77
  self-mastery (*enkrateia*) of, 77–78
Pythia (Delphic oracle), 7, 91, 120,
    200, 221, 223, 234–35
Pythian Games, 120

Ransoming of Hector, The (Dionysius),
    143, 151
Recollections of Socrates (Xenophon),
    68, 69
Revenues (Xenophon), 215–16
Rhodes, 170

Sacred Band, 65, 106, 170, 174, 188,
    199, 208, 210, 235
  ancient accounts of, 3–4
  in Boeotian-Spartan Wars, 53–54,
    57–61
  in Chaeronea battle, 239–41
  Chaeronea burial ground of,
    xiii–xiv, 123, 185, *243*, 253
  as comprising pairs of male lovers,
    xvi, 29, 242, 253
  Corinthians' defeat of, 144–45,
    149
  creation of, 4, 28–29, 85, 109
  erôs and, 4, 29
  in fifth Boeotian invasion of
    Peloponnese, 209
  Gorgidas as commander of, 29,
    53–54, 61
  in Leuctra battle, 97, 101, 115
  organization of, 29

Sacred Band (*cont.*)
 Pelopidas as commander of, 29,
  57–61, 97, 179
 in Peloponnese invasion, 128
 Plato's presumed references to,
  110–11, 112–13
 Plutarch on, 29
 Symonds's tribute to, 123, 124
 in Tegyra victory over Spartans,
  59–61, 89
 thumos and, 29
 Xenophon's scorn for, xvi, 74–75,
  159
Sacred Wars, 221, 229
 against Amphissa, 236–37
 against Phocis, 223–25, 235, 249
sarisas (pikes), 240, 241
Satyrus, tyrannical regime of, 182
Scedasus, 92
Scotussa, Alexander of Pherae's
  massacre of citizens at, 150–51
Sellasia, 129
Semele, 9, 10, 13
Seven against Thebes (Aeschylus), 10
Seventh Letter (Plato), 141
Sicily, 139
Simmias, in solstice plot, 17–18, 19–20,
  110
Socrates, 110
 on chaste male *erôs*, 112
 on Choice of Heracles, 69–70
 as exemplar of *enkrateia* (self-
  mastery), 68–69, 77
 Xenophon as influenced by, 68–69,
  73
"Socrates," Xenophon's version of, on
  male *erôs*, 113–15
solstice plot (379 BC), 39, 44, 85, 109
 Athenian army's reinforcement of,
  26, 235
 Athenian priests' warning to
  polemarchs about, 17, 22
 Caphisias in, 20
 Charon in, 17–19, 21–22
 Chlidon in, 18, 21

 Epaminondas in, 17–18
 Epaminondas's abstention from
  violence in, 20–21, 79
 freeing of prisoners in, 25, 35
 Melôn in, 16, 23, 24–25
 memory of, 247
 ominous dream in, 18
 Pelopidas as leader of, 16, 21–22,
  23–24, 25–26, 28, 57, 58, 79, 179
 Phyllidas in, 17, 20, 22, 25
 Plutarch on, 18, 28
 recapture of Cadmea in, 26, 49
 Simmias in, 17–18, 110
Sophocles, 10
Sophronistêr stone, 11, *12*
Sostratus of Sicyon ("the
  Fingertipper"), 171–72, 173
Sparta, Spartans, *xi*
 agôgê training system of, 74, 98
 Arcadian army slaughtered by,
  149–50
 Artaxerxes as ally of, 153–54
 Asian campaigns of, 39–42, 72
 Athenian alliances with, 131–32, 143
 Athenians' view of, 32
 Boeotia invaded by, 52–61
 Boeotian army on outskirts of,
  129–30
 Boeotian League as threat to, 34–35
 capture of Messene as obsession of,
  163, 205, 207, 235
 celebrated history of, xv
 classes of, 98
 in conference with Corinthians over
  Messene, 163
 declining power of, 97–98
 in destruction and rebuilding of
  Plataea, 83–84
 Dionysius as ally of, 143
 enkrateia (self-mastery) as principle
  of, 68
 Epaminondas's decision to abandon
  first assault on, 132
 Epaminondas's second assault on,
  196

ephors of, *see* ephors

exile of Theban refugees in Athens demanded by, 7

expansionist policies of, 37–38, 39, 48

in failure to pay Amphictyonic Council fine, 221–22

hoplites as main weapon of, 28, 37, 56

in King's Peace treaty with Thebes, 44–48

machtpolitik of, 14, 29, 47

male *erôs* in, 72–73, 74, 115

in Mantinean alliance, 195, 196

money needs of, 204–5

moral rigor of, 32

Philomelus's seizure of Delphi aided by, 222–23

reaction to Leuctra defeat in, 104–5

Theban alliances with, 5, 38

Thebes seized by, 4, 5–6, 13, 15, 48, 78–79

as uninterested in events outside Peloponnese, 235, 249

walls disdained by, 127, 131

Xenophon's bias in favor of, xv–xvi, 67, 73, 74–75, 88–89, 115, 188–89, 216

Spartan Constitution (Xenophon), 74

Spartan navy, 37, 40, 56, 66

Spartiates (full citizens):

declining numbers of, 97–99

Leuctra death toll of, 102, 105

as minority in Spartan army, 97

Spartoi, 8, 200

Sphodrias, 101

acquittal of, 50–51

in failed march on Piraeus, 49–50

Stamatakis, Panagiotis, Chaeronea excavation of, xiii–xiv, 3

stasis (class strife), 117–18, 120

Stateira, 154

Stratagems (Polyaenus), 95

stratêgos, stratêgoi (military commanders), 51, 52, 190–91

strigils, 243–44

Susa, Artaxerxes' court at, 154–56, 157, 164

sword of Damocles, 142

Symonds, John Addington, 185

homosexuality of, 123–25

Jowett and, 123–24, 125

Whitman and, 124–25

Symposium (Plato), 75

on male *erôs*, 11–12, 63, 64–65, 110, 111–12, 123

Symposium (Xenophon), 68, 74–75, 113–15, 174

Syracusan army, in relief of Corinth, 145

Syracuse:

Dionysius as dictator of, 139–40

navy of, 142, 143

Plato in visit to, 141

Tachos, Egyptian pharaoh, 214

Agesilaus's desertion of, 206

Phoenicia invaded by, 205–6

Tanagra, 57

Taygetus mountains, 132

Taylor, George Ledwell, Chaeronea site discovered by, 1–2, *1*, 63

Tearless Battle (368 BC), 149–50

Tegea, 117, 192

anti-Spartan revolt in, 117–18

arrest of Mantineans in, 194

pro-Theban states aligned with, 195, 198–200

Theban aid sought by, 193

Theban garrison at, 193, 194

Tegyra, Battle of (375 BC), 59–61, 89, 159, 179

telmarch (garbage collection supervisor), 80

Ten Thousand, the (Arcadian assembly), 126, 149, 189, 192

antidemocratic faction in, 193–94

use of Olympic funds ended by, 192

Ten Thousand, the (Greek mercenaries in Persia), 37–38, 67, 70–72, 166

Teribazus, 212

Theagenes, as commander of joint
Theban-Athenian forces at
Chaeronea, 239
Theanor, 20–21, 77
Theban navy:
Artaxerxes' funding of, 159, 169, 170
Epaminondas as creator and
commander of, 168–71
Thebe (Alexander of Pherae's wife):
Alexander's abuse of, 210–11
in assassination of Alexander, 211
in meetings with Pelopidas, 146
Pherae regime of, 211, 231
Thebes, Battle of (335 BC), Theban
death toll at, 250
Thebes, Peace of, 159–60, 168, 169,
209
Corinth's signing of, 162–64
Greek cities' rejection of, 161
Pelopidas's role in drafting of, 159,
161, 179
Thebes, Thebans, x, xi, xv, 12
Agesilaus's personal vendetta toward,
36, 40–41, 43, 44, 52, 61, 85
Amphictyonic Council controlled
by, 221–23
annihilation (katalusis) of, 251
in annihilation (katalusis) of
Orchomenus and murder of all
male citizens, 175
anointed by Artaxerxes as leader of
Greeks, 160
antidemocratic government installed
by Philip in, 244
Antigone's Drag Track in, 10–11
anti-Macedonian revolt in, 248
Aphrodisia festival in, 16–17
Arcadian League's fraying alliance
with, 148–49, 160, 161–62
Arcadian League's request for aid
from, 128
Athenian alliances of, 5, 46, 51, 52
Athenian exiles in, 15–16
Atticists in, 17, 19, 38, 46
Cadmea (acropolis) of, see Cadmea

Cadmus as mythical founder of, 7–8
Cassander's rebuilding of, 252
in collaboration with 480 BC Persia
invasion, 32–33
competing proposals for alliance
with Philip or Athens, 237–38
Corinthian alliance with, 42
in decision to ally with Athens
against Philip, 238–39
as democracy, 108, 174
escape of Atticists from, 7
in failed attack on Plataea, 83
failed pro-Spartan coup attempt in,
174–75
food shortages in, 65–66
forgotten history of, xv, xvii
forts built by, 126, 127
fourth-century rise and fall of,
xvi–xvii
Harmonia's cursed necklace in
legends of, 8–9
Jason's alliance with, 108
in King's Peace treaty with Sparta,
44–48
Laconists in, 5, 6, 15, 19, 46–47
Macedonian alliance with, 138
Macedonians mistrusted by, 236
male erôs as viewed by, 4, 11–13,
28–29
Messene founded by, xvi, 133–34,
189, 201
northern alliances of, 116
Orchomenus's rivalry with, 58
overthrow of Spartan rule in, see
solstice plot
Peloponnese garrisons of, 188
Persian alliance with, 159–60
Phalaecus's victories over, 232
Philip as treaty hostage in, 138,
209
Philip's aid to, 232
as pioneering wall builders, 126–27
Plataea razed by, 84–85
pro-democracy forces executed or
exiled from, 244, 247–48

in refusal to join 395 BC Persian
campaign, 40
in rescue of Pelopidas, 146–47
in Sacred War against Phocians,
223–25, 229–33
shifting alliances of, 5, 235–36
Spartan army's abandonment of, 26
Spartan capture of, 4, 5–6, 13, 48,
78–79
Spartan counterattack expected by,
28
Sparta's Peloponnesian War alliance
with, 38
surrender to Alexander of, 250
in Tegean alliance, 195
Thesmophoria festival in, 4–5
tomb of Iolaus in, 11
Xenophon's bias against, xv–xvi, 67,
73, 74–75, 88–89, 115, 188–89,
216
Xenophon's downplaying of
achievements by, xvii
see also Boeotia, Boeotians; Boeotian
League
Theocritus, 19
Theopompus, 59
Thermopylae, x, 120, 138, 174, 235,
236
Philip's control of, 233, 236
Thesmophoria (Theban festival),
4–5
Thespiae, Thespians, x, 15, 57, 85, 228,
249, 253
allowed to withdraw from Leuctra
battle, 99
Praxiteles' Eros given to, 226, 228,
253
shrine of Eros at, 225
Spartan garrison at, 49
Thessalian League, 204
Pelopidas in creation of, 138
Thessaly, Thessalians, x, 149, 150
Alexander of Pherae as tagus of, 136
Alexander of Pherae's subjugation of,
208, 210

Boeotian aid requested by, 137
internecine struggle for control of,
135–36
Jason chosen as tagus of, 119
Jason's desire to become tagus of,
106, 108
navy of, 208
Pelopidas's burial in, 177–78
in struggle with Pherae regime of
Thebe, 231
in Tegean alliance, 195
Thirty, the, 15–16
Thiva, xv
see also Thebes, Thebans
Three Hundred (Elean elite troops),
174
Thucydides, 118, 131
on abuse of power, 187–88
thumos (high-spirited anger, pride),
7, 16, 21, 29, 57–58, 61, 137,
177
Timaea, 37
Timagoras, 158, 159–60
Timoclea, 251–52
Timotheus (Heraclean ruler), 182
Tiridates, 166–67
transmigration of souls, 76
trapezai ("banks"), 203
tresantes (tremblers), Leuctra survivors
as, 105
Trojan War, 40
Trojan Women (Euripides), 136
Tyrant Slayers (Turannoktonoi), 112,
146

Ulrichs, Karl Heinrich, in founding of
gay rights movement, 65

Venus of Arles, 229

warlordism, in fourth-century Greece,
179–80
Whitman, Walt, 186
and male erôs, 64–65, 124–25
Symonds and, 124–25

Wilde, Oscar, 64
  letters to Ives from, 186
  trials and imprisonment of, 185

Xenocrates, 228
Xenopeitheia, 27
Xenophon, 14, 18, 22, 35, 36, 41, 48,
  49, 50, 60, 67, 89, 135, 154, 160,
  161
  as adjutant on Agesilaus's staff, 73
  Agesilaus lionized by, 72, 115
  on Alexander of Pherae, 204
  anti-Theban, pro-Spartan bias of,
    xv–xvi, 67, 73, 74–75, 88–89, 115,
    188–89, 216
  on Arcadian League breakup,
    189–90, 192, 194–200
  Athenian banishment of, 72
  in Corinth, 188
  on Corinthian defeat of Sacred
    Band, 144–45
  on Coronea battle, 42, 43–44
  in Cyrus's army, 70, 166
  debate on Athenian aid to Sparta
    recorded by, 131–32
  Epaminondas's achievements
    disdained by, 189
  on Epaminondas's fourth
    Peloponnese invasion, 195–96
  on Epaminondas's strategic acumen,
    195–96
  on Jason's character and methods,
    107–8
  last years of, 215–16

  leadership of the Ten Thousand
    assumed by, 71–72, 154
  on Leuctra battle, 92, 99
  on male *erôs*, 12, 113–15
  male *erôs* as viewed by, 66–67,
    72–73, 74–75
  on Mantinea battle, 198–200
  on Mantinea cavalry skirmish,
    197–98
  master vs. slave worldview of,
    73
  on Olympia battle, 174
  on Pelopidas's mission to Artaxerxes,
    158–59
  in retirement from military, 74
  in return to Athens, 215
  on role of historian, xvii
  Sacred Band disparaged by, xvi
  Scillus estate of, 74, 133, 144,
    188–89
  Socrates' influence on, 68–69, 73
  on Spartan invasion of Boeotia, 53,
    54
  on Spartans' reaction to Leuctra
    defeat, 105
  Theban achievements downplayed
    by, xvii
  on Thebans' second failure to
    capture Sparta, 196
  Theban victory at Tegyra ignored
    by, 61
  on 371 peace conference, 86, 87

Zeus, 7, 9

About the Author

James Romm is an author, reviewer, and the James H. Otta-
way Jr. Professor of Classics at Bard College in Annandale,
New York. His reviews and essays appear regularly in the *Wall
Street Journal* and the *New York Review of Books*. He currently
oversees the ambitious *Ancient Lives* series recently launched by
Yale University Press.